OAKWOOD LIBRARY OF RAILWAY H

THE GWR AT STOURBRIDGE AND THE BLACK COUNTRY

The Life, the Times, the Men

Volume Two

by
Clive Butcher
(with additional material from C.R. Kendrick et al)

THE OAKWOOD PRESS

© Oakwood Press & Clive Butcher 2005

British Library Cataloguing in Publication Data
A Record for this book is available from the British Library
ISBN 0 85361 630 2

Typeset by Oakwood Graphics.
Repro by Ford Graphics, Ringwood, Hants.
Printed by Pims Print Ltd, Yeovil, Somerset.

GWR 'Bulldog' class 4-4-0 No. 3373 *Sir William Henry* at Stourbridge shed. To the right is '45XX' 2-6-2T No. 4540.   *Rhodes Collection/Kidderminster Railway Museum*

Front cover: 'Castle' class 4-6-0 No. 7012 *Barry Castle* leaves Brierley Hill station with the 5.29 pm Wolverhampton (Low Level)-Worcester (Shrub Hill) service on 26th August, 1961.   *Michael Mensing*

Rear cover, top: 'Hall' class 4-6-0 No. 4974 *Talgarth Hall* pulls away from Brierley Hill station with the 6.05 pm Wolverhampton (Low Level)-Worcester (Shrub Hill) service on 26th August, 1961 which comprised just one auto coach and one van!   *Michael Mensing*

Rear cover, bottom: Class '60' No. 60012 has brought a stone train into the Brierley Hill unloading terminal at Kingswinford Junction on 14th February, 2004.   *Author*

Published by The Oakwood Press (Usk), P.O. Box 13, Usk, Mon., NP15 1YS.
E-mail: sales@oakwoodpress.co.uk
Website: www.oakwoodpress.co.uk

Contents

Hereford-based 'Modified Hall' class No. 6992 *Arborfield Hall* passes through Pedmore on 2nd March, 1957 on a Birmingham-bound express.　　　　*J. Gibbs*

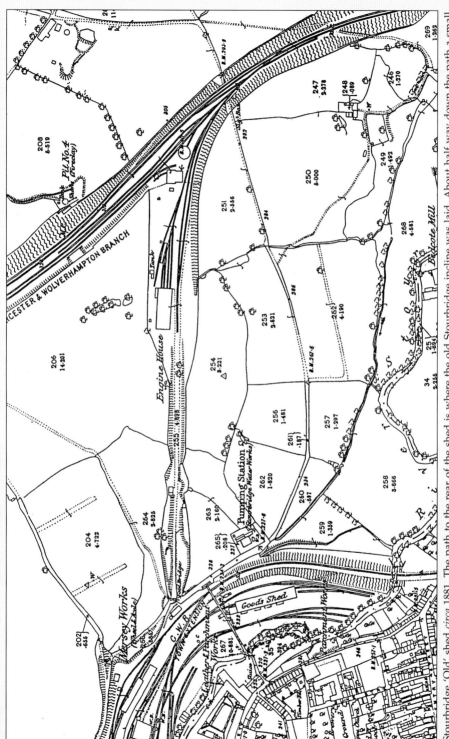

Stourbridge 'Old' shed *circa* 1881. The path to the rear of the shed is where the old Stourbridge incline was laid. About half way down the path a small building can be seen, this was the GWR pumping station that pumped water up to the shed. Originally, the building may have housed the incline's winding engine. The purpose of the building to the left of the turntable is not known.

Reproduced from the 25" Ordnance Survey Map

Chapter One

Stourbridge,
A Black Country Shed

The Oxford, Worcester & Wolverhampton Railway (OWWR) first arrived at Stourbridge in the spring of 1852, the main line station opening to regular passenger traffic on Monday, 3rd May. By late autumn the line had been extended to Dudley, with freight over the section commencing on 6th November, 1852 and passenger traffic on 20th December. The spring of 1854 saw the OWWR finally completed when the line joined up with the London & North Western Railway at Bushbury Junction. In 1863, the OWWR, which was now part of the West Midland Railway, was absorbed by the Great Western Railway Company and it is with this company that the story of Stourbridge engine sheds actually begins.

It would appear that the Great Western Railway (GWR) first considered constructing a facility at Stourbridge two years after the absorption of the OWWR, however, it was not until 1870 that something actually materialised. The shed at Stourbridge was built to replace the two-road wooden building that had been erected by the OWWR at Dudley in 1854, and was located on the west side of the former OWWR main line to Dudley, approximately ½ mile to the north of the original Stourbridge (Junction) station. Engine movements on and off the shed were controlled by Engine House signal box (later Engine Shed signal box). Although the shed was known officially as 'Stourbridge', it was actually to be found in the adjacent district of Amblecote and many local railwaymen knew the shed by this name. Strangely, the shed, especially in the 1960s, was often referred to as 'Stourbridge Junction', a quite erroneous title if a name should bear some relationship to location. In Great Western days the shedcode was STB, changing to 84F with the coming of British Railways in 1948. Later, as a by-product of the takeover of Western Region territory in the West Midlands by the LMR on 1st January, 1963, Stourbridge was allocated the code 2C as from 9th September. Today, the site of the engine sheds has been completely covered by a residential development, although the area's Great Western history has been recorded in the street names with Great Western locomotive superintendents and chief mechanical engineers prominent.

Stourbridge 'Old' shed

Returning to the beginning, Stourbridge shed was erected during 1870*. It was quite a substantial affair with brick-built walls, gable ends and slate roof, and measured about 156 feet long x 52 feet wide (65 feet wide if side buildings are included). Originally, the shed had only an office and a messroom, although during 1898, both a fitting shop and stores were added, the four buildings running the whole length of the outside wall on the north side. When built, the

---

* As yet nothing has been found in the local newspapers supporting this date. The 'papers did tend to report virtually everything which happened locally so it is surprising that the event was not recorded.

shed had four parallel roads terminating inside the building. By the end of the century one of these roads had been extended beyond the rear wall to terminate by what may have been a machine shop. Routine engine maintenance was undertaken on the shed roads, but as there were usually a few 'cripples' awaiting the attention of a fitter or boilersmith, space, to say the least, was at a premium. Each shed road had a short maintenance pit inside the building and a fire-pit outside, the latter usually half full of ash and clinker. As the small maintenance pits were nearly always occupied some enginemen may have been tempted to get under their machines via the fire-pits; if this action was considered it would have been a very risky business given the state that these pits must have been in. The coal-stage had been built just to the right of the shed entrance and was equipped with a hand crane and bucket. This facility was possibly enlarged *c.*1900. Roads ran on either side of the coal-stage, so in all likelihood coaling-up took place on both the right- and left-hand sides. Locomotives were turned on a 45 ft diameter turntable situated at the end of a short line which came off the left-hand through siding, one of two such sidings which were located on the down side of the main line, just to the north of the shed access road (*see plan c.1881*). These through sidings were known as Engine House sidings (later Engine Shed sidings) and were under the control of Engine House signal box. By the beginning of the 20th century the number of through sidings had been increased to five, with access to the northern end from the down main line being controlled by Engine Shed ground frame. The sidings and ground frame were taken out of use during February 1968, but Engine Shed signal box continued in use for a further 15 months until closed on 11th May, 1969.

Coming back to the turntable, by about 1900 the road leading to this had been extended as far as the water tank located just beyond the coal-stage. Later, the south end of Engine House sidings was realigned in such a way as to separate physically the sidings from the turntable road (*see plan page 12*). During the next few years further modifications were carried out to the track layout around the shed including the laying of new sidings and, by about 1921, the replacement of the existing 45 ft turntable with a new 65 ft example which was installed just to the north of the shed. The modified layout has been shown in the accompanying plan for *circa* 1921. The plan shows that the turntable was reached via two roads, one of which was a new one that left the shed road just past the signal box; the other, a short road which branched out from the original, extended turntable road, about half way down. The two lines then merged to form a single approach road to the turntable. With the construction of the roundhouse, much, if not all, of the trackwork forming the turntable roads was lifted, although it is possible that part of the original turntable road could have been retained and used to form the coal siding at the new shed. So what happened to the 65 ft turntable? It is hard to imagine that the GWR would have sited this anywhere else other than the spot where it would later be wanted for the roundhouse. Presumably, therefore, it remained where it was, the new shed being constructed around it.

There are two other questions concerning the 'old' shed which remain unanswered (at least in part); the first of these involves the roads known as 'Klondyke' and 'Newquay'. The author first came across these roads in Rex

Christiansen's *Regional History of the Railways of Great Britain, Volume 7, The West Midlands*. Unfortunately, at the time, further research failed to yield any additional information, nor could any of the former Stourbridge enginemen that were spoken to remember any such roads. It came as a very pleasant surprise to realise that defeat had been accepted far too easily as later investigation has shown that these in fact did exist, even if their precise location has not been identified to the complete satisfaction of the author. Furthermore, how these came to be so named remains a total mystery. The first official mention of 'Klondyke' was during a Local Departmental Committee meeting held on 31st March, 1924 when the dangers of cleaning out fires and leaving hot ashes strewn around the shed sidings were discussed at length, the Committee deciding that disposal should take place between 'Klondyke' road and the back road. It is thought that the back road was also known as 'Newquay'. The two roads have been identified, albeit tentatively, on the accompanying plan for *circa* 1920 (*page 12*). The throwing out of fires was also discussed two years earlier when it was agreed that disposal would be between the two back roads. The late Harry Hardwick, in a newspaper article recalling his memories of life at Stourbridge shed during the 1920s, provided more evidence when he mentioned that engines coming on to shed along 'Klondyke' or 'Newquay' were taken over by the shedmen for turning, coaling, cleaning and maintenance. Finally, reference was made on 20th May, 1931 to the work of No. 1 Bank Train. One of the duties of this service was to transfer traffic away from Engine Shed sidings to the shed yard before taking out wagons from 'Newquay'. Was 'Newquay' the original right-hand coaling road at the 'old' shed? Any information relating to 'Klondyke' and 'Newquay' would indeed be very welcome!

The second mystery involves a building that *c.*1881 existed just beyond the original turntable and was rail connected to one of the through sidings. It was thought that this may have had something to do with the original branch and incline leading down to Amblecote, but it has not been possible to substantiate this. By the end of the 19th century, the building had been demolished. The incline itself formed part of the branch which left the main line almost ¼ mile to the north of Stambermill viaduct, before terminating at Messrs Bradley & Company's iron works on the far side of Amblecote High Street. To reach Amblecote the line had to be constructed on a falling gradient, although it was not until the branch reached the upper end of Powkmore or Parkmoor Hill colliery that the descent proved to be too steep to be negotiated safely by a locomotive. During the opening ceremony on 30th July, 1859 a train was sent down the branch as far as the head of the 1 in 14 incline where the engine was detached and replaced by four powerful horses (probably Shire horses). These took the three wagons, two of which contained pig iron, the other a number of guests, the rest of the way down. Apparently, the trucks were returned in similar fashion. Unfortunately, the description of the event omits to mention how the train was controlled down this very steep gradient. The utilization of horses on the incline probably continued even after the branch had begun to handle regular traffic, although it is unlikely that this situation continued for long, horse power being replaced by a stationary, steam driven winding engine that was installed at the head of the incline. Although horses might have been banished from the incline itself, they would surely have been used to convey trucks from the foot of the incline to the two works served by the branch as it was not until the new branch line into Amblecote goods yard was opened, at the beginning of 1880, that steam locomotives could gain access to the site. However, even then horses were not totally replaced, this form of power continuing in use both within the yard itself (although confined to certain areas), and on the west side of the High Street until the 1930s when a Fordson tractor took over (steam engines were not allowed to cross the road - *see also Chapter Three in Volume One*). Whilst virtually no official information seems to exist relating to the winding engine, in all likelihood this would have been a condensing beam engine. The fact that the boiler off the Shrewsbury & Chester Railway's 0-6-0 No. 1, which had been withdrawn in 1874, was taken to Stourbridge and used as a condenser for the incline engine would appear to support this view. The incline fell into disuse after the new branch opened, but what happened to the winding engine and engine house; did they survive? It is possible that the building lived on to become the GWR pumping station, which according to early Ordnance Survey maps was located approximately 150 yards up from the foot of the former incline. In view of this could the winding engine have been converted to operate the pump which supplied water from the borehole to Stourbridge engine shed?

By about 1920 the increased number of engines at the shed was putting quite a strain on the existing supply, so it is likely, therefore, that to make up any deficiencies in the shed's requirements, the GWR would probably have had to purchase water off the local Water Board. Stourbridge Water Board had sunk a borehole in its Mill Meadow site* as early as *circa* 1856, the pumping station being about 150 yards from the GWR's. Both the GWR and the Water Board boreholes would have been sunk into the Bunter measures of New Red Sandstone that lay beneath the Stour valley. Harry Hardwick, in his book *The Magic of Steam*, mentions that the GWR, at different times, built two pumping stations in Amblecote, although until recently proving the existence of the later facility had not been possible until Albert Homer, who joined the GWR in 1929, pin-pointed its location in Amblecote goods yard. Looking at the 1931 map of the yard (*see Chapter Three*), the pumping station engine house and coal stage can be seen just to the rear of the canal transhipment shed. It is thought that this became the main source of water for the engine shed, the borehole on the old incline only being used if the goods yard pumping engine had broken down or was in need of routine maintenance. In the summer of 1937 the goods yard pumping station was turned over to electric power, the three men employed on the plant being made redundant. Another source of water was the large tank located near to the top of the embankment adjacent to the main line, overlooking the shed yard. This tank dates back to at least the early 1880s and once again it is thanks to Albert Homer for shedding light on what had, hitherto, been a mystery. The water tank over the coal stage was supplied from one of the GWR pumping stations, however, on occasion, the boreholes could not keep up with demand and the water level in the tank would begin to drop.

* The Water Board's pumping station at Mill Meadow employed a single cylinder condensing beam engine from 1896 to 1903 when it was relegated to stand-by duties. In its place was installed a triple expansion Worthington vertical pumping engine. This machine had a much greater pumping capacity than the beam engine which by now simply could not cope with the increasing demand for water.

When the level reached a certain point a bell rang in the shed office warning the running foreman whose immediate reaction was to send one of the shedmen to the far side of the viaduct where there was access to the Stourbridge Water Board's supply via a valve on the pumping main. So when water was in short supply it was on with the valve and the embankment tank would be filled up; with the permission of the Water Board of course. When full, the supply would be automatically cut off, presumably through the use of a ball-cock, and the water would then be fed by gravity to the tank in the yard via an underground pipe which came to the surface in the messroom under the coal-stage. When the yard tank was full, the shedman would return to the water main and shut off the valve.

Returning to the 'old' shed itself, working conditions were indeed quite primitive, lacking many of the facilities later generations of enginemen would take for granted. For example there was no messroom, cooking facilities or hot water, and what the toilets were like must be left to the imagination. Enginemen and shed staff used an old coach or van fitted out with lockers and benches. Office accommodation was also very restricted, the shed foreman's office being just about large enough to hold up to six men if all breathed in together. In the adjacent office were the clerical staff, (chief clerk, roster clerk, etc.) communication between the two offices being via a speaking tube with a whistle at each end. Needless to say the boss rarely needed to blow his whistle twice to command the attention of those working next door!

The expansion of rail traffic throughout the late 19th century had major implications for the shed, especially in respect of servicing the many locomotives which were finding their way into the area. Stourbridge's location in relation to the major coal and iron producing districts, and its position on the Wolverhampton-Worcester-London and the Birmingham-Worcester-Hereford lines, gave it a strategic importance that created demands that could not be easily met by existing facilities. Originally, there was little by way of sidings at the shed, apart from the loco roads themselves and the coal-stage siding. Following the abandonment of the incline the running lines that formerly led to it were probably used as sidings to hold both locomotives and wagons, however, in spite of this, the shed area must still have remained very overcrowded. The answer of course was to provide a new shed, but given the time scale and financial implications associated with such a project a short term solution had to be found and found quickly. As there was some spare land in the vicinity of the former incline it was decided to increase the length of one of the existing sidings, as well as laying two additional ones. Consequently, by around the end of World War I, the area held three dead-end parallel sidings and a shorter fourth parallel siding located between these and No. 1 shed road (the left-hand road looking at the front of the shed from the coal-stage).

Although the 'old' shed was closed on 8th February, 1926, coinciding with the opening of the new roundhouse, it did not stay out of use for long. Coaling-up of the steam railmotors had probably continued at the 'old' shed even after it had 'officially' closed so what better place to keep these machines at the end of a working day? However, the shed really came back to life during World War II when severe overcrowding at the roundhouse forced the authorities in 1944 to reintroduce locomotive servicing at the 'old' shed to relieve some of the congestion. After the war the role of the 'old' shed changed as the increasing use of diesel traction (first the GWR diesel railcars and the newly introduced shunting engines; later BR single and multiple units) required a separate, modified facility which resulted, during the late 1950s, in the shed's partial rebuilding. The original slated, timber-framed roof and wooden doors were replaced, although the side walls and offices were retained. Just outside the shed a fuelling point was provided.

The last shed foreman at the 'old' shed was Tom Dovaston who took over the post from John Preece who retired on 4th January, 1923 having completed 47 years and 5 months in the employment of the Great Western Railway Company. John Preece's career is a very interesting one as it illustrates just how a young man could progress through the ranks to become a middle manager with the company. He first joined the GWR on 7th September, 1875 as an engine cleaner at Shrewsbury shed. In the following April he was transferred to Wolverhampton where he learned to fire. Thirteen years later, in 1889, he moved to Malvern Wells as a passenger fireman. Another transfer in 1892 saw him promoted to goods driver at Bullo Pill (Goods), 12 miles from Gloucester on the line to Lydney. Nine months later he was on the move again, this time to Llanelly. He remained in South Wales until 1896 when another promotion saw him heading back to the West Midlands to take up a post at Bordesley Junction. During his stay at the Birmingham shed he successfully applied for the job of sub-inspector in the Locomotive Department. This was in 1903. Rapid promotion followed, and a year later he was made up to inspector, a position held until 1907 when he was advanced to night foreman at Oxley New Shed in Wolverhampton. Two years later he transferred to Tyseley New Shed as assistant day foreman. The last position to be held by this much travelled, and very experienced, man, was shed foreman at Stourbridge, taking over the reigns of responsibility from T.H. Lodge during August 1910. Mr Lodge had just retired after 50 years' service with the GWR. Replacing John Preece at Tyseley was Samuel Higgins who had been employed as a sub-inspector at Stourbridge for the past 10 to 12 years. The vacant post at Stourbridge shed was subsequently filled by Mr G.H. Mason formerly a sub-inspector at Bordesley Junction. As a fair and reasonable man, John Preece created a particularly good working relationship with the 400 men he had been called upon to supervise, earning their respect and, dare it be said, their admiration over the next 13 years. He was particularly popular with the trade unions, a view which is supported by the following comments made by Mr G. Tyler, acting on behalf of the two unions at the shed, who stated at the retirement dinner held at the Vine Hotel, Stourbridge, on Saturday 27th January, 1923 that 'he (Mr Preece) had been an able servant to the Company and an asset to the men in negotiations. He (the speaker) had differed from Mr Preece many times but they had always been good friends'. This was one of several tributes paid to him during the evening. The trade unions also presented Mr Preece with an illuminated address in a gold mount and heavy dark oak frame.

John Preece's career saw him twice on the footplate as fireman on the Royal Train which conveyed Queen Victoria from the North (Balmoral?) to Windsor.

Presumably he took over the fireman's duties at Bushbury Junction (Wolverhampton) from a London & North Western man. Another memorable firing turn was during the harsh winter of 1881/82, when the snow was so deep that the assistance of the Royal Engineers was required to clear the permanent way. Furthermore, he was fireman on the first engine to cross the new, brick-built, Stambermill viaduct in 1881 along with driver W. Downs. Perhaps it was here that he made up his mind one day to return to Stourbridge on a more permanent basis? During World War I, he was responsible for the smooth handling of the ambulance trains arriving at Stourbridge and was actually present at the arrival of 72 of the 76 trains which conveyed wounded troops from the Front. Yes, John Preece would be sadly missed, but he had a more than able replacement in Tom Dovaston! Mr Dovaston had joined the GWR as an engine cleaner at Wolverhampton. Later he became an engine turner at Oxley shed from where he was transferred to Bordesley Junction in 1910 having been promoted to sub-inspector, replacing G.H. Mason. Tom Dovaston eventually came to Stourbridge in 1915 as assistant foreman in the Locomotive Department. Sadly he died in April 1942 whilst still in office.

Incidentally, the first ambulance train arrived at Stourbridge in the early evening of Sunday 17th October, 1915 followed by a second just after midnight. The staff at Stourbridge Junction were not expecting two trains that night so it came as quite a surprise when at 8.30 pm a message arrived informing them that the second had left Southampton earlier that evening. Not to be put off by such short notice, the local ladies' Voluntary Aid Detachment (VAD) once again swung into action and by 10.00 pm they had made the Town station (at the time closed to normal passenger traffic) as warm and comfortable as possible. It was due mainly to the dedicated efforts of the VAD that these latest wounded soldiers were quickly detrained and made ready for dispatch to Wordsley Military Hospital, the last detachment leaving for the hospital at 4.45 am. The train, free of its sorry cargo, steamed out of the station at 3.15 am. In charge of the railway operation that night was the divisional superintendent F.S. Johnson, ably assisted by chief inspector W.Chandler; district inspector J. Morgan; Stourbridge Junction station master A.E. Arnold, and the former station master at the Town station, F.S. Bolton. Altogether about 400 soldiers arrived that night, and throughout the war somewhere in the region of 11,000-13,000 casualties arrived at the Town station on their way to Wordsley. Possibly the last of these trains arrived at Stourbridge at around midnight on Sunday 12th April, 1919 carrying 229 wounded.

Having mentioned ambulance trains, on Sunday 10th March, 1918 *The County Express* was able to record how these hospitals upon wheels were fitted out:

Officers of the local Voluntary Aid Detachment who assembled on Sunday afternoon to meet an ambulance train, which arrived at Stourbridge Town station at 5.40 and left at 6.45, had a specially interesting time as by the kindness of the officer in charge they were permitted to inspect a wonderful moving hospital. Ambulance train No. 16 is of Great Western stock, beautifully fitted with all modern conveniences. Its officer, who has had two year's experience at the Front, was evidently very proud of his staff and his train, and invited the officials at the station to look through it. There are in the train eight wards for lying down patients, each capable of accommodating 16 men. At the side of

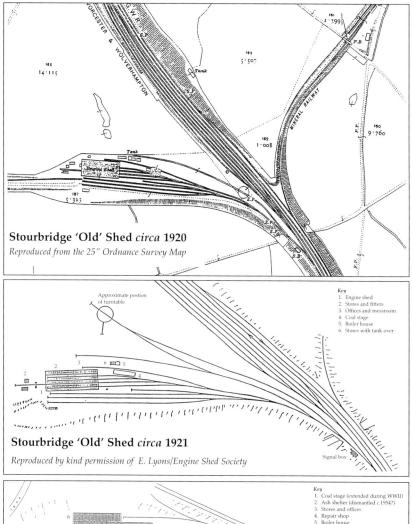

Stourbridge 'Old' Shed *circa* **1920**

Reproduced from the 25" Ordnance Survey Map

Key
1. Engine shed
2. Stores and fitters
3. Offices and messroom
4. Coal stage
5. Boiler house
6. Stores with tank over

Approximate postion of turntable

Stourbridge 'Old' Shed *circa* **1921**

Reproduced by kind permission of E. Lyons/Engine Shed Society

Signal box

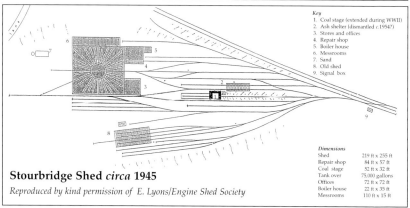

Key
1. Coal stage (extended during WWII)
2. Ash shelter (dismantled c.1954?)
3. Stores and offices
4. Repair shop
5. Boiler house
6. Messrooms
7. Sand
8. Old shed
9. Signal box

Dimensions
Shed — 219 ft x 255 ft
Repair shop — 84 ft x 57 ft
Coal stage — 52 ft x 32 ft
Tank over — 75,000 gallons
Offices — 72 ft x 72 ft
Boiler house — 22 ft x 35 ft
Messrooms — 110 ft x 15 ft

Stourbridge Shed *circa* **1945**

Reproduced by kind permission of E. Lyons/Engine Shed Society each cot is a paper rack and match bracket; all the cots are collapsible and transferable, so that a patient in any particular cot can be carried on that cot direct to the operating room and back again, or transferred on it from the coach to another. In the train there is an operating room, a pharmacy coach, spacious accommodation for the sisters and staff, and every convenience for the suffering patients; a coach for the officer in charge, beautifully fitted and upholstered, with a handsome secretaire, and a gramophone to enliven the waiting hours. The whole of the train is linked up by telephone; there is also excellent office accommodation, with a typewriter, safe, and all modern equipment. The officer, sisters, and staff were so charmed by the scenery on the way to and in the vicinity of Stourbridge that they expressed a desire to see the town, and said they hoped they would be paying another visit. On this occasion, there were in their charge 113 patients, of whom 70 were lying-down cases. These were removed from the train by Stourbridge and Lye Ambulance men, the officers present being Medical Officers Dr G. Russell-Jarvis and Dr H.C. Darby, Supt J. Stacey, Commandant C.S. Hall, Commandant H. Mills and Quartermaster L.J. Cook, the last named in charge of the detachment which went to assist at the Military Hospital. The officer with the train commended the appearance and work of the ambulance men, and also complimented the Ladies VAD (A Section) who were under Commandant Mrs Hall and Quartermaster Miss Sharp.

Stourbridge 'New' Shed

Plans to construct a new motive power depot at Stourbridge had been prepared prior to the outbreak of World War I in 1914. Land for the new shed had been purchased by the GWR in 1913 and by the beginning of May 1914 work had begun on levelling the site. The contract for the job had been awarded to Messrs Muirhead & Company of Westminster whose 'Steam Navvy' (a steam driven bucket and crane) caused quite a stir amongst local people. It was expected that once the project had begun it would take around 4-5 months to complete. However, after war was declared, the GWR decided that capital projects such as Stourbridge shed, which had still to be started, should be temporarily postponed until the conflict in Europe had ended and a more favourable climate had been created. Unfortunately, the European war lasted for four long, bloody years and even after hostilities ceased it took a considerable time for life to get back to normal. However, on Friday 9th February, 1923 a number of projects were authorised and on the next day it was announced that one of these would be the new locomotive depot at Stourbridge. The authorisation of these schemes was the GWR's response to a request by the Government to accelerate its works programme in an attempt to combat rising unemployment. In the middle of May 1923 Mr C.B. Collett, chief mechanical engineer of the Great Western Railway, confirmed the decision to build the shed and in the same year the go-ahead was given to obtain estimates for the work. On 16th August, 1924 it was reported locally that the total cost of the whole undertaking would be in the region of £118,000 (the actual figure may have been slightly higher at £119,230).

The contract to erect the shed itself was awarded to the Amblecote firm of A.M. Guest Ltd whose successful tender was almost £30,000 (Ian Sixsmith in his article entitled 'Stourbridge Shed' - *British Railways Illustrated* Vol. 8, June 1999, states that this was later revised downwards to £24,414). By this time the

GWR '2301' 'Dean Goods' class 0-6-0 No. 2569 in Stourbridge shed on 1st October, 1933.
C.F.H. Oldham/Kidderminster Railway Museum

Ex-GWR '28XX' class 2-8-0 No. 2857 at Stourbridge shed on 18th June, 1950.
P. Bingham/Kidderminster Railway Museum

original pre-war scheme for two roundhouses had been shelved and replaced by a new one for a single roundhouse. The work of preparing the ground and laying the track began early in 1924, but a strike in the construction industry put building plans way behind schedule. The dispute was resolved around the end of August 1924 so it is presumed that building work began at this time. It was subsequently envisaged that the shed would be completed in about 12 months, the task providing employment for 100 men. In the event, the new engine shed at Stourbridge opened for business on 8th February, 1926 the last roundhouse to be built by the GWR.

The building itself measured 219 ft by 255 ft, the brick built walls carrying a composite roof of boarding and poilite slating, supported by wooden rafters and purlins, held together by iron ties. In the shed roof were built smokechutes, whilst under the maintenance roads large pits had been dug, these gave enginemen more room than they were used to at the 'old' shed to carry out their routine maintenance. This task, though, was still a pretty unpleasant one, especially in the dead of winter.

At the front of the shed, on the left-hand side of the entrance road, were to be found offices and stores, the former including the booking-on point. Nearby, the shed foreman (Tom Dovaston being the first; the last A.E. Gregory) and clerks had their offices, whilst inside the shed, against the left-hand wall, were a number of offices for the other foremen and chargehands (in the early days of the new shed's operation, Harry Perkins was chargehand boilersmith). Moving to the other side of the shed, on the right-hand side of the main reception road, was the fitting shop or, as it was originally known, the lifting and repair shop (ensuring that everything ran smoothly after opening was probably Alf Cartwright). This building measured 84 ft x 57 ft with a 68 ft-long inspection pit under the shop road. Later, a second road was added, but this terminated immediately outside, adjacent to the boiler house. Inside the fitting shop could be found a wide range of equipment, for example there were blacksmiths' and coppersmiths' hearths (the former being driven by a compressor); a heavy duty metal planer; lathes, including a wheel lathe; a radial drilling machine, and a shaping machine. Much of the equipment was powered by friction belts attached to a large shaft which in turn was driven by a two-cylinder compound steam engine. Also in the shop was a sheer hoist used for lifting a boiler away from a locomotive's wheels. When a boiler lift was required, the locomotive would be shunted along the fitting shop road until it was in position under the hoist. The boiler would then be lifted to allow the wheel sets to be rolled out. If for some reason power to the hoist was unavailable, the hoist would have to be operated by hand which necessitated two or three fitters turning a large hand-wheel which slowly eased the boiler into the air.

At the front of the fitting shop was the boiler house which accommodated two old locomotive boilers. The origin of the boilers in place when the roundhouse was opened is unknown, but it is thought that in later years these were replaced by two that had been taken off a couple of withdrawn 'Dean Goods' freight engines. The boilers provided the steam for the fitting shop engine, as well as any other equipment to be found in the rest of the shed, including a modern boilerwashing plant. On the right-hand wall of the shed

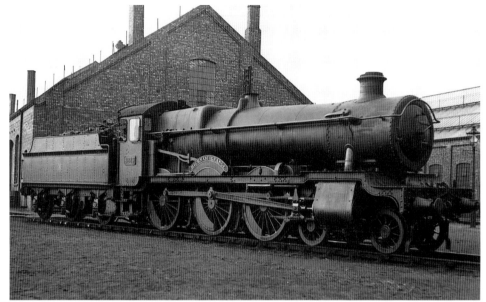

'Grange' class 4-6-0 No. 6819 *Highnam Grange* outside Stourbridge shed on 12th March, 1939.
R. Carpenter Collection

Stourbridge shed in 1958 with 0-6-0PT '57XX' class No. 9613 in the foreground.
D.K. Jones Collection

were a number of lean-to type cabins which housed a kitchen fitted out with stoves and, that wonder of wonders, running hot water, together with mess-rooms for enginemen, fitters and shed staff. In March 1926 Harry Chapman was appointed messroom attendant at 50 shillings per week.

As stated earlier, the shed was built around a 65 ft turntable that was used to direct locomotives on to any one of 28 engine storage and maintenance roads, with No. 14 road continuing beyond the rear shed wall to terminate alongside the sand furnace just outside. Dry sand would be obtained from here and carried in buckets to the engines where their sanding equipment would be replenished. In the 1940s, a second doorway was constructed in the rear wall enabling No. 12 road to be extended outside. Track was then laid from this extension, along the south-west wall of the shed to form a connection with nearby sidings, thereby providing an emergency escape route for locomotives if the main entrance road ever became blocked, which it was on at least one occasion following a derailment. The lengths of the roads ranged from 41 ft to 100 ft. The engine holding capacity is difficult to assess accurately, but probably it varied between 40 and 70 locomotives, depending on the size and type. Initially, the central turntable was manually operated and was long enough to accommodate a 'Castle'. With the locomotive properly balanced, two turntable men were able to rotate it to the appropriate road. However, by the beginning of 1956, the condition of the turntable was giving rise to concern. It had been repaired on numerous occasions, but turning it was becoming so difficult that some of the more elderly shedmen were threatening to refuse to operate it unless help was provided. A new turntable had been promised for some time, but clearly this had still not been installed. Eventually, something was done, a Ransom Rapier electric turntable replacing the old hand-operated one around July/August 1959.

The work of removing the old turntable had begun about five months earlier and as a result it had not been possible to stable engines inside the shed until the work had been completed. Consequently, to ensure that routine locomotive maintenance was properly carried out and that all engines were available for their rostered duties, three temporary supervisory posts were created so that outside work could be closely monitored for as long as the turntable was out of action. These 'outside foremen' were recruited from the four man panel that was normally used to provide a replacement for a running foremen who was either sick or on holiday, or who was deputising for the shedmaster. On this occasion, all four panel members were upgraded to the minimum running foreman's rate, working a rotating three man shift system with one man acting as relief. The panel at this time comprised Albert Homer, Billy Cooper, Albert Wood and Mel Jenkins. The 'outside foremen' were required to: a) make a note of all incoming locomotives and ensure that they were disposed of correctly; b) to see that engine preparation was carried out, and c) to arrange for engines to be marshalled on the appropriate roads. Passenger engines would be stabled in the roundhouse yard separate from the freight engines, the 'old' shed yard also being used for the latter. Locomotives on the early turns were always placed at the front of the line in order to enable them to get away quickly first thing in the morning, whilst spare engines would be stabled on the siding outside the boiler

No. 6828 *Trellech Grange* arrived at Stourbridge *circa* June 1948 along with classmate No. 6857 *Tudor Grange*. An early photograph of the former shows it outside the old shed *circa* 1948.

E. Potts-Perkins Collection

Ex-GWR 'Aberdare' class 2-6-0 No. 2655 at Stourbridge shed on 21st November, 1948. The locomotive is still in GWR livery.   *L.B. Lapper Collection/Kidderminster Railway Museum*

Ex-GWR '2182' class 0-6-0PT No. 2186 in Stourbridge roundhouse on 18th June, 1950.
P. Bingham/Kidderminster Railway Museum

Collett '51XX' class 2-6-2T No. 4104 in the yard at Stourbridge shed on 16th August, 1952.
L.W. Perkins/A. Wycherley/Kidderminster Railway Museum

'56XX' class 0-6-2T No. 6678 outside Stourbridge shed *circa* 1954. This engine arrived at Stourbridge around 1948 and stayed until withdrawal 16 years later.   *D.K. Jones Collection*

'51XX' class 2-6-2T No. 5199 in steam at Stourbridge shed with 0-6-0PT No. 9613 behind on 25th September, 1960. Partially obscured in the background is the breakdown crane.

R.H.W. Whitworth/Kidderminster Railway Museum

house and on the loop leading to the north end of Engine Shed sidings. To make sure that engines were allocated to their correct places on the line, and in the right order, either for traffic or for maintenance purposes, the 'outside foremen' had to closely liaise with the running foremen inside the shed who were responsible for allocating engines to particular jobs and identifying those for repair by the fitters or due for boiler washouts. This information would then be posted on the engine board located inside the shed. Accuracy in this sort of situation was essential, and running foremen had to be kept continually informed of changes to engine requirements and/or their availability for work. Usually, up to two engines booked for a boiler washout would be stabled on the shed entrance road.

Although the formal opening of the shed occurred in 1926, the shed's coal-stage may have come into operation earlier. The existing bucket and crane type coal-stage situated at the 'old' shed probably fell into disuse as one of a more modern design came on stream around 5th July, 1925 (presumably, a new coal-stage would not have been built at a shed that would shortly close, so the plant referred to would be the one that would later serve the needs of engines at the roundhouse). Interestingly, the coalmen working at the 'old' shed were paid at day-work rates, unlike many of their contemporaries at other sheds in Great Western territory whose pay was determined by the piece-work system. Piece-work was a form of payment by results and was related to the number of tons of coal delivered to the shed. However, with the introduction of the new coal-stage imminent, it was proposed on 11th May, 1925 that the six men to be employed on engine coaling would be paid a piece-work rate of 27 minutes per ton delivered. This rate though, was three minutes per ton lower than that given to men working on the majority of modern installations elsewhere on the Great Western (in December 1924 only Westbury, Gloucester and Pontypool Road were paid less than 30 minutes per ton), a fact that was quickly seized upon by the men's union. As a result, the rate was increased to 30 minutes per ton delivered soon after the plant was opened, the reason for the increase being that the majority of engines to be coaled were bunker fitted rather than tender engines. On 29th August, 1925 it was confirmed that piece-work earnings of the coalmen would not be less than the basic time worked, calculated at the existing day-rate of 8 shillings and 8 pence. Added to the piece-work wage would be any night-rate, overtime and Sunday working as appropriate. Incidentally, firedroppers (and probably other grades in the shed) were also on piece-work, the payment being calculated on the number of engines attended to. Prior to April 1957 the rate was 60 minutes per locomotive; this was now increased to 65 minutes, which included cleaning out the firebox, ashpan and smokebox, as well as the fire-dropping pit, and lifting the ashes to ground level. Disposal of the ashes to the wagons was carried out by the shed labourers. Returning to the coal-stage, this was extended during World War II thereby enabling locomotives to be coaled from both left- and right-hand sides. The coal-stage was located about 120 yards away from the main shed building.

Obviously, a coal-fired steam engine cannot perform its primary role without a good supply of fuel. Furthermore, to get the best out of that engine not only must it have a skilful crew on the footplate, but also the coal must be of the right

Royal train engines 'Castle' class Nos. 7001 *Sir James Milne* and 7027 *Thornbury Castle* outside Stourbridge shed on 23rd April, 1957.

E. Payton

'Castle' class 4-6-0 No. 7024 *Powis Castle* inside Stourbridge shed minus rear driving wheels and front bogie on 10th November, 1963. The mechanical foreman's office is on the right.

Joe Moss/R.S. Carpenter

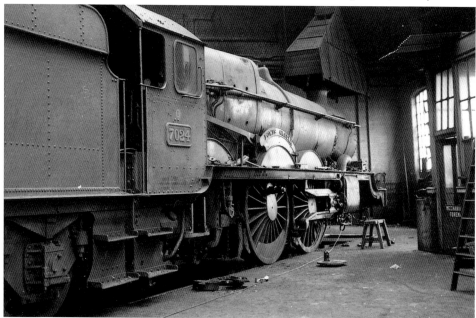

'Hall' class 4-6-0 No. 5912 *Queen's Hall* at Stourbridge shed on 8th July, 1962. On the far right is ex-LMS Stanier class '8F' 2-8-0 No. 48475.   *R.H.W. Witworth/Kidderminster Railway Museum*

'28XX' class 2-8-0 No. 3854 adjacent to the coal stacking area at Stourbridge shed in the 1960s.
T. Lawrence

A general view of Stourbridge shed on 13th March, 1960. To the left a pair of ex-GWR railcars are stabled in the yard with BR diesel units in the old shed. The coal-stage is in the centre with the roundhouse to the right. All the steam locomotives seen in this view are of GWR origin.

W. Potter/Kidderminster Railway Museum

A Stourbridge shedplate. The shed was classified as '84F' by British Railways Western Region until reorganisation when it became '2C', a London Midland Region code, in 1963.   *Author*

type and quality. It would appear that at Stourbridge there were a number of occasions when the fuel supplied failed to meet expectations. For example, during World War I, there were, at times, grave shortages of top quality Welsh steam coal with the result that footplate crews were experiencing major difficulties with their engines. Certainly, during the late Autumn of 1915, whatever coal was being supplied was leading to excessive fire cleaning and producing very little steam. One example involved driver Gardener who, on 28th September, was working a Government chain special through Didcot when poor steaming forced him to come off the main line and seek sanctuary in a nearby loop. Here he lost 45 minutes cleaning out the fire. Problems also arose closer to home and on 4th November, Stourbridge's class '1016' 0-6-0PT No. 1047, could only raise 40 lb. per square inch of steam pressure even after the fire had been cleaned. A few days later, on 13th November, driver Horton, after banking two passenger trains from Stourbridge Junction and Cradley respectively, was unable to continue without regular attention to the fire. Even after this had been cleaned, steam pressure remained so low that his engine could not even perform the lightest of shunting duties.

Management was of course sympathetic to the plight of the footplatemen and promised to arrange delivery to Stourbridge of as much South Wales steam coal as possible. Employees, though, were reminded that in view of the continuing conflict in Europe, no guarantees could be given in respect of restoring supplies to their earlier levels. Between the wars, very little was said about the coal situation at the shed, so it must be assumed that in the main, everyone was happy with what was being delivered. The only problem worth recording occurred in the spring of 1924 when 'Whitwick' coal was considered to be totally unsuitable. Unfortunately, nothing more is known about this particular type of fuel or what action was taken to remedy the problem.

After World War II, at a time when coal was once again in short supply, one of the shed's 'Aberdare' 2-6-0 heavy freight engines was involved in an unusual fuel experiment. Instead of normal steam coal, the tender was one day filled with coke. The trial proved to be a very embarrassing failure as Stan Lawrence, who was firing on that day recalls: 'We were on a Bordesley Junction pick-up freight. The coke burnt like paper and at Langley Green (on the return journey) we had run out'. The final criticism involving the quality of coal happened during April 1950. At this time the shed's needs were being accommodated, at least in part, by the colliery at Walsall Wood. Apparently, much of this coal arrived as rather large lumps which tended to block the bunkers of tank locomotives. This made life particularly difficult for firemen working on these engines.

Although Stourbridge was on the very edge of a huge coal producing area, the type of fuel mined by local collieries was not really suitable for Great Western engines which had been designed to perform best on a diet of soft Welsh steam coal. Consequently, considerable quantities of this fuel were brought into the area by mineral trains from South Wales, many of these beginning their journey to the Black Country from Pontypool Road. An example of one such working was the 5.25 am class 'H' ex-Pontypool Road which was scheduled to arrive at Stourbridge Junction at 12.05 pm. This train was usually headed by a class '28XX'

'51XX' class 2-6-2T No. 5136 on the left-hand side of the coal-stage at Stourbridge. This side was brought into operation during World War II. The locomotive was withdrawn on 1st October, 1951 whilst still allocated to Stourbridge.   *D.K. Jones Collection*

'43XX' class 2-6-0 No. 5332 standing by the coal-stage at Stourbridge shed with piles of ash around it on 25th September, 1960.   *R.H.W. Whitworth/Kidderminster Railway Museum*

'51XX' class 2-6-2T No. 4141 at Stourbridge shed with the coal-stage to the rear on 25th September, 1960.   *R.H.W. Whitworth/Kidderminster Railway Museum*

'57XX' class 0-6-0PT No. 3619 outside Stourbridge shed *circa* 1966 with the coal-stage in the background.   *C.R. Kendrick*

Ex-GWR diesel railcars Nos. W15W and W8 at Stourbridge shed on 13th March, 1960. No. W8 has some windows missing.   *W. Potter/Kidderminster Railway Museum*

Diesel multiple units (dmus) at the new fuelling point at Stourbridge shed *circa* 1966. *C.R. Kendrick*

2-8-0 or ROD 2-8-0. However, irrespective of where the coal originated, once the trucks containing the loco-coal had been delivered they would have to be shunted over to the coal-stage and coal sidings. At the former, some of the full trucks would be propelled up the 1 in 30 single elevated road to the staging area where they would be emptied, the coal being put into wheeled tubs ready for tipping into the tenders or bunkers of engines waiting on the coaling road below. Through the staging area itself the incline of the road reduced to 1 in 80, the line continuing out to the rear of the building where empty wagons were held until such time that they could be returned to the sidings to eventually make up a return working. Built into the coal-stage roof was a two-compartment water tank measuring 52 ft square by 8 ft deep with a capacity to hold a total of almost 75,000 gallons. The obvious advantage of constructing the tank in this way was that one compartment could be cleaned and painted whilst the other remained in use.

To the left of the coal-stage were located the coal sidings, one of which continued to form four dead-end sidings serving the coal stacking ground where up to 4,000 tons of locomotive coal could be stockpiled. To the right of the coal-stage, running parallel with the coaling road, was the ash loading siding where steel bodied wagons were filled with the (sometimes) still hot material. Adjacent this siding were two ash-pit roads which, along with the coaling road, came together to form the shed access road. In the ash-pit road nearest the coal-stage there was one 240 ft-long pit; the second ash-pit road had a pit half that length. During World War II an ash shelter was built over these pits so that fires could be dropped without being seen by enemy aircraft flying overhead. As an added precaution, cleaners armed with hoses would spray water over the glowing embers. This shelter was later demolished. Incidentally, the shed may have been the target of one air attack, a bomb landing by the down main line between Stambermill viaduct and Engine Shed signal box in 1940. However, whether the shed or the main line had been the intentional target is unknown. There were several air raid alerts, a 'yellow' warning indicated that an air raid was imminent, whilst a 'red' warning meant that a raid was in progress and all lights had to be extinguished. One night a fitter's mate, gauge lamp in hand, ran through the shed shouting 'red warning'. Consequently all the lights went out. Unfortunately, the man fell into one of the inspection pits. Having quickly got out he promptly fell into another. He then wisely decided to stop where he was until the 'all clear' was sounded.

During April 1961 new offices and canteen were opened in an amenities block situated on ground to the rear of the shed, opposite the old canteen that had been built *circa* 1944, however, it did not have a very long working life. Both 'old' and 'new' sheds closed to steam on 11th July, 1966 although what had for many years been known as the 'old' shed (also called the 'railmotor' shed) continued in use to stable dmus until 6th May, 1968 whilst the roundhouse was used to stable diesel locomotives. Furthermore, footplate crews continued to book on and off there until they were found alternative accommodation at Stourbridge Junction (a new prefabricated administration block had been planned). The roundhouse also played host to a couple of steam locomotives which, during 1967, were on their way into preservation on the Severn Valley Railway. It is thought that fuelling and inspection of diesel locomotives and

A line-up of withdrawn ex-GWR pannier tanks of '64XX' and '74XX' class 0-6-0PTs outside Stourbridge shed. The locomotives are, *from left to right*, Nos. 7443, 7418, 7413, 6434, 7414, 7432 and 6424.   *Brian Moone/Kidderminster Railway Museum*

A view inside Stourbridge roundhouse just before closure with BR Standard class '9F' 2-10-0 No. 92132 on the right and an ex-LMS Stanier locomotive to the left.   *C.R. Kendrick*

multiple units was withdrawn from Stourbridge sheds *circa* 3rd March, 1969; by June of the same year, the buildings had been demolished. Although the sheds had gone, Stourbridge Junction remained a major stabling point until the 1980s with diesel locomotives and units using the sidings on the down side of the main line between the station and Stourbridge North Junction.

After the closure of the sheds to steam, Stourbridge train crews were to have moved into a new prefabricated adminstration block that was to be built adjacent to the Junction station. However, construction of the building appears not to have been started until around February 1967, consequently, train crews continued to book on and off at the roundhouse. Eventually, with little information coming from management as to when the new block would be completed, attitudes began to harden and the taking of some sort of industrial action became a real possibility. However, this was as far as the dispute went for shortly afterwards the station manager, Henry Holloway, confirmed that the building ought to be finished by the end of August 1967, and that it would then be handed over early in the following month. As it turned out this forecast was a little optimistic for it appears that the staff did not move into the block until 11th December, 1967. But still the problems continued, for it was argued that the building had only been designed to accommodate 167 staff in total; this was less than the actual number employed (apparently, there were 167 Sectional Council No. 2 employees alone, i.e. 120 drivers and 47 secondmen. It appears that someone may have overlooked the conciliation staff). As nothing else seems to have been said on the matter, the issue must have been amicably resolved. The new prefabricated building was located on the left-hand side of the main entrance to the station car park and continued to be used by train crews until the end of the 1980s when, after prolonged negotiations between the men's representatives and the London Midland Region management, Stourbridge Train Crew Depot (TCD) was closed on 9th July, 1988. This resulted in the remaining 49 railwaymen employed at the depot, that is, 27 drivers, 18 guards, three train crew supervisors and one messroom attendant (plus two guards from Kidderminster sub-depot) being made redundant or redeployed. Over the last few years of operation there had been a drastic reduction in the amount of work undertaken by Stourbridge men, however, what really hammered home the final nail into the depot's coffin was the decision not to train footplate staff on the class '150' 'Sprinters' or the recently introduced class '155s'. After closure, the building was taken over by the permanent way gang and is still in use today, the contractor working for Network Rail, Jarvis, occupying the site.

The Mutual Improvement Class

In common with most sheds around Britain, Stourbridge had its own 'Mutual Improvement Class' (MIC) which was run on a voluntary basis from an old carriage body located to the rear of the shed. It was here that on a Sunday morning, firemen, keen to listen and learn from older hands with years of experience behind them, acquired the skills and knowledge vital to the furtherance of their career on the footplate. What a valuable mechanism this class was, especially when there were men of the calibre of Bob Brown, Arthur Brookes, Lew Brettall and Walter Cooper (recalled by Harry Hardwick in *The Magic of Steam*)*, just four of the many drivers who, over the years, were willing to spend their spare time passing on 'the tricks of the trade' to their would-be successors. Little wonder that Stourbridge firemen achieved a very high pass rate when tested for advancement to driver. In addition to driving skills, Harry Hardwick also remembers that some firemen even gained knowledge of dismantling valves and coupling rods to prepare them for a failure of this mechanism whilst out on the road, these men benefiting from the skills of one particular fitter by the name of Bert Parry. However, this sort of tuition was probably the exception rather than the rule. Furthermore, back in 1926, the class of that year even clubbed together to buy a model of a two-cylinder locomotive for the sum of £26 which was subsequently used by instructors to demonstrate the more complex workings of the steam engine. The model used by Stourbridge MIC is now in Swindon Railway Museum.

The Mutual Improvement Class had quite a long history behind it and it is believed that at Stourbridge its existence went back to at least the last decade of the 19th century. This has been borne out by some very interesting remarks made by a Stourbridge driver, Bernard Corcoran, speaking at the annual dinner held for the Stourbridge Improvement Class at the Talbot Hotel, Stourbridge on 31st March, 1923. According to Mr Corcoran, the Stourbridge class, under the leadership of Harry Simpson, was the first to be formed in the country. The class gained a very good reputation and was so successful that it was said that Stourbridge had fewest failures at examinations of any station in the country. Mr Corcoran first attended a dinner for the class over 30 years before which suggests that the MIC had been formed as early as 1893 and probably earlier. Other surviving records seem to indicate that the Improvement Class had been suspended sometime around the turn of the century. This decision, however, seemed to be deeply unpopular with Stourbridge footplate crews. By 1906 the demand for the reintroduction of the MIC had gathered such momentum that by 29th April a deputation of senior enginemen had been formed whose aim was to persuade management of the value of the class and to identify and inspect a cabin in which the MIC could be held. These enginemen were C. Smith; C. Broughton; E. Andrews; A. Smout; L. Read; F. Mumford and F. Hull. Evidently these gentlemen argued their case very effectively for the Mutual Improvement Class was resurrected shortly afterwards. By 3rd February, 1926 the employees were pressing for a carriage body to be supplied, for use by the MIC, as a permanent location for their training sessions. The company though appeared reluctant to agree to this proposal and it was not until 2nd September, 1926 that they came up with an alternative which was to clean out and equip the mechanical staff's mess-room. Although not too popular with the men it would appear that this did become the MIC's classroom, at least until after the war. The room in question was located at the front of the line of cabins built on the right-hand side of the shed's outer wall. Besides this messroom

---

* The first two were certainly employed at the shed in the late 1930s, Bob Brown being the shed specialist on four-cylinder engines such as the 'Castles' and 'Stars' although neither class was ever represented on the allocation. The last two drivers go back even further, both were on the books in 1909, if not earlier.

there were, from front to rear, the enginemen's cabin; the fitters' and cleaners' cabin; the cookhouse; the boilerwashers' and tube cleaners' cabin, and at the far end, the toilets. By 25th June, 1946 the MIC had vacated this cabin, which subsequently became the first aid room, and moved into a redundant carriage that had been sited at the back of the shed. The main instructor after the war was Eric Webb, as Ray Kendrick recalls:

> What a man! It was said that if you could satisfy Eric on your competency the Sunday before you went to Swindon to pass out as a driver then you had little to fear when faced by the inspector. A lot of Stourbridge men owe a debt of gratitude to Eric for all the help he gave them.

In steam days two of the last instructors were Walter Smith and Bill Rowlands. Walter was an expert on slide valve locomotives; also the rules and regulations relating to railway operation. Bill, on the other hand, knew four-cylinder engines inside out.

As far as it is known the 'steam' class continued at Stourbridge shed until well into the 1960s, although late on numbers had decreased dramatically. Such was the situation that in December 1965 the MIC instructors were so concerned that young firemen were losing interest in attending classes that the subject had to be raised at a Local Departmental Committee (LDC) meeting. The employee representatives believed, probably correctly, that many firemen saw little future in remaining in an industry where depot closures and the introduction of single manning seemed to indicate that the railways had very little to offer by way of job security. With so few firemen taking the driver's examination the worry was that there would not be enough passed firemen at the shed to provide adequate cover for the remaining steam turns (steam was to be withdrawn from Stourbridge in July 1966).

Although interest in the 'steam' MIC had declined appreciably by the early 1960s there was, at the same time, an increasing demand for training on the non-driving elements of steam's successor at Stourbridge, the diesel locomotive and dmu. This sort of tuition had probably been carried out at the shed since the late 1950s when diesel shunters and diesel multiple units began to make a serious impact upon the number of steam turns worked by the shed. Certainly by the mid-1960s regular classes were being held at the 'old' shed on Thursday evenings with special classes on Sunday mornings, each session lasting for approximately 2 hours. One of these classes would study rules and regulations, the other, aspects of dieselisation. However, as more and more jobs were being turned over to diesel traction demand from the remaining footplate personnel for appropriate tuition began to outstrip the training resources available. In 1966 there had been just two instructors at the shed, a fact brought up at an LDC meeting that same year. Clearly management were sympathetic to the men's arguments as by the end of the year two more Stourbridge drivers, H. Attwood and V. Chapman, had been trained-up as instructors thereby easing the pressure on their colleagues. Unfortunately, pressures of a different sort were mounting as the MIC instructors were offered, in their opinion, totally inadequate classroom accommodation at Stourbridge Junction when all train crew were transferred there following closure of the steam sheds.

Post War Organisation Chart of Stourbridge Shed (84F)

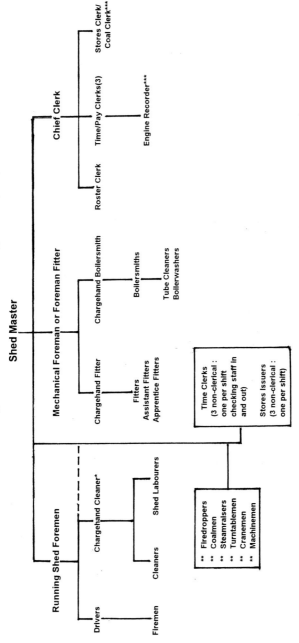

Shed Master

Running Shed Foremen

Drivers

Firemen

Chargehand Cleaner*

Cleaners

Shed Labourers

Time Clerks
(3 non-clerical :
one per shift
checking staff in
and out)

Stores Issuers
(3 non-clerical :
one per shift)

** Firedroppers
** Coalmen
** Steamraisers
** Turntablemen
** Cranemen
** Machinemen

Mechanical Foreman or Foreman Fitter

Chargehand Fitter

Fitters
Assistant Fitters
Apprentice Fitters

Chargehand Boilersmith

Boilersmiths

Tube Cleaners
Boilerwashers

Chief Clerk

Roster Clerk

Time/Pay Clerks(3)

Engine Recorder***

Stores Clerk/
Coal Clerk***

*In the early 1950s there were two posts covering early and late shifts, but with fewer cleaners, only one position was probably filled later in the decade (?)

**It is not totally clear as to whom these groups, and the two non-clerical groups, were officially responsible to. It is thought that it might have been the Shed Master, but operational necessity probably meant that in practice it was one of the foremen.

***These two posts may have been dispensed with by the early 1950s, the coal clerk's duties being taken over by the stores clerk (?)

Produced with the help of C.R.Kendrick and D.Beech

Grandfather and grandson (perhaps) stand in front of 'Modified Hall' class 4-6-0 No. 7922 *Salford Hall* in Stourbridge roundhouse on 10th November, 1963.

Joe Moss/R.S. Carpenter

As early as January 1965 it had been proposed that a classroom be included in the new administrative block to be built at Stourbridge Junction, however, after the closure of the shed, work had still not begun on the new building, consequently the MIC had to be found temporary accommodation (presumably at the shed). By November 1966 there still had not been a decision as to where the MIC was to be held although shortly afterwards Management did suggest the conference room in the new block and whilst this was far from ideal it was at least a start, although the LDC was soon campaigning for somewhere more suitable. To back up their arguments the chairman of the MIC, J.H. Thatcher, was invited to address an LDC meeting held on 24th February, 1967. It was pointed out that the class ideally required two rooms each measuring 15 feet by 12 feet, the conference room being too small to accommodate the increasing number of staff now wishing to attend the classes. Shortly afterwards the class was given the redundant office in the old marshalling yard. However, as the yard area was being redeveloped this was only a temporary measure and soon the class was on the move again. Henry Holloway, the station manager, suggested the now empty district inspector's office on the station platform and although this was agreed it is not clear if this was ever used. As no more information has been found relating to any further travels of the MIC it may be assumed that the instructors accepted their lot and decided to make the best out of a bad job.

Signalling at the Shed

Engine movements into and out of Stourbridge engine sheds were controlled by Engine Shed signal box located on the down side of the main line just to the south of Engine Shed sidings and the engine shed reception lines. The signal box was open continuously and controlled the sections between Brettell Lane and Stourbridge North Junction which included both up and down main lines; the carriage sidings; the engine shed lines themselves; the up goods loop, and John Hall's sidings. The box held 33 levers which operated all points, post-mounted signals, and ground signals apart from two up distant signals positioned beneath the up main starting and up main advanced starting signals which were controlled by the Stourbridge North signalman. The signalman at Engine Shed box was responsible for five home or starting signals controlling traffic on both main lines as well as a left-hand bracket signal guarding the entrance to the up goods loop and a left-hand bracket signal at the entrance to the down sidings. He also worked two distant signals, one at 434 yards on the down side, the other at 880 yards on the up side. Some 378 yards beyond the up worked distant was a fixed distant positioned below Brettell Lane's up main starter. *Circa* April 1961 this signal, plus Engine Shed's up main worked distant, were replaced by a single, three aspect colour light signal located at 1,158 yards from Engine Shed box. In addition to the main line signals there were three that controlled engine movements in the downside sidings and the locomotive yard and a starting signal at the end of the up goods loop where there was a head shunt. There was also a shunt-ahead arm fixed below the up main advanced starting signal at 234 yards.

In addition to the post-mounted signals were 10 ground signals including two on both up and down main lines in which each pair were operated by a single lever (levers 24 and 11 respectively). Lever No. 24, for example, activated the ground signals which allowed movements from up main to up goods loop (Stourbridge Junction end) or from up main to down main (crossover) or to down sidings. There were also nine sets of points, the two facing points on the main lines being guarded by facing point locks, each lock being operated by a separate lever. In March 1961 John Hall's siding was closed and the points and the siding's ground signal were taken out of use. Levers 25 and 27 were therefore 'spare'. On the up and down main lines, just to the north of the signal box, were two detonator placers operated by a small two-lever ground frame. The points allowing access from the north end of Engine Shed sidings to the down main line were also controlled by a ground frame. This was kept locked, the key having to be obtained from the signalman at Engine Shed signal box. In the late 1960s a number of changes took place which eventually eliminated the need for a signal box at Engine Shed sidings. First, all five carriage sidings were taken out of use on 21st February, 1968. This was followed by the removal in 1969 of fuelling and stabling facilities from the engine sheds. Finally, the up goods loop was taken out of use on 11th May, 1969 the same day that Engine Shed signal box was closed down.

Chapter Two

Shed and Footplate Staff

A Career on the Footplate

In the days of steam it was the dream of many a young lad to become an engine driver. But what was the attraction of the job? Was it the outward glamour of being in charge of a powerful and shining steam engine that could effortlessly convey its train to some distant city or resort? Perhaps it was its shape and design; or the sound as it pulled away from the station; it might have been the sight and smell of steam and smoke? Could anyone wish for a more exciting career than being on the footplate of such an awesome beast? Perhaps not, but the truth of the matter was that engine driving was not the glamorous occupation young minds thought it was; far from it in fact. The picture that engine driving conjured up in many young minds was more romantic than real and, for the majority of drivers, being on the footplate of some prestigious express engine was an event only enjoyed by a relative few. But whether it was a humble freight engine or a powerful 'Pacific' these drivers certainly had one thing in common: they had all learnt their trade over many years, gaining an essential depth of experience as their careers passed through a number of different stages. Those that did decide to join the industry, and had set their sights upon a career on the footplate, soon found that any romantic notions that may have lingered from childhood were swept away by the harsh realities of life on the railway. Prospective engine drivers faced a long and hard apprenticeship, one that began on the bottommost rung of the promotion ladder. This chapter examines, amongst other things, the first stage of that engineman's apprenticeship : the years as an engine cleaner.

The first step taken by the would-be engine driver was to be appointed to a cleaning vacancy in the Locomotive Department at one of the local engine sheds. This was, in effect, the start of the apprenticeship for it was here that the basic skills of the engineman were learnt. New entrants to the service had to be under 18 years of age and all were subject to interview and a very strict eyesight test. It would not do for young men with poor eyesight to be employed as in a locomotive shed lurked many dangers: engines on the move; deep inspection pits; badly lit walkways often obstructed with tools and equipment, and other hazards which those that have experienced the dimly lit confines of a shed such as Stourbridge could readily identify. The new cleaner had to be physically fit and had to undergo a comprehensive medical examination to prove it. When all the formalities had been satisfied, his career began to take shape. If the lad showed promise he would soon be allowed on to the footplate to learn about steam engines and how to fire them. Then, after getting a few firing turns under his belt, he would be ready to take the first step up the promotion ladder to fireman and a permanent job on the footplate. On promotion to firemen it was usual to take the first vacancy which arose even if this was far from the 'home' shed. When a fireman was required to move away he was allowed to make an

'Bulldog' class 4-4-0 No. 3405 *Mauritius* outside Stourbridge shed *circa* 1928. Shedmaster Mr Dovaston is second from the right.

E. Potts-Perkins Collection

application to return as soon as a position arose as will be seen later in Ray Kendrick's narrative of his own firing experiences. However, promotion to driver remained for most many years in the future. But the years of working with skilled men paid off for this produced the next generation of equally skilled footplatemen. Ray Kendrick was a Stourbridge driver who spent most of his working life at the shed and later, the train crew depot. Ray began his career as a cleaner at Stourbridge in the dark days of World War II; it is his story that will open the chapter.

Cleaning Days at Stourbridge - A young man's story

Having left school at the age of 14, my first job was with D. & F. Fellows in Stourbridge. However, I decided that the railway was to be the career for me and in December 1941 I applied for a cleaning job at Stourbridge engine shed. Just gone 15, I was a little nervous when I went into shedmaster Tom Dovaston's office for the interview. I must have acquitted myself well, for having answered his questions and successfully passing the eyesight test (this consisted of distinguishing different colour wools to determine colour blindness and reading letters on a wall-chart) I was offered a job. So on 28th December, 1941 off I went down to Swindon to take the medical. Unfortunately, the medical officer was unaware that the minimum age for a cleaner was soon to be dropped to 15 so on arrival I was promptly told that I was too young! Returning to Stourbridge was a tedious affair; trains were running late due to the war, and a missed connection caused me to spend a night on Snow Hill station during an air raid. Next morning, tired and dispirited, I eventually arrived home to relate to my worried parents the events of the previous day. I was now without a job, but thankfully not for long as in January the GWR officially reduced the starting age for cleaners to 15 due to manpower shortages brought about by men being called-up for the armed forces. So although I had yet to be formally passed medically fit, Tom Dovaston allowed me to start on 2nd February, 1942. Two weeks later, Swindon sent for me again and this time I took the medical and having been passed fit, I paid my five shillings dues to join the Great Western Railway Enginemen's and Firemen's Mutual Assurance Sick and Superannuation Society (quite a mouthful) or to put it a little more succinctly, the railwaymen's pension fund. With my GWR issue overalls tucked under my arm, I returned to Stourbridge in much better spirits than on the last occasion; I was now to begin a career that was to span the rest of my working life.

On the first morning I met up with another cleaner, Ray Perks, who accompanied me across Stambermill viaduct into the shed and over to the booking-on point where I was introduced to the time clerk who handed me a brass disc with a number on it, this was my official employee registration number. The time clerk, having booked me on, emphasised that this disc had to be returned when I booked off in order that my hours could be recorded. The formalities completed, I was taken over to the cleaners' cabin to meet my new work mates (at around this time there were about 26 cleaners on the books working two shifts); many of these lads continued as colleagues for the next 46 years. Introductions over, I was taken to the chargeman cleaner's office where Alf Weedner, a bit of a hard one by all accounts, was waiting to allocate my first job. This done, and armed with the cleaner's standard equipment, a ½ lb piece of oily cotton waste, I was set to work cleaning the motion and frames on No. 5136, a 2-6-2 Prairie tank that had first arrived at the shed during 1939. However, not long after starting at the shed I found that I was being called upon to carry out other duties, some quite far removed from engine cleaning. Why I was picked I don't know, but it certainly added some variety to the working day. During my time away from cleaning I was at times assigned messenger duties taking notes to footplatemen advising them of a change of turn or booking-on time; there were no telephones then! On other occasions I would help out booking men on and off. This and other general office duties occupied me, off and on, for about the next 12 months, until female clerks took over the work and I was reassigned to engine cleaning. During my time in the office I usually could be found working to the instructions of the chief clerk, Harry Whitehouse, or Bob Reynolds, the roster clerk. Also in the offices in 1942 was Bill Reynolds, one of the pay and time clerks; Alf Walker, who helped out when not too busy mending watches; and Frank Steele, who would later become chief clerk (there also may have been a Mr Read). Sadly, in 1942, Tom Dovaston died at the age of 63 and was succeeded by Walter Morris. Tom Dovaston was buried at Stourbridge churchyard not far from his predecessor, John Preece, who died in 1931 at the age of 73. In the office I worked a 12 hour shift, 6.00 am to 6.00 pm and at one time I did this for three months running, every day including Sundays without having a day off! The night shift clerk in the office worked the same hours and at the time this duty was carried out by F. Goddard. As I was still 15 years of age I was only allowed to do the day shift. I wonder what today's 15 year olds would think of these hours?

The stint in the offices finished early in 1943 and I rejoined my mates on the cleaning side working a normal 40 hour week, Monday to Friday, plus a 4 hour shift on Saturday morning. At this time cleaners always worked in teams of four and if we were working upon a 2-6-2T, we were allowed one hour to do the whole engine, and two hours if it was a tender engine. The team would be split into two, one set would work on the motion and frames whilst the others would be up above cleaning the boiler, cab, bunker or tender. However, roles would be reversed on the next engine. Sometimes a driver might ask one of us to go under the engine and do the oiling. This saved him from getting dirty whilst the cleaner got absolutely filthy. I probably didn't think it at the time but on reflection it was all part of the learning process, as was climbing onto the footplate to help the fireman prepare the fire. Some of the senior drivers still retained their 'own' engines and most took great pride in the appearance of these machines and it was not unusual for them to insist on cleaners paying special attention to the brass safety valves, whistles, and the copper rings around the chimney, getting them not only clean but sparkling. If we did a good job the driver might reward us with a shilling, quite a lot in those days.

Although, of course, I was officially an engine cleaner, on occasion the management at the shed decided that other jobs took priority, especially if there was a shortage of labour, as there often was during the war. As a result, my fellow cleaners and I were regularly called upon to carry out a wide variety of tasks. For example, one of the jobs that would be given to us was the particularly dirty one of cleaning out the ash pits. Usually, two cleaners were instructed to assist two labourers to load, by hand, the wagons on the ash pit road. Here, the dropped fires of around 25 to 30 engines had to be cleared, as well as the material from ash pans and smokeboxes. All this in an 8 hour shift. I think some of the older hands would take advantage of the inexperienced cleaner who could often find himself doing a little more than his fair share of the work! Another job involved coal stacking. This was a task for the summer months in case of a coal shortage later on in the year caused by bad weather, or perhaps even a coal strike. This work developed a young cleaner's muscles, each of us being expected to move about 12 tons per day from the coal wagons to the stack. Although this was very hard work for a 15 or 16 year old it certainly prepared us for the rigours of firing, building up stamina and teaching us to use a shovel with either hand. Cleaners employed on this job would be supervised by a shedman and be paid a labourer's rate, a small but welcome increase on our meagre cleaner's wages. In the shed, two night shift cleaners might fill locomotive water tanks using a hose attached to a stand pipe. This meant that engines would not have to wait at the water columns and could therefore get off shed a lot quicker next morning. On the night shift, cleaners worked from 10.00 pm to 7.00 am (including a one hour meal break). During the war there was always a fear of enemy air raids, consequently, these lads would be on stand-by ready to damp down fires dropped into the ash pit so that the glow would not be spotted by any sharp-eyed German pilot who happened to be flying overhead. It was during the war that ladies were employed on shed duties, in particular cleaning up around the shed. In 1944, Italian POWs were drafted in to work as labourers. This led to a rumour or two suggesting that their activities were more inclined towards sweeping the ladies off their feet rather than sweeping the shed floor. At busy times cleaners might help the coalmen working on the 'new' coalstage; this was another hard job and after a shift of loading coal into the tubs and tipping them into bunkers or tenders, or emptying the coal wagons, the lads really had earned their corn! We also used to crack the large lumps of coal with a coal pick so that they would not block the shovelling hole, a problem often encountered on bunker-fitted engines. However the warmest job was undoubtedly going into an engine's firebox to replace fire bars that had been lifted up when the fire had been cleaned. Unless the engine was stone cold, a cleaner would emerge soaked with sweat, for it would only take a small amount of steam in the boiler to make the firebox hot and claustrophobic. Can you imagine what it was like, on a bitterly cold winter's night, to be one minute working in the sticky and confined space of a firebox, then immediately afterwards to be told that you were needed outside, up on the coal-stage?

In the winter months cleaners were often required to keep an eye on the braziers which were put near the water columns in the shed yard in an attempt to stop them freezing up. This was usually a fireman's responsibility, but if there were none available, cleaners did the work. However, even if the fires were well maintained the water bags would sometimes freeze solid, making it very difficult to put them into the tanks. To soften them up we would hit them with coal picks. In general all the cleaners were asked to perform a wide range of duties: assisting the storemen, fitters, boilerwashers, coalmen, firedroppers, steamraisers, tube cleaners and the turntable men, in fact becoming a 'jack of all trades' (but master of none); it did though ensure that much valuable knowledge would be gained which would hold us in good stead in later years.

Meal breaks were usually taken 'on shed' and this was an opportunity to sample some of the delights provided in the cookhouse next to the cleaners' cabin. When bacon and eggs were brought to work (not too often due to wartime shortages) these would be fried by the resident cook Joe Garrat. In those days there were few rules governing the handling and preparing of food and no one objected to Joe standing over his frying pan, often with a cigarette in his mouth, and ash falling into the fat, in a far from spotless cookhouse. I don't think it did us too much harm; perhaps we were hardened to it after working in the grime and smoke of the shed? We also provided potatoes, these often coming from illicit forays into nearby fields. Forsaking the skills of Joe in the cookhouse, these potatoes would be roasted on the stove or even on an engine's safety valves if a loco in steam happened to be nearby. We also cooked onions this way. However, using the safety valves to cook our meals was a little risky, especially if the engine in question got up too much steam. Then the valves would lift depositing our supper onto the underside of the shed roof. Nearby farmers also provided supplies of milk, although they did not, of course, know it. If this commodity was in short supply in the messroom, someone with the necessary know-how would be dispatched to the nearest field containing a cow or two to furtively milk the beasts!

Cleaners were also employed on the 'call-up', that is the practice of going round to the houses of footplate crews on early morning turns to ensure that they got up in time to book on. This task fell to the night shift cleaners and those on this work would have to start at midnight on Sunday calling-up footplate crews for the early Monday morning turns. There were four areas covered: Wollaston; Brettell Lane; The Bank (Enville Street/Beauty

Bank and all the Stourbridge men); and Lye, one 'call-up' to an area. Each call-boy would knock on the door until they received a response. However, this was no guarantee that the men would not go back to sleep, which sometimes did happen with the result that the call-up lad would get the blame for a driver or fireman arriving late for his turn. One chap had his own system for proving that he had called. This was to wake up the next door neighbour and tell him that he had called the driver or fireman in question. Obviously, this did not make this particular call-boy very popular. By and large, the 'call-up' was quite an efficient system for getting men to work on time and, with about 20 calls to be made per round on a busy night, there was rarely time to hang around; but sometimes we did. Being on 'call up' duties was quite lonely, however we soon got to know any night-watchman in the area and we would stop for a chat and, if we were lucky, a hot cup of tea. In bad weather, call-boys were issued with cape and leggings, whilst two of the rounds were each allocated a company bicycle, not always the most reliable of machines, especially the paraffin lamps which were always going out. This often got us into trouble with the local beat 'bobby' who would regularly report us for riding without lights.

I seem to recall a story that in the 1920s, a bicycle was issued to the call-boy who worked the Lye area. By the winter of 1924, this machine was badly in need of repair. Although the management agreed to the repairs, they did so in the hope that the machine would be better looked after in the future. Apparently, three years later, in September 1927, the company reached into its pockets again and provided a second bicycle; such generosity! In the 1940s any repairs to these bicycles, such as punctures etc, would be carried out by Bill Lane who was a shedman at the time. He was also one of the men in charge of the two stationary boilers that provided all the power to the shed's machinery, as well as hot water for boiler washing. If Bill was for some reason called away, and was therefore unable to maintain the boilers, the task was allocated to a fireman. Unfortunately, on occasion, Bill's replacement would not be up to the task and consequently would make a bit of a hash of firing these boilers. This did not do the man's firing reputation any good at all with the result that his ability to fire 'out on the road' would be called into question.

There were some compensations for the call-boy, especially if there was an orchard on the round. These would be subject to many a night time visit from call-boys anxious to supplement the sandwiches their mothers had provided. One night, one of my fellow cleaners, Reg Hill, had gone scrumping and when he returned to the shed he offered an apple to toolman Joe Smith. Joe took a couple of bites and said to Reg 'nice, but not as good as mine'. What he did not know was that they *were* his! Joe never worked out why some of us had knowing grins on our faces for the rest of the shift. Lads do tend to play tricks and cleaners at Stourbridge were no exception. I well remember one chap having his shoe laces tied together and a piece of smouldering paper shoved under his nose. The response was of course very comical to those in the know. Another trick was to drop a detonator down the chimney on the stove. As soon as that unmistakable rattle was heard there would be a mad scramble for the door as anyone left in the cabin when the detonator went off would be covered in soot and ash. At the time the culprit had little thought for the consequences of his actions especially the possibility of setting fire to the cabin. I also have known cleaners locked in the fireboxes of engines; very frightening, claustrophobic, dark and dirty!

Considering the environment there were relatively few accidents to employees in the shed, however, some did occur, but as most were minor they could usually be treated in the first aid room. In the event of a fire on shed, a very real possibility given the nature of the work, a 'Merryweather' fire engine was on stand-by to deal with it, although 'deal with it' are perhaps not quite the right words. This piece of fire equipment was in fact steam powered and when there was a fire drill it would take quite some time to get it ready for action. I often wondered if it was put to the test, whether or not the blaze would have burned itself out before sufficient steam power could be raised to make the equipment work?

After a time, and having got to know my way around, I was asked one evening by the shed driver to climb up onto the footplate and get some experience stabling locomotives; under very close supervision of course, for great care had to be taken because accidents could easily happen even if engines were in the hands of experienced men. When a cleaner had accumulated sufficient experience to be considered for promotion, then, and only then, would he be allowed to move an engine without supervision. Helping the fireman to prepare his engine for the road was also part of a young cleaner's education, in particular how to make up a fire; its shape, and how to feed coal onto it, thereby learning how to get the best results from a particular type of firebox. Firing was an art in itself and it was not just a case of shovelling coal willy nilly and hoping for the best! Cleaners also became familiar with the function of dampers, blower, steam injectors, fire irons, etc. so when we ventured out on our first firing turns at least we would have a reasonable idea what the driver was referring to when an instruction came to 'drop the dampers' or 'put the injector on' or 'use the blower'. Some drivers, and as far as I can recall these were the exceptions, were not always tolerant of a novice fireman's efforts; most, though, were sympathetic and took time and trouble to put a struggling cleaner right. They remembered that they too had had to learn!!

Seniority was at the centre of any railwayman's career and this was as true for cleaners as any other footplate grade. After about six months in the shed, cleaners could be called upon to carry out a firing turn on a 'Jacko' (shunting engine), if the regular fireman was absent or covering another turn. However, it was seniority which decided which cleaner would take the first turn. These firing opportunities provided both extra pay and invaluable experience. Shunting work was all that the cleaner did before passing out as a fireman, in my case at the age of 17 which was the minimum age agreed, I think, in July 1943. The railway company was very keen on firemen gaining experience on shunting work; it provided essential training and prepared them for the main line. I seem to recall that during the war, the company was very concerned that firemen were going out onto the main line with very little experience behind them. Cleaning was the railway's equivalent of the first stage of an apprenticeship. Once this was satisfactorily completed, usually after about two years, a cleaner would have accumulated sufficent knowledge and expertise to be considered for promotion onto the next rung of the ladder. In 1944, I passed out as a fireman following a medical examination taken at Cardiff; the next chapter of my career on the footplate was about to begin.

Ray Kendrick's story provides a detailed insight into what life was like for cleaners during and after World War II. However, it is also possible to turn the clock back even further to obtain a glimpse of engine cleaning at Stourbridge some 20 odd years earlier. For this it is necessary to refer to some surviving records and the little known book written by the late Harry Hardwick, one of Stourbridge's best known enginemen. Life for the cleaners at Stourbridge, and at any other shed for that matter, was clearly hard, tiring and dirty, with long and unsociable hours. Harry Hardwick, who joined the railway in April 1918 as a 17-year-old cleaner at Stourbridge shed, remembers that cleaning duties just after the 1914-1918 war comprised a day and a night shift, each shift rotating on a fortnightly basis. Before the eight hour day was introduced in 1919, the early shift worked from 7.00 am to 5.30 pm, Monday to Friday, and 7.00 am to 12.30 pm Saturday (including meal breaks). The night shift worked from 7.00 pm to 6.00 am, Monday evening to Saturday morning. On Saturday nights two call-boys were on duty for the Sunday morning calls. When on nights the junior cleaners were utilised on the 'call-up', visiting homes of drivers and firemen between the hours of midnight and 6.00 am. Reg Lamb, who joined the Great

Above: '57XX' class 0-6-0T No. 4646 outside Stourbridge shed *circa* 1960s. Driver Ray Kendrick (*right*) is accompanied on the footplate by fireman Steve Totney. *Ray Kendrick Collection*

Right: Reg Lamb on the footplate of '28XX' 2-8-0 No. 3838 in the carriage sidings adjacent to Stourbridge engine shed *circa* 1960. *R. Lamb Collection*

Western Railway at the age of 16½, also remembers acting as call-boy when employed as a cleaner between 1930 and 1936 at Stourbridge shed:

One night a senior cleaner, Joe Broughton, said to me, 'Come on Reg, I'll get you used to the dark'. I was just 18 and was soon to go out on my first 'call-up' turn. The night shift was from 10.00 pm to 7.00 am, with a one hour meal break taken between two and three o'clock in the morning, although those on the 'call-up' started at 11.00 pm and worked through to 7.00 am without an official break. Anyway, back to my expedition with Joe. We got our coats and off we went, out of the shed and along the main line to the 'Good Friday' bridge (a wooden structure in those days, not the one that's there today) and up to the 'Birch Tree' public house. There were few if any street lamps in those days and in the blackness of the night it was quite an experience fumbling along at this unearthly hour. Still, as Joe said, it got me used to the night. One 'call-up' was with a lad called George Evans. We were walking back through the new council housing estate off Park Road; many of the houses were complete but unoccupied and as we were very cold, we decided to go into one of them and light a fire in the grate. As we sat there trying to get some warmth into our bones, the local 'Bobby' poked his head into the room giving us quite a scare. Luckily, he was an understanding bloke and knew we were doing no harm; he just told us to keep a look-out for the sergeant. I often wondered what the builders thought when they came to work next morning to find the cold embers of our fire still lying in the grate. Before going out on the 'call-up' we would go into the office and see the clerk to get our list of 'calls'. As well as 'calling-up' our own drivers and firemen, we also had to go to the lodgings to get the visiting crews up. One such crew worked a Pontypool Road double home turn which would leave Stourbridge Junction between 2.30 and 3.00 in the morning.

The tools provided for the cleaner were very basic, just a piece of cotton waste soaked in paraffin, and occasionally a scraper for those difficult jobs on the motion. From this fairly primitive equipment some drivers expected very high standards to be achieved. One particularly onerous cleaning job recalled by Harry Hardwick was that involving No. 940, a class '927' 0-6-0 tender engine allocated to Stourbridge shed *circa* 1910. According to Harry this engine had a dome as big as St Paul's which took a lot of 'elbow grease' to reach the high standard of cleanliness insisted upon by the engine's regular driver, Arthur Aimes. Apparently Arthur also insisted that his fireman polished the fall-plate between engine and tender even though out on the road it would soon be covered in coal dust! As mentioned above, cleaners would also be employed on other duties besides engine cleaning. Harry Hardwick in his book *The Magic of Steam* remembered a couple of jobs cleaners did when the regular staff were not available:

Cleaners were often used for other shed duties if the permanent shed staff were off through sickness, holidays etc. That meant an extra penny or two an hour so it was the senior cleaners who had these jobs, jobs such as shovelling ashes out of engine smoke boxes, getting into fire boxes to put the firebars back into place after the fire dropper had knocked the fire out through the ashpan. That was indeed a very hot few minutes and they were always glad to scramble out through the firehole.

Reg Lamb also recalls a couple of tasks he was asked to do:

One day boilersmith Billy Horton asked me if I would help him out. It was not unusual for cleaners to assist the boilersmiths, or for that matter the boilerwashers, tubecleaners

Harry Hardwick at Stourbridge Junction in June 1964.   *Birmingham Post & Mail*

Driver Albert Homer of Stourbridge shed leans out of the cab of 'Grange' class 4-6-0 No. 6837
Forthampton Grange on an excursion to Rhyl at Dudley on 18th May, 1964.   *G. Bennett*

etc. as it was all part of our training, however, what Bill asked me to do was too much even for a willing hand like myself. In the early 1930s, Stourbridge shed still had a few steam railmotors. These machines had a vertical boiler in the firing compartment and the firebox had quite a small firing hole. Bill, I think, had to do a job on the tube plate and wanted someone else to get into the firebox to carry it out. When I saw the size of the hole he wanted me to clamber through I was far from happy. Bill was quite a small man; much more suited to the job than me and that is what I told him. On the subject of the railmotors, my father used to drive these machines on the Stourbridge Town branch. I would be 7 or 8 at the time, and I would accompany him in the firing compartment. I could then easily hide behind the boiler if anyone in authority happened to be around when we drew into the Town or Junction platforms.

Ernie Payton and Albert Homer who started at the shed in 1934 and 1929 respectively, also remember some non-engine cleaning jobs they had to do:

When the shed had its steam railmotors, cleaners on the night shift sometimes helped the coalmen to coal these over at the stage at the 'old' shed. These machines could not be coaled in the usual way so the company had to have built a special coal-stage whose platform was level with the floor of the boiler compartment of the motor. The coal was delivered by wagon and had to be unloaded by hand.

Ernie also recalls: 'Another task was to throw sand on the line to Amblecote goods yard in the winter as this was such a steep gradient'. Albert though, found himself occasionally assisting the shed's water fitter, Tommy Dance:

One job was the maintenance and repair of water columns, the type with the cylindrical tank attached. Tommy used to climb up the ladder and do what was necessary while I stood underneath passing up the tools. I think there were at least six of this type of column in the area; one at Dudley; Rowley; Old Hill station; Amblecote goods yard, and two in Stourbridge yard [see The Railways of Stourbridge pp. 29, 30, 96, 102 and 252].

Reg Lamb continues:

One very hot summer a couple of us were asked to clean the inside of the water tank on top of the coal-stage and paint it with red oxide. We had to climb up the long metal ladder that was attached to the outside and then walk round the top of the tank to the hatch. Inside the tank was another ladder which we had to climb down. It was so hot in there that the paint dried as soon as it was applied. The atmosphere was awful and we had to take regular breaks. I think that was the worst job I was given as a cleaner. Another bad job, but for totally different reasons, was having to go to Corbett hospital to collect some personal effects. These had belonged to Mr Fletcher, a Stourbridge driver who had been knocked down and killed on the main line. He was walking to the shed to start his shift when he was hit by auto-engine No. 2158 which was returning after working the Town service.

By August 1919 agreement had been reached to pay cleaners 16 years and under 4 shillings per day; those 17 years and under 5 shillings per day; 18 and 19 year olds received 6 shillings per day and those 20 and over 7 shillings per day. In the same year, the company agreed to supply overalls to their footplate crews although it was much longer before this concession was extended to cleaners. Consequently, cleaners had to provide their own working clothes and these came in all shapes and sizes, many were of course cast-offs from other male members of the family. As Ray Kendrick points out above, cleaners were usually considered for promotion to fireman after around two years, however, there were in the 1920s some major exceptions. Many demobilised soldiers recruited after the end of the war, because of their age, were often promoted after only a few months cleaning. Moreover, during the depression of the late 1920s and early 1930s, promotion slowed down greatly and with the shortage of jobs many men opted to remain cleaners for the rest of their time in the service. Reg Lamb has already mentioned Joe Broughton who joined the company as a cleaner at Stourbridge in 1921. Joe remained in that post for the next 13 years when, in 1934, he was made up to fireman. One long time cleaner, Stan Bates, had a nice little side line. Apparently he owned a horse and flat bed cart which he used for delivering fruit and veg in the Amblecote area when not engaged upon cleaning duties. At night he would graze the horse on some waste land near the MIC coach. On the late shift, some of the young cleaners decided to play a joke on the chargehand cleaner who was fast asleep in his office. Untying Stan's horse, they led the animal through the shed and into the office. The air was blue when he awoke to find that he had been sharing his dreams with Stan's old cart horse.

It was rare for an engine from another shed to be cleaned by Stourbridge men but Harry Hardwick does remember this happening on one occasion. It was probably in 1918, Harry's first year as a cleaner, when an ambulance train arrived at Stourbridge headed by 'Atbara' 4-4-0 No. 4138, the name *White* and the engine's number proudly displayed on an oval-shaped plate fixed to the sides of the cab. Harry states: 'I think the foreman cleaner Alf Weedner was rather sentimental and had it cleaned because it was pulling an ambulance train'. Whatever the reason, it would have been a nice gesture as *White* would undoubtedly have left with another ambulance train full of convalescing troops on their way home from a spell in Wordsley Military Hospital.

Circa 1920 and Stourbridge shed was experiencing such a severe shortage of cleaning staff that the management had become inundated with complaints about dirty engines, some of which had gone as long as a week without an 'oily patch' (cotton waste soaked in paraffin) being laid upon them. Apparently, only about half of Stourbridge's cleaning posts were filled which meant that there were about 19 vacancies. To fill these jobs, men from all over the Great Western were recruited, several coming from such sheds as Banbury and Oxford (to combat the shortages the GWR attempted to recruit demobilised servicemen up to the age of 24). The beginning of 1924 saw an experiment carried out which was aimed at improving the efficiency of the cleaning staff. It would seem that the late shift, covering afternoon and early evenings, was suspended and replaced by a night shift (presumably the latter had been withdrawn in favour of the former earlier in the decade?). The new shift pattern began at midnight Sunday to 9.00 am Monday and then 10.00 pm to 7.00 am Monday to Friday with a one hour meal break. Introduced on 3rd February, 1924 the experiment was seen to be a success with engines being cleaned to a much higher standard. These arrangements possibly only lasted until late November 1927 when a Stourbridge LDC proposal to review the cleaners' hours was agreed by Mr

Giles, the divisional superintendent at Wolverhampton. The new working arrangements involved a day shift from 6.00 am to 3.30 pm, Monday to Friday, with one hour for lunch, and 6.00 am to noon on Saturday with ½ hour meal break (48 hours per week). The late turn (this replaced the night shift) would come on at 3.00 pm and work to midnight, Monday to Saturday with one hour meal break. This too represented a 48 hour week. By the beginning of the 1930s rail traffic handled by the GWR was in decline, thereby forcing the company to take a long hard look at manning levels at its locomotive sheds. There was a proposal to make many cleaners redundant and demoting junior firemen to cleaning and junior drivers to firemen. However, after much discussion and negotiation an alternative plan was adopted whereby senior drivers over 60 years of age would be gradually retired. Whilst this process lost to Stourbridge a considerable number of its skilled and experienced men, it did protect cleaning jobs and there was no demotion of footplate crews. Reg Lamb remembers firing to the last Stourbridge driver to retire under this scheme, Gus Drury.

Firemen and Drivers

Every fireman began his career on the footplate of the shunting engines where he would learn how to shape the fire so that it burnt in such a way as to generate the necessary amount of steam to drive the engine. Different engines had to be fired in different ways and the young fireman would pick up these ways by watching the driver handle the shovel or listening to his verbal instructions. On the shunting engines the fireman would also be shown how to regulate the quantity of air passing into the firebox so as to minimize smoke emission by burning it rather than blasting it out from the chimney into the atmosphere. The production of black smoke was certainly frowned upon; it was evidence of bad firing practice and the perpetrator would be subject to a few critical comments. However, if dirty smoke was picked up by a loco inspector travelling on the footplate the crew could find themselves in trouble. Whilst the inspector might say very little to the driver directly, he could decide to report the incident with the result that the driver would have his knuckles rapped.The fireman would not be too popular either. As well as having his firing technique improved, the fireman would often receive instruction from the driver on how the engine actually worked, this tuition being formalized through the depot's Mutual Improvement Class.

Reg Lamb was a fireman at Stourbridge in the 1930s as he now recalls:

I passed as a fireman in 1936 having gained experience firing whilst working as a cleaner in the six years prior to my promotion. I started in the shunting link, then the bank links, the double home link and eventually I was firing in the passenger link to such men as George Bennett, a senior driver whose engine was No. 5160 a 2-6-2T Prairie, a lovely engine which he kept in immaculate condition. I fired to George for a long time working local passenger trains to Worcester, Birmingham (Snow Hill), Leamington Spa, Stratford-upon-Avon, Wolverhampton, and even Wellington. When George retired he said to his fellow drivers, 'You can forget about the water, and you'll never need to

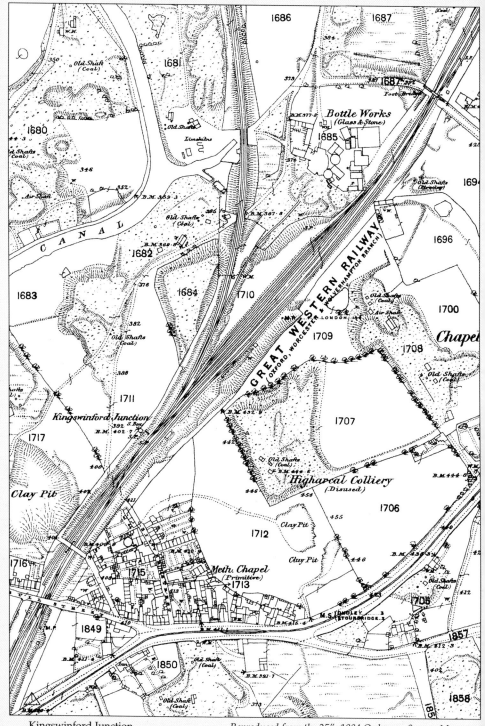

Kingswinford Junction.

Reproduced from the 25", 1884 Ordnance Survey Map

check the gauges, Reg will always tell you if there's a problem'. Another driver I fired to was Fred Tonks and one day we were on the Tenbury Wells goods train which also conveyed empty cattle wagons. Now Fred was also a good driver who made sure that his fireman fired to his liking. On this occasion I think we had a '5700' and he said to me, 'Remember Reg, one in each corner followed by four in the middle'. I once tried to put an extra one on but Fred saw me and gave the shovel a kick. I obeyed his instructions to the letter from then on. This was often a long job from early in the morning until late at night. On arrival at Tenbury Wells (the cattle market operated fortnightly) we had to shunt two or three wagons into the cattle sidings for the drovers to fill up. We would then pull them out and put another two or three in until the train had been made up. On the way back we might drop off at Kidderminster before continuing to Stourbridge yard. One driver who taught me a lot about how engines actually worked was Harold Taylor. He always managed to find the time to answer my questions with patience and understanding. If he couldn't explain a particular point on the footplate he would, at the first convenient location, get down from the cab and show me at the track-side. When I became a driver, I always tried to teach my firemen in the same way that I had been taught. Drivers, such as those mentioned above, were excellent men to work with; they taught me a lot. It was their methods which I passed on to my firemen.

Shunting the many yards and railway connected works such as John Hall's brickworks, located opposite Stourbridge shed, and the Dreadnought tile works in Pensnett, represented a significant proportion of the turns worked by the shed and of course there were the marshalling yards at Kingswinford Junction and Stourbridge Junction to shunt as well. One job which Ray Williams remembers was the Himley trip working and the works along the way:

We used to go into the Dreadnought tile works and have our tea cans filled for ½d., as well as being able to get a good cheap meal. However, going into the brickworks could be a horrendous experience for a young fireman like me just up from the country. The women in there were very intimidating. (The 'brickworks wenches' had a formidable reputation and it would be a brave man indeed who took them on in a verbal exchange.)

Shunting Round Oak was not one of Ray William's favourite jobs, the work was monotonous, and the engine, '16XX' 0-6-0T No. 1621, was small and cramped. The Round Oak shunter was not always top of Albert Homer's list either:

I passed as a fireman in 1936 after six years as a cleaner, although for three of those years I worked in the office. One of my first jobs in the shunting link was at Round Oak where I fired to the most miserable driver I have ever met, Bill Harmon; not even a 'good morning', just a grunt. On the other hand, 'Buff' Owen, who was also a driver on the Round Oak shunting engine, was a real gentleman and a pleasure to work with.

As will be seen later, Stourbridge Junction yards alone counted for three shunting engines, working 24 hours a day Monday to Saturday, as well as part of Sunday, trains coming and going at very regular intervals. Harry Hardwick remembers the many coal and coke trains that used to call at the yards on their way to and from South Wales, and the busy nights as through trains stopped to drop off or pick up traffic for locations throughout the network (see Volume One, Chapter Two). After serving in the shunting link, the fireman would move up to the bottom or junior bank link. There were two bank links engaged mainly on the movement of local freight. Jobs in these links took the fireman to every yard in the area and a few beyond it, dropping off wagons here, picking up wagons there; in fact considerable tonnages were conveyed by these trains to and from the yards at Brettell Lane, Kingswinford Junction, Round Oak, Blowers Green, Dudley, Lye, Cradley, Old Hill, Oldbury, Rowley Regis, Halesowen, Amblecote and Stourbridge. Furthermore, traffic would have to be conveyed over the Hayes Lane branch, the Corngreaves branch, the Kingswinford branch, and the Netherton branch, as well as to Kidderminster, Hartlebury and Elmley Lovett sidings in the one direction, Bilston West and Priestfield in another, or over to Longbridge, or Handsworth and Queen's Head. The bank links also carried out some yard shunting, in particular at Amblecote goods yard and Halesowen, as well as providing assistance to trains struggling to master the fierce gradients in the area. Harry Hardwick recalled in *The Magic of Steam* one job which tested the engine and crew almost to the limit:

I remember on one occasion my driver, Sam Winnall, and I were sent to work an iron ore train from Stourbridge to Round Oak, the engine being a 4-4-0 with a combined oval-shaped number and nameplate on the cab. It was more a passenger engine than a goods and what a trip we had. There was a nasty rail at the time and when we were going up Brettell Lane bank the engine slipped and slipped as the sand boxes were empty. Well I wonder the tyres did not wear out that night for it took us over an hour to pass Brettell Lane. The engine was *Primrose*, number 4167, and what a primrose it was! *

After serving in the bank links it was into the double home link and finally the passenger links, No. 1 being free of the very late night/very early morning turns that were part and parcel of the shunting and freight links. As well as firing, a senior fireman would also be called upon to carry out temporary driving duties. However, before being able to take over the controls he would be subjected to a very strict test of everything he had learned about the rules and the way an engine worked, this knowledge having been gained informally on the footplate and more formally at the shed's MIC. The test was carried out at Swindon by a locomotive inspector who certainly made sure the intending driver knew his stuff. Having convinced the inspector that he was fit for driving duties the fireman would be graded 'passed fireman' and would be ready to take his place at the controls of engines in the shunting link. Reg Lamb remembers his early days as a driver:

I became a passed fireman in 1946 and two years later I got my driving job. In that short time I accumulated over 300 driving turns, so many in fact, that I went straight on to the second year driving rate. I started off in the shunting link and by the time I retired in 1974 having taken early retirement, I had progressed to the No. 1 Passenger Link driving dmus on local passenger services. One amusing incident happened when I was shunting John Hall's sidings just opposite the engine sheds in Amblecote. It was during the summer and the grass adjacent the line was bone dry. Suddenly, the grass burst into flame as sparks from the engine set it alight. We jumped off the footplate immediately and started stamping out the flames. One of our running foremen noticed the smoke and

---

* No. 4167 *Primrose* was a 'Flower' class locomotive withdrawn in July 1929. The train referred to may have been an Adderbury to Wolverhampton class 'K' ironstone or a class 'H' Banbury/Kingham to Wolverhampton ironstone, conveying raw materials for 'Stewarts & Lloyds', Bilston.

came over to assist us. Finally the fire was extinguished and we returned to our duties. At the end of the shift I was called into the foreman's office where he was waiting for us. 'Look at this Reg', he said, rolling up his trousers to reveal two very black legs, 'that's through helping you stamp out that bloody fire!' It was then that I looked at mine, yes, they too, were in a similar state.

A passed fireman was paid the bottom driver's rate when carrying out a driving turn, a rate retained after completing 313 driving turns whether or not he was firing or driving. Before being promoted to permanent driver, the passed fireman would again have to make the journey to Swindon to be grilled on his knowledge by the inspector. Reg Lamb became a driver after 18 years whilst Harry Hardwick had an even longer apprenticeship, 22 years in fact!

The newly promoted driver also began his career in the shunting link before moving through into the bank links and then the double home link. As mentioned above, working Amblecote goods yard was a bank train duty, No. 3 Bank, and it was whilst shunting in the yard that Albert Homer came to grief:

One incident I can never forget was when I was involved in a derailment in the late 1940s. I had been shunting the gas work's siding with 0-6-0T No. 2712 and was in the process of leaving with a train of empties when the accident occurred. The points at the end of the siding should have been set to give access to the single goods line to the Town; unfortunately, for some reason, they had not been pulled over all the way. As the engine hit the half open points it was derailed blocking the goods line completely. Behind the engine was the shunter's truck carrying Charlie, the yard shunter. He realised what was happening just in time and jumped clear, his truck careering up and over the engine to land on top of the cab roof. Luckily, neither my fireman, George Spally, nor myself were injured so we were able to get off the engine and inspect the damage. I sent George back to the Junction on foot with the single line staff, as without it the breakdown gang could not reach us. One of the first men to arrive on the scene was Frank Barlow, the running inspector from Wolverhampton who was on a visit to the shed. 'Quite a mess, Albert', he said. I was hardly in a position to disagree. The breakdown gang duly arrived led by Harry Allsop, the foreman fitter, and they set to work clearing up and jacking the engine back onto the rails. It was a long job, nearly eight hours, and no traffic could leave or enter the yard until the job had been done.

Before drivers could work the longer distance jobs in the double home link they either had to re-acquaint themselves with routes that they may not have worked since their firing days, or learn routes that they had never travelled over at all. This process involved accompanying a regular driver on the footplate during daylight hours and noting the position of signals, stations, gradients etc., as well as listening to the advice of the man who already knew the line like the back of his hand. Once a driver felt that he had sufficient knowledge of a route to allow him to work a train safely, he would sign the Road Book. Apparently one Stourbridge driver went to extraordinary lengths to ensure that he knew the road. Not satisfied with what he had seen and heard on the footplate, he would walk the length and breadth of the goods yards he would be working into to ensure that he knew every inch of their layout. Road knowledge was a very important element and drivers had to sign for the road every six months. Where their knowledge had lapsed, a 'refresher' might be allowed, otherwise the road would have to be deleted. Reg Lamb signed for a number of roads,

'56XX' class 0-6-2T No. 6674 on a light down freight between Cradley Heath and Lye on 14th June, 1958.   *Michael Mensing*

'56XX' class 0-6-2T No. 6678 on an up freight from the Windmill End branch climbing through Old Hill station on 30th May, 1959.   *Michael Mensing*

'51XX' class No. 5152 takes water at the north end of Stourbridge Junction station in October 1962. Despite the date the locomotive still carries the early large BR totem. Driver Len Shingles opens the valve for fireman Roy Gwillam (standing on top of the engine) to top up the tanks.

Kidderminster Railway Museum

Driver Len Noke and fireman Mick Brant, also known as 'Flash', on '74XX' class 0-6-0PT No. 7430 *circa* 1963. *M. Noke Collection*

including Cardiff and Paddington, route learning on these, and other routes, taking several weeks before he was ready to put his name against them. Reg recalls working over some of these routes:

I once went up to Paddington on a Cup Final special travelling via Dudley, Great Bridge and Birmingham (Snow Hill). The train was double-headed with two 0-6-0s, a '2301' class and a '2251' class as we could not use a 4-6-0 due to a weight restriction over the Great Bridge section. I also signed the route to Basingstoke, particularly useful as we had a long distance excursion to Portsmouth on Easter Sundays. However, as no one knew the road from Basingstoke to Portsmouth we had to have a Southern pilotman for the rest of the journey. The route to Cardiff was also signed for and I regularly worked an empty tank train down to the Welsh capital from Rowley Regis. Route knowledge also allowed me to sample the delights of driving that excellent engine, the 'Castle'. One day I was booked for pilotman duties on an 'Ian Allan Locospotters' Special' to Banbury. It was an eight-coach train which No. 7029 *Clun Castle* managed with ease and what a pleasure it was to drive. It was a pity that I had to be relieved at Banbury and come back on a passenger service. Weston-super-Mare was another destination, and even after steam, route knowledge proved invaluable, as I was able to take a class '47' diesel-electric-hauled excursion, carrying Hagley school boys and their friends and relatives, to this south-west holiday resort.

Albert Homer also had extensive route knowledge and he too drove the Portsmouth excursion:

One of our best workings was the trip to Portsmouth. One day Barry Shillingsford and myself had No. 4930 *Hagley Hall*, a good engine and we did not anticipate any problems. The journey down to Basingstoke was uneventful and we continued to Portsmouth Harbour with a Southern pilotman. At the Harbour station there wasn't a run-round loop so engine and carriages had to be hauled out by a Southern shunting engine. It was only when we reached Fratton shed that we were able to uncouple the engine and turn it. Before we went off duty Barry cleaned the fire and everything was left ready for our return journey. We had to be back at Fratton a couple of hours before our booked departure time and after a wet day out in Pompey we duly arrived back at the shed with time to spare. After checking over the engine we backed on to the stock and once again a Southern engine was summoned, this time to pull us down into the station platform. On the footplate with our pilotman we waited for the signal and having got the road the guard signalled us off. As usual I offered the pilotman the regulator. 'I'm not taking that', he snapped. I looked at Barry in disbelief. 'But you're the pilot', I said. 'I know, but I'm not driving this Western engine'. He was clearly not going to take over, so to avoid delay I took hold of the regulator and taking my usual position on the right-hand side of the cab, I eased the train out of the station, the pilotman standing at my shoulder. Beyond Eastleigh and up to Basingstoke was a bit of a haul and our pilotman was obviously worried that we would lose time; he was, of course, quite wrong.

It is thought that special and excursion jobs were confined to double home and senior bank link drivers, whilst firemen could be used from any link on and above the junior bank link.

The last rung on the engineman's promotion ladder was the passenger link; to get into the top link really crowned his career. However, at Stourbridge there were no long distance passenger trains; no famous named expresses! In fact, with the exception of excursions such as those mentioned above, all the steam passenger jobs were local, virtually all of them working over the lines to and from Wolverhampton, Birmingham, Leamington Spa, Stratford-upon-Avon, and Worcester, as well as the Stourbridge Town shuttle service, the Dudley to Old Hill workings over the Windmill End branch, and the Dudley to Birmingham (Snow Hill) trains that ran via Great Bridge. However, with the end of steam, and even before that when most of the local lines were closed between 1962 and 1964, many of Stourbridge's passenger jobs were lost, and by *c.*1970 the remaining turns were confined to the Worcester-Kidderminster-Stourbridge Junction-Birmingham (New Street)-Lichfield City corridor, and of course the Stourbridge Town branch.

In the days of steam there were three passenger links, the top passenger link drivers having their own engines, a situation which continued until the 1950s when dmus began to make their presence felt. By 1960 drivers in the passenger links were mainly booked to work diesel trains only, although due to poor availability of the new dmus, some services had to revert temporarily to steam haulage (*see below*). There were though still a number of scheduled steam passenger workings and these were manned by men from both No. 2 Passenger link and the Auto link, the latter working branch line trains over the Windmill End branch; the Great Bridge line; and to and from Stourbridge Town (up to 1958 this link also manned the Longbridge workmen's trains). For No. 2 link it is thought that if there was not a booked return passenger service for the steam crew the turn would often be completed with a freight working scheduled to call at yards on the Stourbridge Extension. Steam passenger jobs by 1962-63 were largely confined to the Stourbridge Junction-Birmingham (Snow Hill)-Shirley line and the Dudley-Old Hill services, the latter continuing until passenger traffic was withdrawn on Saturday 13th June, 1964 when driver Joe Carden and fireman Geoff Walters took non-auto-fitted No. 7418 with auto-coach No. W254 over the line for the last time. The auto-coach was well filled with enthusiasts for the journey from Dudley and at Old Hill even more joined the train for the farewell run. To say the train was full is perhaps an under-statement and a number of passengers had to be squeezed into the guard's compartment. The next day scheduled passenger services between Dudley and Birmingham, now operated by dmus, also ran for the last time.

The other regular steam passenger jobs in 1962-63 were the 7.15 am Saturdays Excepted (SX) departure from Stourbridge Junction to Birmingham (Snow Hill) (the 5.40 pm from Snow Hill to Stourbridge Junction was also booked for steam haulage but it is not known if this was a Stourbridge job), whilst from Dudley to Birmingham (Snow Hill) the 6.59 am and 7.26 am departures were booked for steam haulage Monday to Friday and dmu on Saturdays, the former continuing from Birmingham (Snow Hill) as the 7.38 am to Shirley. On occasion, shortage of the booked diesel traction would result in a steam substitution, for example on 14th January, 1963 'Grange' class No. 6832 *Brockton Grange* was on the 7.30 am local from Stourbridge Junction to Snow Hill. With 220 tons on the draw-bar, driver Charles Lawrence and fireman G. Evans had the satisfaction of arriving a minute early against the booked time of 8.11 am. During the early part of 1963 Charles Lawrence was also at the controls of the 7.15 am from the Junction and the 6.59 am from Dudley. The survival of his driver's log has meant that a closer look at these turns can be taken.

'74XX' class 0-6-0PT No. 7418 with auto-coach No. W254 at Old Hill ready to depart with the last Old Hill to Dudley passenger service on 13th June, 1964.

G. Bennett

From left to right, fireman Barry Shillingsford, driver Len Noke and guard I. Jones with '2251' class 0-6-0 No. 2232 *circa* 1952.

M. Noke Collection

Charles Lawrence on the footplate of '57XX' class 0-6-0PT No. 8791.

T. Lawrence Collection

The 6.59 am from Dudley usually comprised four carriages (124 tons) and would run via Great Bridge South and Swan Village arriving at Snow Hill at around 7.30 am. It would then continue as the 7.38 am to Spring Road before running empty to Shirley (on the line to Henley-in-Arden and Stratford) arriving 8.00 am. The empty stock then formed the 8.35 am local to Birmingham (Moor Street), arriving at 8.55 am. From Moor Street the empty stock was conveyed to Tyseley carriage sidings. Having disposed of the stock it was over to Bordesley Junction to pick up a return freight working which called as required at Rowley Regis, Cradley and Lye, before continuing to Stourbridge Junction engine and van. At the time '51XX' class 2-6-2T No. 4140 was a regular engine on this job, although '56XX' class 0-6-2T No. 6667 also made an appearance on 31st January, 1963. The 7.15 am departure was, as to be expected, a heavier load, usually six carriages (187 tons). The train was booked to arrive at 7.55 am and on four days during week beginning 14th January, 1963 the engine was 'Grange' class No. 6827 *Llanfrechfa Grange*. At Snow Hill an additional four vehicles would be attached to form a 10 carriage empty stock train bound for Tyseley carriage sidings. The engine would then be taken to the shed sidings where it would probably take on water before returning to Stourbridge shed. However, it would appear that on at least two days per week engine and crew would be required to work part of the way back to Stourbridge Junction with a freight train. When this was the case the crew, after uncoupling the engine from the empty stock, would move the engine to the shed sidings as usual waiting there for their return working to arrive. It would then be coupled up in the down loop and at around 11.00 am the train would leave for Langley Green via Bordesley Junction (this might have been a fuel-oil train from Acton?).

To round off this section, a step back in time to the early years of the GWR when promotions were made in relation to the needs of the service and bonus was paid to drivers who kept coal and oil consumption to a minimum. From around 1879 until the end of World War I, Great Western firemen and drivers were graded 3rd, 2nd, and 1st class, the grade being determined by the type of work each man was employed upon, e.g. shunting, etc. (where driving was concerned there may have been a pilotmen's grade which was below 3rd class driver). Men gained promotion from one grade to another by transferring to other sheds, implying that a cleaner would have to make as many as six moves to reach 1st class grade driver. This was known as the 'all-line' system of promotion. It was also Great Western practice for a cleaner promoted to 3rd class fireman to take the first vacancy that arose even if this meant moving to another part of the company's empire. However, following promotion to 3rd class fireman, it is presumed that the man would be able to choose the next vacancy he wanted to apply for, although his advancement would probably be quicker if he was prepared to relocate anywhere within the company's network. Many footplatemen did try and return eventually to their original station, but this course of action could often mean a lengthy wait until an appropriate job turned up on the vacancy list. What possibly happened is that men returned to their home station gradually, each move bringing their return that much closer. Although promotion often meant a compulsory move it is thought that some internal regradings might have taken place. These, though, could have been

Ex-LMS 'Jubilee' class 4-6-0 No. 45742 *Connaught* on an excursion being piloted by an unidentified ex-GWR '51XX' class 2-6-2T *circa* 1960. The footplate crew standing near the locomotive with their backs to the photographer are driver Alan Cartwright (*left*) and fireman Malcolm Richards (*right*). *T. Lawrence*

Driver Len Noke waves to the photographer from the cab of ex-LMS '8F' class 2-8-0 No. 48430 on a Hednesfield-Hartlebury train pictured on the Hednesfield side of Ryecroft Junction in 1960. *M. Noke Collection*

confined to just a few advancements from 2nd to 1st class driver. Promotions to Stourbridge shed, for example during 1912, resulted in 36 men being regraded: C.R. Holloway, a cleaner at Banbury, was promoted to the shed as a 3rd class fireman (no more examples of cleaner promotions have been discovered for 1912 although a number of 3rd class firemen were re-graded thereby creating vacancies); twelve 3rd class firemen were promoted to 2nd class fireman; eleven 2nd class firemen to 1st class firemen, and ten 1st class firemen to 3rd class drivers including G.H. Holloway from Old Oak Common; T.H. Jones (ex-Shrewsbury); A. Bradburn (ex-Tyseley); G.W. Hill (ex-Banbury); T.J. Wootton (ex-Leamington); and Charles Goddard from Aylesbury (it is thought that Charles drew up the Bank Link scheme of 1929 as mentioned in Chapter Three). Drivers' promotions were as follows: from 3rd class to 2nd class, driver Arthur Aimes; from 2nd to 1st class, driver A. Clements.

Also up until the end of World War I drivers on the GWR were paid a bonus based upon the quantity of coal and oil used in any given month. Consequently, some drivers became particularly keen to receive this additional income which often meant that a fireman's life would sometimes become very difficult indeed as the driver would usually be watching every move he made. One of the few Stourbridge drivers to earn this type of bonus was Tom Smith whose regular engine was No. 132, a '131' class 0-6-0. One day Tom had quite a row with the shed foreman (John Preece?) about his engine as Harry Hardwick recalled in *The Magic of Steam*. At this time Harry must still have been a young cleaner as No. 132 was withdrawn in August 1924:

> . . . 132, a small tender engine that he (Tom Smith) worked on double home jobs to Birkenhead, Crewe and other stations. He was one of the few enginemen who earned a bonus for low consumption of coal and oil, and so that his engine would not have to be coaled at Birkenhead and Crewe, he got his mate to place iron plates round the sides and back of the tender so that it would hold more coal. It looked rather ugly as the foreman cleaner would not let his chaps clean the iron plates. One day the boss had a dickens of a row with Tom and to show that he was boss, he had the plates taken off the tender which meant a loss of about two tons of coal to Tom. Tom's fireman was named Sid Byng and I can well believe he had a miserable time with Tom watching every shovelful of coal used.

Dieselisation and the Effects upon Footplate Staff at Stourbridge

Although it is believed that Stourbridge shed had at one time as many as 195 drivers and 186 firemen, records supporting these counts have so far not been discovered. However, in October 1953 it can be shown that the shed had 191 drivers and 171 firemen (14 less than required). With the introduction of diesel traction, numbers rapidly shrank and by December 1963 the shed had 154 drivers and just 88 firemen. Eight months later, on 10th August, 1964 Kidderminster shed closed and this necessitated the transfer to Stourbridge of 11 drivers and 11 firemen. These men covered nine operational turns and two spare turns. Apparently Kidderminster still retained a booking on/off point at the station for nine drivers and two firemen. Prior to closure Kidderminster shed possessed two main line links, plus a shunting link and a firemen's link.

Right: Len Noke looks out of the cab of Brush type '4' (later class '47') while undergoing driver training.
M. Noke Collection

Below: Driver Ray Kendrick with guard Jim Perry at Stourbridge Junction in February 1973.   *Birmingham Post & Mail*

No. 1 Link was the senior passenger link, whilst No. 2 Link, in 1959/60, probably included the following turns:

4.20 am	Stourport to Alveley Colliery sidings and its 10.30 am relief
5.15 am	Hartlebury to Stourport trip working and its 1.00 pm relief
5.15 am	Worcester Shrub Hill passenger (8.19 am TC to London)
5.25 am	Kidderminster to Solihull passenger
6.00 am	Passenger shunting
10.30 am	Kidderminster to Tenbury and Woofferton goods
Midday	Spare turn
4.00 pm and 11.00 pm	Shed duties

During the sugar beet season (from autumn to early spring) Kidderminster shed worked three turns, the first of which commenced at 5.00 am, on the trip workings between the yard and the processing plant taking loaded wagons in and bringing the empties out.

When Stourbridge shed closed on 11th June, 1966 there were 135 drivers and 62 firemen. Of the 135 drivers, 124 were on main line duties; nine on yard shunting, one was on union duties and one (for medical reasons) was employed in the shed. So at the closure of the shed, the total number of footplatemen was considerably down on the numbers formerly employed at the height of the shed's activities in the early 1950s. Unfortunately, the reduction in numbers continued after the shed's closure as the availablility of work for Stourbridge men steadily declined. This brought with it the very real threat of redundancy.

The end of steam was accompanied by the loss of the firemen's grade and the introduction of secondmen or drivers' assistants; it also heralded huge reductions in the number of footplate staff employed at Stourbridge as work reduced and the need for double manning was gradually eliminated. A taste of things to come was a proposal made on 31st October, 1966 to reduce the depot's complement to 106 drivers (70 on diagrammed work; 8 rest day relief (rdr); 20 spare; 6 on diesel traction learning and 2 on road learning) and 44 secondmen, 32 of which would be employed on diagrams, 3 rdr and 9 spare, as opposed to what was possibly the actual complement of 122 drivers and 46 secondmen. However, by 1968 the threatened reductions had begun to take place and by 1970 the number of footplatemen employed at the depot had reduced to 74 drivers and 27 secondmen. Between 1970 and the end of 1972 the number of drivers at Stourbridge reduced still further, to 69 in fact. The number of secondmen also fell during the same period, from 27 to 16. Of the 69 drivers in post on 1st January, 1973 42 were on Crewe diagrams. There were also 12 drivers at the depot on spare turns plus 4 rdr. One was even allocated to Kidderminster on 'frost precautions' for the three winter months. The remaining drivers were employed either on ferry jobs (the movement of empty diesel units), the few remaining trip workings, Control turns, or acting as spares for the rest of the Division.

Kidderminster Booking-On Point closed as from Monday 14th February, 1972 the existing footplate staff being presented with three options: 1. leaving the service under the Redundancy and Resettlement Arrangements; 2. transferring with identifiable work; and 3. applying for vacancies advertised on the January 1972 Footplate Staff Vacancy List. At the time there were 11 positions for drivers at Stourbridge and a number of Kidderminster men (including, as will be seen later, Ramon Williams) were successful at securing a position. The closure of Kidderminster meant that some, if not all of the work carried out by this depot was transferred to Stourbridge. Ramon Williams recalls a few of the jobs undertaken by Kidderminster:

> When I went to Kidderminster for my driving job the booking-on point was on the down platform and all the jobs were either passenger dmus, diesel shunting or trip workings. We had a diesel shunting job in the carriage sidings and yards. There was also a shunting job at Hartlebury from where we tripped coal trains to Stourport power station. There was also a trip to the oil terminal at Leapgate sidings not far from the village of Wilden. The one job I used to change turns for was a dmu which left Kidderminster in the afternoon about 4.00 pm for Birmingham (Snow Hill) and then on to Stratford-upon-Avon. We were then stood inside at Evesham for some time, before returning to Kidderminster via Worcester (Shrub Hill).

Returning to Stourbridge, the reductions continued throughout the 1980s with losses proposed every year. However, whilst the Local Departmental Committee accepted that job losses were inevitable, they tried their hardest to keep them to a minimum, and the proposals were fought 'tooth and nail'. Unfortunately, management were clearly intent upon closing the train crew depot and with little support from colleagues at the larger depots, the men at Stourbridge TCD were fighting a losing battle as the following illustrates:

	Drivers	Drivers Assistants
December 1980	52	12
January 1982	50	12
July 1983	38	9
May 1984	33	9
April 1986	31	5
July 1988	23	3

According to an official document published a few months prior to closure, 27 footplatemen, 18 guards, three train crew supervisors and one messroom attendant were to be withdrawn from Stourbridge train crew depot, together with the two remaining guards from the sub-depot at Kidderminster. At this time the clerical officer was due to remain. When closure did come on 9th July, 1988 the vast majority decided to take the terms offered, although a few of the younger men decided to accept a move elsewhere; it was a sad end to a once important railway centre.

So how did railwaymen view redundancy? Ramon Williams, who left the service in 1972, moved from Stourbridge to Kidderminster in 1968 after 20 years at the former serving first as a cleaner then fireman. This is his view:

> Redundancy came as a great shock to me. I thought that when I joined the railway in 1948 I would have a job for life. However, the early 1970s put paid to that. In December, 1971 I was told that I had lost my driver's job and that I had been 'put back'. Then, on 3rd January, 1972 I received two letters from the Divisional Manager at Birmingham, the first announced the closure of Kidderminster MPD on Monday, 14th February, 1972; the other informed me that I would be given an opportunity of naming an alternative depot to which I would wish to transfer. In this letter it stated that there were 11 driving posts at Stourbridge. I applied

and got one of these posts. I was delighted to be returning to a depot where I knew virtually all of the locomotivemen; unfortunately my delight did not last long! On 1st March, 1972 I received a letter telling me that I would be made redundant as a driver at Stourbridge and would either have to apply for a transfer or be reduced to 'driver put back'. I chose the latter and on 10th May, a letter arrived confirming that I was now classified 'driver put back'. However, almost immediately I received another letter telling me that I was redundant in that position and if I was not willing to transfer within my existing grade to another depot I would be discharged from the service. On 14th July, 1972 eight other 'put back' drivers and myself applied for three posts at Saltley. I was unsuccessful and given until 16.30 hours on Wednesday, 19th July to revise my choice. I selected Cricklewood and went down to London with another former Kidderminster driver, Ray Goulding. However, having looked at the property in the area I found that housing was so much more expensive than in the West Midlands and after being told that I would have to spend 4½ years there before I could apply for a transfer back to Birmingham (New Street), I knew that I would have to think very carefully before I accepted the job. Having talked it over with my family, I decided to leave the railway service. So on 19th August, 1972, after 24 years and three days, my career on the railway came to an end. Being made redundant so often in such a short space of time left me thoroughly disenchanted with the service and I felt very bitter about the way I had been treated.

The Fitters and the 'other' grades

Stourbridge shed, in common with other depots of similar size, was a place where locomotives were maintained, repaired and serviced and it was these jobs that fell to a group of men who rarely get the recognition their skills deserve, that is the fitters and their assistants. The fitting shop itself has already been described in Chapter One, however, it will be the intention of the following to introduce the reader, in some small way, to the work of the shop and the men whose primary task was to keep the engines running.

During the middle to late 1950s the fitting shop at Stourbridge included the following personnel. The mechanical foreman was also responsible for the boilersmiths, tubecleaners and boilerwashers:

Mechanical Foreman	Harry Allsop
Chargehand Fitter	Howard Wollaston
Fitters	L. Toombs, B. Castle, R. Highway, W. Hillman, C. Parton, B. Farmer, B. Chance, G. Skelding, L. Holloway, H. Bartlett, F. Hall, F. Garbett, J. Barrett and J. Sokel.
Assistant Fitters	G. Russell, L. Chandler, E. Potts-Perkins, G. Smith, S. Prosser, J. Wood, A. Highway, R. Malpass, G. Sansoni, T. Hughes, F. Hargreaves, T. Pearson, N. Knott and R. Sokel.
Fitter/Machine Operator	J. Skelding (NUR shop steward)
Apprentice Fitters	The number varied over the years but in 1954 there was just one, Henry Caffrey. Other apprentices were John Jones, M. Skinner, Tony Watson, Fred Watkins and John Stevens. The last apprentice to be employed at the shed was Bob Price in 1962.

Each fitter was usually allocated a permanent fitter's assistant, although the chargehand fitter, Howard Wollaston, worked alone in the 'old' shed looking

Fitting shop staff with '43XX' class 2-6-0 No. 6346. From left to right; ?, F. Garbett, R. Malpass,
T. Hughes and B. Sokel.   *E. Potts-Perkins Collection*

after and repairing the diesel shunters and cars. In fact it was Howard Wollaston who was responsible for maintaining the GWR diesel railcars from at least 1946. Earlier, from around the end of 1943, oiling of the cars had been carried out by the night toolman and the night shift foreman cleaner. This was only a short term arrangement, all diesel maintenance duties eventually passing to the fitting shop.

The fitting shop would have been manned around the clock Monday to Sunday, continuous cover being provided by a complex arrangement of shifts combined with overtime. In the late 1950s there was in operation three basic shifts, although these differed significantly from the more usual shift pattern of 6 am to 2 pm; 2 pm to 10 pm; and 10 pm to 6 am worked elsewhere. Around 50 per cent of the fitting shop personnel were employed on the day shift from 8 am to 5 pm (including a one hour meal break) Monday to Friday, and from 8 am until midday on Saturday. In addition to the day shift was both a night shift and an intermediate shift and with the exception of two (*see below*) all fitters and assistant fitters were expected to work each shift in rotation. The night shift consisted of two fitters and two assistant fitters, as did the intermediate shift (usually known as the afternoon shift) which apparently came on during the late morning and continued into the mid-evening. As the afternoon men booked off well before the night (or late) shift officially arrived, the pairings on 'lates' would take it in turns to book on early so as to provide cover over the intervening period. Interestingly, the fitting shop also had one set of men working permanent days; this was fitter L. Toombs and assistant fitter G. Russell. These two men worked an extended shift from 6 am to 5 pm (including a one hour meal break) Monday to Friday, and presumably on Saturday from 6 am to midday. The reason for the additional two hours first thing in the morning was to again provide cover between shifts, that is from the time the night shift booked off at 6 am to the arrival of the day men at 8 am. After the last shift finished on the Saturday all remaining hours up to 10 pm Sunday, when the night shift came on, would be covered in overtime. It would seem that men on 'lates' worked exceptionally long hours, Sunday to Sunday by all accounts; very lucrative but a very protracted working week! (In view of the complex nature of the shift pattern it has not been possible to describe in full the working arrangements employed by the fitting shop to ensure 24 hour cover seven days a week. However, if any reader has anything to add, the author would be only too pleased to hear from them.)

With the increasing use of diesels after 1955 one of the day shift pairings was transferred to the diesel depot (the 'old' shed) to assist chargehand fitter Howard Wollaston. With the arrival of the dmus in 1957 the existing diesel fitters found themselves inundated with work. Consequently, a night shift fitter and assistant fitter had to be permanently transferred from the steam shed to the diesel depot. Following the closure of the steam and diesel depots, and the transfer of all staff to Stourbridge Junction, two fitters and three assistant fitters were allocated to the stabling point at the Junction to carry out light repairs and maintenance to diesel units and locos. These men were accommodated in a small hut in the marshalling yards. When maintenance was finally withdrawn from Stourbridge all remaining fitting staff received redundancy notices.

The fitting shop's principal role was to carry out routine maintenance and running repairs; it was not designed or equipped to carry out major overhauls, this was left to the works. Consequently, where attention was needed to a locomotive's brakes, pistons or valves, then Stourbridge fitters would undertake the work. They would also attend to a range of other jobs including blown injector joints, blocked top feed trays, worn brake cylinders and blocked sand trays, to name but a few. Furthermore, general welding to frames, cab sides and tender bodies was also carried out. The largest job that could be handled in the shop was the removal of the wheel sets, often necessitated by the detection of a hot box and the need to remetal bearings. To remove the wheel sets the chain lift had to be fitted under the front buffer beam whilst large wooden blocks were placed under the rear of the cab to act as packing. The front of the engine would then be lifted and the front wheel sets rolled out, and if necessary, the middle set. To get the rear set out, the cab end would be lifted, the packing being placed under the front buffer beam. Replacing the side connecting rods was a heavy job as was the replacement of the buffers. A special carriage was used to move the buffers around the shop, but they had to be lifted to the buffer beam by hand and there was always a sigh of relief when the retaining bolts had been slotted into place. Readers may remember No. 60532 *Blue Peter* suffering major damage to its motion and pistons when, on 1st October, 1994, it was involved in an uncontrollable wheel slip incident whilst engaged upon a railtour. A similar incident happened at Stourbridge as former apprentice fitter Henry Caffrey recalls:

Work was being carried out on a Standard 4-6-0 '75XXX' when the regulator overrode the regulator valve and jammed wide open. I remember that there was a huge roaring noise and the wheels were turning so fast that the connecting rods were just a blur. Both Harry Bartlett and Harry Allsop were on the footplate hitting the regulator handle with sledge hammers trying to free it. It was absolutely frightening.

Henry continues:

On the subject of regulators, the night shift cleaners would sometimes get onto the footplate of an engine and act out the role of a driver. Unfortunately, the actions of one of these lads may have led to an incident involving an engine running away in the fitting shop. The engine had been removed from the shed to the cripple road outside the shop in preparation for a wheel lift. The road into the shop was on a slight downhill gradient; just enough to enable an engine to pick up a bit of speed if it was allowed to roll forward. One day this was exactly what happened and the engine smashed through the fitting shop doors before coming to rest against the rear wall. So how did the accident happen? It was thought that one of the cleaners must have got onto the footplate and opened both the regulator and the cylinder drain cocks. When the loco was drawn out of the shed, the movement of the pistons drew air into the boiler through the open drain cocks and regulator valve. Once onto the cripple line someone probably noticed that the regulator and drain cocks were open and immediately closed them. One of the apprentices later went onto the footplate and after taking off the hand brake opened the regulator allowing partially compressed air to enter the cylinder. There must have been sufficient air pressure to move the piston and with the hand brake off the engine started forward.This incident illustrates just how a simple act can have very serious consequences in an engine shed.

Another unfortunate incident involved the shed drivers. Len Shutt was bringing a Prairie tank into the roundhouse from the coal stage and was clearly under the impression that the turntable had been set for him; unfortunately, his mate had set it to allow another engine to leave. As a result Len's engine plunged into the turntable pit. Immediately the shed went to emergency working and all engines in steam that were now blocked in had to have their fires thrown out. Meanwhile the breakdown gang set to work 'jacking and packing' the front end of the stranded tank engine. Eventually, after about four to five hours, the engine had been lifted level with the road and was pulled to safety. There were, of course, less serious incidents. A labourer, Stan Bates, kept livestock at the rear of the depot and one day one of his goats decided to wander off into the shed. The attempts to catch it merely panicked the animal who leapt into the turntable pit. Cyril Harris, one of Stan's colleagues, jumped in after it. Then, holding a guard's red flag and urged on by a growing crowd of onlookers, Cyril gave a masterful impression of a Spanish matador whilst the excited goat reluctantly played the bull.

Finally, Henry remembers a very embarrassing trip home with Fred Hargreaves:

Having finished work at 5.00 pm it was customary for men living near Stourbridge Junction to try and get a lift from the shed in a passing train or engine. Freddie Hargreaves and myself happened to be leading a group out of the shed yard when we saw a freight standing in the up goods loop. Just then the signal cleared and the freight began to move out, however, Fred and I managed to jump aboard the guard's van. We thought we had better make our presence known to the guard and we went into the van. The guard was of course a little surprised to see us, but nowhere near as surprised as we were when told that the train was not stopping at Stourbridge Junction but was booked straight through to Hereford. By now the train was travelling too quickly for us to jump off so we decided to wait until it reached Hagley bank where the gradient would slow it down. Unfortunately, we hadn't reckoned with the power of the '28XX' on the front.

The breakdown gang re-rail a Collett 0-4-2T outside Stourbridge shed in 1954.

E. Potts-Perkins Collection

A derailed diesel shunter at Dudley station requires the assistance of the Stourbridge breakdown gang *circa* 1963. The breakdown vans are on this occasion headed by 0-6-0PT No. 9446.   *G. Bennett*

A 350 hp diesel shunter receives attention from the breakdown gang at Dudley in *circa* 1963.
        G. Bennett

Up Hagley bank it went with the two of us standing helplessly on the van's platform; we certainly weren't going to risk jumping off at that speed! Luckily, the train was put inside at Droitwich so we were able to make a more dignified exit from the guard's van. We eventually returned to Stourbridge via a passenger service; 2½ hours after we had finished our shift! Obviously our mates had seen our departure and were eager to know what happened. I managed to avoid telling them for a couple of days but eventually broke down under pressure and admitted everything. It was quite some time before we were able to live this incident down.

One of the fitters at the shed was Bert Chance who one day found himself in a terrible mess. Bert was in the breakdown gang called to an incident outside the portal of Dudley tunnel. The train conveying Chipperfield's circus had become derailed and the Stourbridge breakdown gang had been summoned to put things right. This they did using jacks to ease the wagons back onto the rails. Obviously, some of these wagons contained the animals who had, during the journey, obeyed the call of nature with the result that the floors of many of the vans had become quite messy and wet. During the rerailing operation Bert was working under the van containing the elephants and was still underneath when the wagon moved depositing its watery contents all over him. Needless to say none of his colleagues were very keen to keep him company on the way back to Stourbridge. On arrival back at the shed Bert stripped off his overalls and threw them into the stationary boiler. Luckily he had a spare pair, so it was on with these and off home on his bike to a welcoming hot bath.

The Stourbridge breakdown gang was usually manned by fitting shop personnel, although in an emergency men from the conciliation grades at the shed, e.g. shed labourers, boiler washers etc. would be called upon to lend a hand if required. In the event of a call out the gang, comprising five or six men, would travel to the scene in the shed's special train. This train was made up of two vans. The first was a messroom van, where the crew ate and cleaned up, whilst the second conveyed all the equipment necessary to deal with the trouble. Stourbridge was not equipped with heavy lifting gear, this being provided by Stafford Road shed, Wolverhampton, although '84F' did possess a 6 ton maximum lift, hand-operated, breakdown crane.

By the middle 1950s the number of shed staff (excluding footplatemen, fitting shop personnel, and the 18 or so cleaners) at Stourbridge would have been as follows:

1	Chargehand boilersmith - Eric Hossacks
3	Boilersmiths - Fred Laite, Jimmy Bull and Alan Broad (also Jack Glaister)
3	Boilersmiths' mates - Julius Jones, Joe Perkins and Charlie Green
1	Chargehand cleaner - Tom Kitsell (the second chargehand, Billy Lane, retired in 1955)
3	Non clerical stores issuers - Bob Mooney, Fred Parker and Jim Hobbs
2	Boilerwashers - Ted Aston and Albert Amphlett (also G. Williams)
4	Steamraisers - Ted Sloper, George Stainsby, W. Prosser and N. Jones
3	Coalmen - Bill Such, A. Davies, and (?) Adams
2	Tube cleaners - John Woods and Bill Perkins
3	Toolmen - C. Pritchard, J. Chapman, J. Hobbs (later a stores issuer)
3	Firedroppers - R. Weaver, F. Draycott and T. Jenkins
3	Messroom attendants - L. Chandler; the others are unknown
6	Turntable men - R. Hawkins, W. Craddock, F. Potts, A. Barlett, R. Wall and F. Bailey
1	Machinery Attendant - Wilf Green

1   Craneman - H. Shilvock (later acted as machinery attendant)
3   Non clerical timekeepers - E. Aston, J. Bromyard, and E.A. Wall
6   Shedmen - E. Eggington, S. Bates, C. Harris, J. Atkins, I. Watts and S. Landers
7   Spare posts (RDR & sickness)
1   Water fitter - Ron Shakespeare
1   Diesel Electrician - Jack Withers

There has been a great deal of discussion as to who filled which post in what year, something which has been further complicated by the fact that some members of staff at the shed moved from one post to another, so if any reader can help out in this matter the author would be most grateful. Prior to the introduction of diesel traction in 1955, a number of grades mentioned above would have had more men in them. There were once six coalmen, and possibly as many boilerwashers, steamraisers, and firedroppers; even, perhaps, a third tube cleaner? By 11th June, 1966 the shed's complement was as follows (actual in brackets):

1   Chargehand cleaner (0)
3   Stores issuers (2 - R. Mooney & J. Hobbs)
2   Boilerwashers (1 - J. Poole)
4   Steamraisers (3 - E. Sloper, G Stainsby, W. Prosser)
3   Coalmen (1 - A. Shields)
2   Tubecleaners (0)
3   Toolmen (1 - C. Pritchard)
3   Firedroppers (2 - R. Weaver and F. Draycott)
3   Messroom attendants (1 - L. Chandler)

'51XX' class 2-6-2T No. 4173 on the turntable in Stourbridge roundhouse on 10th November, 1963. At the turntable is shed driver Fred Bailey with possibly M. Noke on the footplate.   *Joe Moss/R.S. Carpenter*

6   Shedmen (6 - T. Kitsell, H. Nott, J. Atkins, E. Wall, I. Watts and S. Landers)
1   Machinery attendant (2 - W. Green and E. Sheppard)
1   Craneman (1 - H. Shilvock)
3   Timekeepers (2 - E. Aston and J. Bromyard)
7   RDR/sickness relief (0)

Total 42 (22).

However, despite the reduction to 22 men actually in post, the withdrawal of steam meant that only 19 vacancies existed for shed staff in the new set-up. Also on 11th June there were just 135 drivers, 62 fireman and 0 cleaners.

The management of the shed was in the hands of the shedmaster assisted by his running foremen, a mechanical foreman and a chief clerk, the latter responsible for the roster clerk, three time & pay clerks, and the stores clerk. Some of these men have been shown below:

Shedmaster		Running Foremen	Chief Clerk
T.H. Lodge	-1910	Unknown	Unknown
Jack Preece	1910-1923	Tom Dovaston, Levi Wooldridge	George Flowers
Tom Dovaston	1923-1942	Jack Guy, Joe Holloway, Alf Page	R. Reynolds
Walter Morris	1942-c.1946	Sam Holland, Bert Lane, Bill Underwood	Harry Whitehouse
Harry Brown	c.1946-c.1960	Harry Griffiths, Jack Guy, Dai Williams	Bob Reynolds
		Bill Brooks, Bert Lane, Les Jones	John Jones
Albert Gregory	c.1960 until	John Wardle, Ray Powers, Stan Phillips	Frank Steel
	closure	Bill Davies	

On occasion the shedmaster would not be available and therefore someone would have to deputize. An article appearing in one of the railway magazines mentions an assistant foreman at Stourbridge, although one former driver, who had considerable knowledge of the shed's organisation, could not recall such a post. Interestingly, Tom Dovaston was appointed as an assistant foreman in 1915, so this post existed in Great Western days. However, in the British Railways era at Stourbridge, in the absence of the shedmaster the day shift running foreman would deputize and certainly Bert Lane and Bill Brooks were recalled carrying out the shedmaster's duties. Perhaps these men were known informally as the assistant foremen? To cover the running foreman's job, one of the 'panel' men (*see Chapter One*) would be temporarily upgraded, but unlike the time when these men worked as 'outside foremen', they would be paid the same rate as the man for whom they were deputizing.

'36XX' class 2-4-2T No. 3610 on an up Birmingham train made up of 4-wheeled stock at Stourbridge.

GWR steam railcars No. 40 (*left*) and 93 (*right*) stand outside the old shed at Stourbridge on 24th April, 1932.   *W. Potter/Kidderminster Railway Museum*

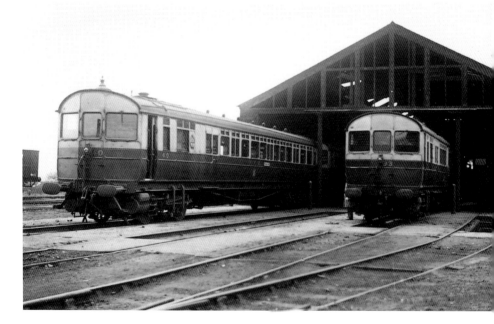

Chapter Three

Through the Links

Links and Turns Between the Wars

Stourbridge shed operated passenger, freight and shunting links. Unfortunately, information relating to the work carried out before World War II has been difficult to come by and that which has been found leaves many questions unanswered. However, despite the difficulties, an attempt has been made to provide the reader with a reasonably detailed picture of footplate working arrangements at the shed, both before and after World War II, beginning with the period 1920 to 1945.

A look through surviving records has yielded a number of references to passenger workings carried out in the 1920s. In 1922 there appeared to be three passenger links numbered 1, 2 and 3, the third being the 'Longbridge' link which presumably worked the public and workmen's services over the GWR's branch between Old Hill and Halesowen, and the Joint Line as far as Longbridge. However, it is thought that in the late 1920s the 'Longbridge' link was abolished, perhaps after the withdrawal of public passenger trains between Old Hill and Halesowen on 5th December, 1927, leaving just the workmen's trains running between Old Hill, Halesowen, and Longbridge (the steam railmotor workmen's services between Old Hill and Halesowen were withdrawn on 31st March, 1928 - *see Volume 1, Chapter 5, p. 97*). Passenger links 1 and 2 were also known, respectively, as the 'Big Engine' link and the 'Small Engine' link. Up to *circa* 1929 they were also referred to as the '36XX' link and the 'Metropolitan' link, although after 1929 the term '36XX' disappeared from the records. On the other hand 'Metro' continued in fairly common usage right up to World War II. It was believed that these names derived from the usual motive power employed by the links, that is, the class '36XX' 2-4-2T and the class '455' or 'Metropolitan' 2-4-0T. However, former Stourbridge drivers Reg Lamb and Albert Homer both recall that in their early days (post 1929) No. 1 Passenger link was sometimes referred to as the 'Metro' link, not No. 2 as implied above. It is possible that the terms did originally stem from engine types as both classes were at Stourbridge in the 1920s. After '36XX' had fallen into disuse perhaps 'Metro' simply evolved into an alternative name for No. 1 Passenger possibly because the main destination for the Top link was Birmingham? Anyway, by August 1928 the '36XX' link comprised 11 turns; the 'Metro' link 12. One of these links would probably have operated the workmen's specials between Old Hill and Longbridge and the short-lived steam railmotor services that worked over the Wombourn branch between 1925 and 1932.

Below No. 1 and 2 passenger links was the double home link comprising 10 or more sets of men (possibly no more than 12) responsible for working long distance freight jobs, a few passenger trips and some local goods workings. On the longer distance turns footplatemen would often find themselves finishing their shift far away from Stourbridge shed, as a result they would have had to stay in lodgings near the yard or station until their return working was scheduled to leave. These lodging turns regularly implied long periods away from home and were therefore not always very popular, as the reader will see in the chapter relating to the work of the Local Departmental Committee. However, driver Harry Hardwick found the work 'varied, straightforward and interesting, though at times hard'. The financial rewards were not that great either. Known pre-war double home turns involved workings to London, Crewe, Cardiff and Pontypool Road. In 1924 the double home link appeared to comprise the following turns:

8.15 am No. 1 Bank Train and 3.30 pm No. 1 Bank Train Relief; 1.50 am and 4.05 am Crewe (the former was probably a Mondays Excepted (MX) working whilst the latter could have been the Mondays Only (MO) equivalent); 10.00 am and 1.00 pm Pontypool Road (both of these may have been ex-Wolverhampton); 7.30 am Rowley Regis to Droitwich; 1.25pm Passenger Relief and a daily London working.

The London working referred to was probably a class 'C' express freight originating at Kidderminster. During the 1920s this train became known as 'The Carpet' when the GWR allocated names to some of its more prestigious goods services. At this time the Stourbridge crew worked to Kidderminster light engine, however, by the 1930s there was a handy local passenger service between Stourbridge and Kidderminster which would be worked by the double home crew who would stable the empty coaching stock at Kidderminster before preparing the engine for the freight to Paddington. The 'Carpet' departed at 8.20 pm, and stops were made at Hartlebury (probably to pick up traffic off the Severn Valley line); Worcester; Evesham, which generated a large number of heavily laden vans especially in the fruit growing season; Honeybourne, where a banking engine would be attached as far as Campden; Moreton-in-Marsh, to top up with water; Oxford; and finally Paddington just after 3.00 am (Tuesday to Saturday). In the 1930s the Moreton stop was 'as required' as it was no longer necessary to stop for water as the tender tank could be replenished via the troughs. Harry Hardwick mentions that this train was usually in the hands of a 'Hall'. This being the case it would not have been a Stourbridge engine, as this class of locomotive was not allocated to the shed until 1958.

At the end of the shift the engine crew lodged in London, presumably somewhere near Old Oak Common shed, until returning with the 12.10 am (Tu-Sun only) Paddington to Birkenhead passenger and mail train which stopped only at Oxford, Banbury and Leamington Spa before arriving in Snow Hill at around 3.50 am. The Stourbridge men came off the footplate at Birmingham; they would then work the first passenger train to Kidderminster which arrived at Stourbridge Junction at around 6.25 am. However, on Saturday evenings, instead of returning with the 12.10 am Sunday mails, the crew worked the 11.05 pm class 'C' express freight from Paddington to Stourbridge Junction booked to arrive at 5.41 am Sunday. Apparently this train called at Park Royal, to pick up several wagons of Guinness, and Hockley (plus a non-working halt at Snow Hill) where it was due to arrive at

3.59 am. From Hockley the train proceeded to Stourbridge Junction under 'E' headlamps calling at Oldbury & Langley Green, Rowley Regis and Cradley Heath & Cradley. This working was booked for a class '47XX', 2-8-0 heavy freight engine. As the 8.20 pm goods from Kidderminster only ran Monday (pm) to Friday (pm), the double home crew may have had to work the Sunday evening passenger service to Paddington over the 'old road' via Oxford so that they would be available to bring back the 12.10 am on Tuesday. Harry Hardwick recalls firing on several 'Saints', the usual class of engine to be found on the 8.20 pm Sunday express, amongst them Nos. 2918 *Saint Catherine*, 2939 *Croome Court*, 2981 *Ivanhoe*, 2989 *Talisman* and 2971 *Albion*. Harry found these engines quite speedy but tended to rock and roll. However, coming up to London on the Sunday did mean an exceptionally long stay in the capital.

Reg Lamb passed out as a fireman in 1936 and after gaining experience in the shunting link, moved up to the bank links and then the double home link. One double home job Reg remembers well was with Archie Thomas, a nice bloke and a good driver:

It was to Crewe via the Wombourn line and Market Drayton with a freight headed by one of the old 2-6-0 'Aberdares'. I was deputising for Archie's regular mate and was a little anxious as Archie was well known for being very conscientious with regard to the amount of coal he used. At Market Drayton we stopped and he took a look at the fire. Fearing the worst, I waited for the judgement. I needn't have worried for what he saw clearly pleased him for he said 'I don't think you'll need to put much more in there, we have enough to get us to Crewe'. So it was off with the brake and on to Crewe where we picked up the firedropper at the entrance to Crewe Gresty Lane, then a sub-shed of Wellington. At the shed the Crewe man opened the firebox doors to see how much work he had in front of him. Seeing the state of the grate he looked back at us in surprise. 'Where's the fire?' he asked. Archie looked at me and with a grin replied, 'We always bring 'em in like that mate'. The fire had practically burnt itself out and with plenty of steam and a full boiler, the firedropper and the other shed men had little to do. No wonder Crewe shed looked forward to engines driven by Archie Thomas! We returned to the shed at around 8 pm and left shortly afterwards. It was a good pull from Crewe to Nantwich and Archie kept a close eye on the fire. 'You've done well Reg; better than my usual mate'. That was indeed praise!

Reg also fired on the Pontypool Road double home jobs. One was a loose-coupled freight with a '28XX' class 2-8-0 on the front. This time it was driver Jack Edmunds at the controls:

This was a long run at the best of times, but on this occasion it took us over 12 hours to complete the journey. We booked on at 8 am and left about an hour later; at about 9.30 pm we arrived at Pontypool Road. I can't remember why it took so long, but time would soon be lost if we were put inside to allow an express to pass us. The return was, I think, at about 8 am (it is likely that this was the 9 am class 'H' freight from Pontypool Road) and it usually took us about nine or ten hours. On the way we would normally stop at Hereford and possibly Worcester where traffic would be put off and picked up; I quite enjoyed the Pontypool Road run.

Rostered Turns of Duty - Stourbridge Shed

Date	Passenger (Steam)	Passenger (Diesel)	Freight	Shunt (Steam)	Shunt (Diesel)	Banking	Shed	Zone	Loco Relief	Specials	Annual Leave	Rest Day Relief	Total Sets	No. of Driving Turns	No. of Firing Turns	No. of Drivers at shed	No. of Firemen at shed
Oct-53	26	5	63	36	0	7	9	7	3	0	18	16	190	190	185	191	171
Nov-55	27	6	56	35	0	6	9	5	2	2	12	15	175	175	169	nk	nk
Feb-56	27	6	57	25	9	6	9	5	2	2	12	15	175	175	160	nk	nk
Aug-56	27	6	55	25	9	7	9	5	2	2	12	15	174	174	159	175	155
Jun-57	17	22	58	25	9	6	11	5	3 Spare		12	15	183	183	146	182	153
Dec-60	7	22	42	10	37	4 Ferry	7	1 Pilot		3 Prep	20 Spare	21	174	174	nk	177	nk
Apl-64	5	23	20	35 *	33	3 Ferry	8				nk	nk	nk	159	94	154	88

nk = not known

* This includes freight trip workings.

Below the double home link were the bank links; Nos. 1 and 2 : the senior and junior links. These two links provided the engine crews for the majority of the Bank Trains, those local pick-up freights that plied their trade between the yards and sidings on the former OWWR as far as Dudley and Tipton, and also the Stourbridge Extension up to Rowley Regis and Langley Green. At some places, in particular Rowley Regis, Corngreaves sidings, Old Hill (goods), and Halesowen, Bank Train engines also worked lengthy shunting stints as well as conveying traffic to and from local yards. At Amblecote goods yard No. 3 Bank Train worked trips to and from Stourbridge Junction in addition to carrying out all shunting duties. The senior link (No. 1 Bank Link) also had a number of passenger turns whilst the junior link (No. 2 Bank Link) carried out most of the train banking duties. The passenger turns covered by No. 1 Bank Link appear to have been confined to auto-trains and steam railmotors, although there was possibly one loco-hauled to Birmingham (Snow Hill) whilst No. 16 Bank worked an afternoon Longbridge workmen's special. The auto turns were probably on the Dudley-Old Hill services whilst the railmotors would have been employed on the Town shuttle. Railmotor turns were allocated to the link as early as January 1925. In January 1929 the men's representatives put forward a proposal that would have seen a number of services moved to different links. However, at the formal Local Departmental Committee held on 9th January, 1929 these changes were only agreed in part and that was on condition that both No. 1 and No. 2 Bank links were revised. During 1929 it would appear that at least No. 1 Bank underwent a major restructuring, the link being divided into two evenly balanced sections (A and B), each section being of equal importance.

During the war a number of GWR diesel railcars were allocated to Stourbridge shed. By 1943 it had been agreed that a diesel link be formed which would comprise three diesel car turns and five goods turns, the link being placed, at least temporarily, between the double home link and the senior bank link. As a result the links at this time were probably arranged as follows: Nos. 1 and 2 Passenger links (No. 3 Passenger link - a.k.a. the 'Longbridge' link - had probably been abolished); Double Home link; Diesel Car link; No. 1(A & B) & 2 Bank links; Shunting link, and lastly the Shed or Old Men's link (after 1937 this may have been known as the Medical link).

Post-war turns and manning levels

Although records exist relating to the post-war period, and these are more comprehensive than those pre-war, they are far from complete. In particular, it has been difficult to identity many of the jobs shown alphanumerically in the rostered turns of duty. However, in spite of these difficulties, it has still been possible to produce a fairly detailed picture of the manning levels at the shed and the work carried out. Consequently, there has been included opposite and overleaf two charts the first of which shows a breakdown of the rostered turns of duty for various dates over a 10 year period. It is not complete, but it does show how the shed's workload was structured, for example in October 1953

Stourbridge Link Working as at 31st December, 1960

Link No.	Operation	Diesel Turns	Steam Turns	Ferry Turns	Pilot Turns	Engine Prep.	Shed Turns	Rest Day Relief	Spare	Total
One	Passenger	14						2		16
Two	Passenger	6						1		8
Three	Dual/Auto*	2	7	1				2	2	16
Four	Double Home (Goods)		11	3				2	3	16
Five	Senior Bank		18					3	3	24
Six	Junior Bank		13		1		1	3	6	24
Seven	Train Banking*	9	10			3		4		32
Eight	Yard Shunting	28						4		32
Nine	Shed (Medical)						6			6
Totals		59	59	4	1	3	7	21	20	174

Number of drivers employed at the shed   177
Number of firemen employed at the shed   110

* It is thought that in practice the turns shown against the Train Banking link were included within the duties of the Junior (Bottom) Bank link and perhaps even the Senior (Top) Bank link . This structure, therefore, is probably a proposal aimed at redistributing jobs using a well defined mathematical basis (with the exception of No. 9 all other links are multiples of eight) over a greater number of links. It is also noticeable that the proposal balances steam turns against diesel turns and removes from the Passenger links all steam turns. Unfortunately, no details have been discovered regarding the background to this plan so if any reader has further information the author will be only to happy to hear from them. Oddly, as there do not appear to be nine links in operation at Stourbridge in 1955 it is strange that No. 9 link was referred to. Perhaps the shunting link was originally subdivided into a 'diesel shunting link' and a 'steam shunting link'.

there were 26 passenger turns; five diesel car passenger turns (single manned); 63 freight turns including double home jobs, bank trains and local pick-up freights not covered by the bank trains; 36 steam shunting turns (there were no diesel engine shunting turns at this time); seven train banking turns; nine shed turns; seven zone turns (working to the instructions of Control), and three loco relief turns. Each turn, except where stated, required one set of men. To cover for sickness and holidays there were 18 sets of men, whilst 16 sets of men were available for rest day relief etc. Although the second chart appears to give a detailed breakdown of link manning as at 31st December, 1960, in view of the inclusion of 'Dual' and 'Train Banking' links, it is thought that this may have been a proposal and not a working example. Further information would be most welcome.

Every turn at the shed was known by a number often followed by a letter, unfortunately, although complete records of turn numbers exist, it is not always clear which specific job each one relates to, although it has been possible to tentatively identify a substantial minority. On the chart for 'Rostered Turns of Duty' for November 1955 it will be seen that there were six diesel passenger turns; these turns were 40, 40a, 40b, 41, 41a and 41b, each set of three representing a complete daily job. It is thought that turn 40 began by taking an empty car from Stourbridge at 5.50 am, arriving Dudley at 6.10 am. From there it was the 6.24 am 'all stations' to Old Hill arriving at 6.38 am, the return being the 6.48 am to Dudley. This was the pattern of work throughout the day continuing as turns 40a and 40b. The car returned empty to Stourbridge shed from Dudley at 10.22 pm. Turn 41 would be the second diesel car which began the day as the 6.03 am empty working to Dudley, before forming the 6.39 am to Old Hill which returned at 7.00 am. At the end of the day this too returned empty to Stourbridge shed from Dudley, but at 11.22 pm. Unfortunately, many of the other turns are less easy to identify, however, Ray Kendrick's driving log has helped enormously. On the jobs mentioned below, Ray was accompanied by a different fireman on almost every occasion. These firemen were George Poole, G. Whittingham, R. Thomas, A. Webb, P. Cook, J.L. Roberts, S. Hudson, D.G. Thomas, J. Watkins and M. Grosvenor.

In addition to the diesel passenger turns, there were, until 1956, as many as 27 steam passenger jobs starting at No. 20, however, from 1957, as dieselisation began to make inroads into the shed's steam workings, these reduced dramatically. At the time of writing, only two steam passenger turns have so far been identified: No. 28 and No. 51. The latter was a Stourbridge Junction to Birmingham (Snow Hill) working, returning with a pick-up freight from Bordesley Junction. It is thought that this particular passenger service began at Worcester (Shrub Hill) and on 2nd June, 1958 driver Ray Kendrick and fireman George Poole took over the train at 10.30 pm, before departing for Birmingham at 10.35 pm. On the front was Stourbridge's class '51XX' 2-6-2T No. 4146. This service was booked to stop at all stations and was due into Snow Hill at 11.15 pm. The train was on time. The crew left Snow Hill for Tyseley carriage sidings at 11.35 pm and after dropping off the empty stock proceeded light engine to Bordesley Junction arriving at 12.45 am. The engine

'64XX' class 0-6-0PT No. 6422 and its auto-trailer awaits departure from Old Hill probably with a service to Dudley *c*.1955.   *T.J. Edgington*

No. 6418 with auto-trailer No. 83 at Old Hill on 15th September, 1956.   *H.C. Casserley*

left Bordesley Junction at 1.50 am with a class 'K' freight (probably train No. 162), arriving at Stourbridge Junction up yard at 3.10 am (six minutes behind the booked time). After uncoupling, it was back to Stourbridge shed where the crew booked off at 3.30 am. Turn No. 28 was a Stourbridge Junction local passenger service to and from Wolverhampton (Low Level). On 2nd May, 1958 this job was worked by class '57XX' 0-6-0PT No. 9719 (*see page 125*).

By far the most numerous turns were, of course, freight jobs and between 1953 and 1960 the shed averaged around 55 turns. Freight turns appear to fall into three different groups, those beginning with 6(00); 7(00) and 8(00). In October 1953 the shed had 21 6(00) jobs; 24 7(00) jobs and 17 8(00) plus one other. It is believed that the 6(00) turns were mainly long distance freights, certainly in 1950 turn No. 618 seems to have been a Stourbridge Junction to Pontypool Road working, possibly the 8.36 am class 'H' goods. The Stourbridge crew would be relieved at Hereford returning to home ground 'on the cushions'. Another Stourbridge turn was No. 614, a Pontypool Road class 'H' freight scheduled to depart at 1.30 pm. On 8th July, 1958 the men booked for this job had charge of Pontypool Road's 'Grange' class 4-6-0 No. 6872 *Crawley Grange*. The engine left Stourbridge shed at 1.25 pm and with '32 on' departed the up yard at 1.50 pm. Arriving at Worcester Rainbow Hill Junction at 3.10 pm, driver and fireman were relieved by a local crew. It was then a walk back to Worcester Tunnel Junction to pick up the 9.45 am ex-Pontypool Road class 'H' freight headed by Newport's 2-8-0 WD No. 90676. The train departed at 4.15 pm and arrived at Stourbridge down yard at 6.20 pm. Their job done, engine and crew made their way along the main line to Stourbridge shed, finishing at 6.40 pm. Turn 627 was the 3.10 am Cardiff-bound freight manned by Stourbridge footplatemen as far as Hereford (Barton). This train often had a Pontypool Road ex-GWR 2-8-0 on the front, for example Nos. 3826 and 3828, although on one occasion Oxley's 'Grange' class No. 6863 *Dolhywel Grange* was used instead. On Monday 4th May, 1959 turn No. 612 also involved a Pontypool Road 2-8-0, but this time on the return working. The job began with the (ex-Bordesley Junction), 11.00 pm freight from Stourbridge yard to Worcester headed by the latter's class '94XX' 0-6-0PT No. 8427. The train consisted of 46 wagons and was scheduled to stop at Hartlebury where just one wagon was dropped off. The crew reached Worcester yard at 12.25 am and after dropping off the rest of the train it was back to Worcester shed where the men enjoyed a well earned break. By 3.00 am they were ready to relieve the Hereford crew on an incoming 32 wagon freight from South Wales headed by 2-8-0 No. 3818 and by 4.05 am they were on the way back to Stourbridge Junction yard. The following day driver and fireman were booked on the same turn, but this time the up working was aboard Worcester shed's '43XX' class 2-6-0 No. 7338. On this occasion there was no return working from Worcester, the crew having to go back to Stourbridge 'on the cushions'.

Turns numbered in the 7(00) range covered all manner of jobs, as did those numbered 8(00). One such job was turn 742a which was a Kingswinford Junction/Baggeridge Junction trip working. On 2nd October, 1958 the job was in the hands of class '56XX' No. 6678 and a summary of the day's work follows on page 86:

Reproduced from the 25", 1919 Ordnance Survey Map

Netherton Junction, later renamed Blowers Green.

Dudley station. On the left-hand side of the picture an 0-6-0PT is shunting wagons probably on the up goods loop. These wagons may be heading for the marshalling yard. On the right-hand side another 0-6-0PT stands on the down main perhaps with the Old Hill auto-train.

H.C. Casserley

Blowers Green station looking north. BR Standard class '2MT' 2-6-0 No. 78008 on the 4.20 pm from Stourbridge to Wolverhampton on 16th June, 1962. The local passenger service was withdrawn on 30th July, 1962.   *Kidderminster Railway Museum*

Leave shed 5.45 am	Arrive Stourbridge Jn 5.50 am
Leave Stourbridge Jn 6.05 (engine and van)	Arrive Kingswinford Jn 6.15 am
Shunt yard until 8.40, then Cradley (engine & van)	Arrive 9.25 am
Leave Cradley for Lye (15 on)	Arrive 9.45 am
Leave Lye for Stourbridge (engine and van)	Arrive 10.00 am
Leave Stourbridge for Kingswinford Jn (9 on)	Arrive 11.00 am
Leave Kingswinford for Round Oak (18 on)	Arrive 11.30 am
Leave Round Oak for Baggeridge Jn (24 on)	Arrive 12.30 pm
Leave Baggeridge Jn for Stourbridge Jn (E.&V.)	Arrive 1.00 pm
Leave Stourbridge Jn for shed	Arrive 1.20 pm

One 8(00) turn was 816, the Brettell Lane trip working between the yard and Kingswinford Junction and on 1st April, 1958 this was the job allocated to class '16XX' 0-6-0PT No. 1619. At 6.35 am it was off shed and down to Engine Shed Sidings signal box and out onto the down main line. Arriving at Brettell Lane at around 6.40 am, the yard was shunted for about an hour, before making a trip to Kingswinford Junction yards. On this particular day the crew made two round trips to Kingswinford Junction, the second entailing a three hour shunting stint before returning to Brettell Lane where four wagons were detached. The crew booked off at Stourbridge shed at 1.30 pm. Other 8(00) turns covered many of the 18 or so Stourbridge Bank Trains some of which were single turns, whilst others were double. It is thought that turn 866 was No. 14 Bank, the Halesowen and Canal Basin afternoon engine, whilst turn 887 was No. 15 Bank, the Cradley, Rowley Regis, and Oldbury service that normally worked a goods train back to Dudley before running engine and van to Great Bridge LMR to form the 3.17 am to Hartlebury. However, turns 783a and 783b were probably the early and late turns of No. 13 Bank, the Lye and Hayes Lane service (principally a shunting job at Lye goods yard). The early turn began at 5.45 am when engine and crew left Stourbridge shed for Lye goods yard arriving at 5.55 am. Here they would stay until 12.30 pm when they returned to shed. On Monday to Friday, turn 783b left the shed for Lye goods yard at 3.15 pm. At around 3.45 pm there was a trip down the Hayes Lane branch and after shunting there for about an hour, and clearing out any outstanding traffic, it would be back to Lye, the rest of the shift being spent shunting the goods yard. On Saturdays, the crew on turn 783a would be relieved immediately on their return to Stourbridge shed at around 12.45 pm.

Another Bank Train job was turn 871, Bank Train No. 17, the Halesowen to Longbridge service. The turn began with driver and fireman arriving at Old Hill at about 5.15 pm, having travelled up from Stourbridge Junction on one of the frequent local services to Birmingham (Snow Hill). At 5.45 pm on 1st July, 1958 they took over one of Stourbridge's class '74XX' 0-6-0 pannier tanks, No. 7420, which at 45 tons and 9 cwt was a member of the only class of Great Western engines now based at Stourbridge that was allowed over Dowery Dell viaduct. Arriving at Halesowen yard, eight wagons and a brake van were attached and at 6.25 pm (five minutes behind the booked departure time) the train left the main line sidings, past the old Halesowen passenger station closed in 1928, and along the single line to Longbridge situated just before Halesowen Junction on the LMR main line to Birmingham (New Street). After detaching the wagons and reattaching the brake van, No. 7420 left Longbridge at 7.10 pm (10 minutes early) for Halesowen. However, the run back entailed a call at Rubery to pick up traffic for Halesowen and Old Hill and on this particular occasion 21 wagons were added. No. 17 Bank was scheduled to leave Rubery as soon as the class 'K', 7.20 pm ex-Longbridge service, which conveyed traffic from the LMR, had cleared the section. Later, No. 17 Bank engine assisted No. 16 Bank engine (the latter also worked the Longbridge workmen's train) as far as Old Hill with a heavy freight for Dudley. There was also another round trip to Longbridge scheduled, but the driver's log does not show this. At 11.05 pm, 45 minutes ahead of booked departure time, No. 7420 left Halesowen at the head of 19 wagons. This train would probably have been assisted as far as Old Hill by No. 14 Bank engine, the Halesowen and Canal Basin afternoon engine. After completing another round trip between Old Hill and Halesowen, it was down to Stourbridge Junction via Cradley and Lye. At Cradley the crew would both drop off and pick up traffic, the latter, together with any other wagons, being conveyed as far as Lye yard. All down traffic at Lye would subsequently be cleared by No. 8 Bank, the Halesowen evening service, presumably on the way back to Stourbridge Junction with wagons and vans picked-up at Queen's Head and Handsworth. Leaving Lye, No. 7420 ran light engine to Stourbridge Junction where it would cross over to the down main before running to the shed where the crew booked off at 12.55 am.

Having mentioned No. 14 Bank, driver Ray Kendrick and fireman D.G. Thomas worked this turn (No. 866) one Saturday in April 1958. Normally this entailed assisting No. 10 Bank with the 8.15 pm Halesowen to Rowley Regis service, and No. 17 Bank on the 11.50 pm Halesowen to Old Hill, returning if necessary to Canal Basin goods shed to berth empty wagons (if required to carry out this job the engine would be designated Halesowen No. 2 shunting engine). Monday to Friday the crew would then work light engine either from Old Hill or Canal Basin to Stourbridge shed, however on Saturdays there was a trip booked at 6.35 pm from Halesowen to Rowley Regis, engine and van returning to Halesowen to assist No. 8 Bank. On the Saturday in question class '57XX' 0-6-0PT No. 3743 was allocated to the job which began at Halesowen sidings at 3.40 pm. At 3.50 pm eight wagons were 'tripped' to Canal Basin sidings and six returned, the train arriving back in Halesowen at 4.30 pm. After shunting the yard and making up a train of 23 wagons, the trip left Halesowen at 6.40 pm arriving at Rowley at around 7.00 pm. On this occasion four wagons were put on for Old Hill sidings and having arrived at the yard at 7.55 pm engine and crew stayed there until 8.45 pm before running to Halesowen with the van. The remaining duty was to assist No. 8 Bank to Old Hill (the 9.00 pm Halesowen to Queen's Head) where at 9.15 pm No. 3743 was detached, returning to Stourbridge light engine at 9.45 pm.

Between 1953 and 1956 the number of Stourbridge shunting turns remained fairly constant at around 35. These turns were usually given numbers between 740 and 790, and between 800 to 890. Where a job comprised more than one turn the appropriate number was suffixed by the letter 'a', 'b', or 'c' (and, rarely, 'd') thereby denoting that the job comprised early, middle, and late shifts. Existing records appear to indicate that most jobs such as Stourbridge

Junction marshalling yards, Brettell Lane goods yard, Kingswinford Junction, Dudley goods yard, and Oldbury & Langley Green, were probably known by a permanent set of turn numbers, the only variations occurring if a shift was lost or gained. However, it has been noted that some numbers normally associated with freight turns did appear, at various times, in the shunting list. For example, in 1953 turns 754b and 783a were classified as freight turns, however, by November 1955 both turns had been reclassified as shunting duties. These variations were probably brought about by changes in the nature of the work carried out at the yard concerned, for instance the principal duty of turn 754b was now shunting tank traffic. However, changes in the workload of the shed would also impact upon the turn numbering system. If a turn was lost the number would be withdrawn presumably only reappearing if the job was reinstated, or if it had been reallocated to new or additional work. On 16th April, 1958 turn 784a was definitely a Cradley goods yard shunting job as it was Ray Kendrick and fireman P. Cook who worked this duty with class '64XX' 0-6-0T No. 6428. The crew left Stourbridge shed at 6.55 am, arriving at Cradley at 7.10 am. Shunting then continued until 12.45 pm when the crew returned to Stourbridge to book off at 1.20 pm. Other identifiable shunting turns were 746a and 746b, Kingswinford Junction; 751a and b, 752a and b, and 753a, b and c, all Oldbury; 755a, b, c and d were Dudley yard, as were 756a, b and c. Round Oak yard was possibly covered by two turns, 792a and 792b. Shunting the carriage sidings at Stourbridge Junction in the Spring of 1958 was turn 785, a job usually employing a class '51XX' 2-6-2T, e.g. Nos. 5176/5180. By 1956, the duty list began to show diesel shunting turns separately, these being 759a, b and c; 760a, b and c; and 761a, b and c : all would have been Stourbridge marshalling yard turns. After 1957 diesel shunting increased rapidly and soon turns at Round Oak, Kingswinford Junction, Dudley 1 and 2 engines, and Oldbury 1 and 2 engines, had all been turned over to diesel traction.

The remaining turns covered by Stourbridge can be broken down into four groups; (a) train banking; (b) shed; (c) zone, and (d) loco relief. Between 1953 and 1957 the shed operated six or seven banking turns, covering banking targets 18, 19 and 20 (there were other banking targets, but these had not been operational for some years). In 1955/56 banking turns were numbered 742b, 747a and b; 748a and b; 749b (list for August 1956 only), and 801. On 20th June, 1958 No. 19 banking target was a job for class '56XX' No. 6698. From 3.50 pm to 6.40 pm the crew worked in the vicinity of Stourbridge Junction before being called upon to carry out banking duties over the Stourbridge Extension to Cradley and Rowley Regis. Later that same evening, at 8.45 pm, it was over to Coxes Lane on the Windmill End branch where what was possibly a class 'H' freight from Oldbury & Langley Green goods yard to Crewe was to be banked as far as Blowers Green Junction. At 10.45 pm it was back to Coxes Lane to assist a second booked service, No. 16 Bank, that was scheduled to arrive from Halesowen at 11.09 pm. On this evening it was a few minutes early, and was able to depart, banked by No. 6698, at 11.05 pm. Once again banking continued as far as Blowers Green where the engine 'dropped off'. Being the last duty of the shift it was straight back to Stourbridge shed.

Between 1953 and 1963 the shed had on average nine shed turns, the nine which existed between 1953 and 1956 being Nos. 921 to 929. These turns involved moving locomotives around the shed and yard, although it is thought that Nos. 927-929 were the early, middle, and late shifts employed upon wagon shunting at the coal-stage. It is believed that these last three turns were permanent driving jobs for men no longer fit for main line duties and in the 1950s Frank Winnall, Harry Cook and H. Williams were the drivers working these turns.

In addition to the shed turns there were usually two or three loco relief turns, these normally being numbers 910, 911 and 912. One of these turns, No. 910, certainly undertook light engine movements between Stourbridge and Stafford Road, Wolverhampton. One day this involved taking Hereford's 0-6-0 No. 2274 to Wolverhampton, the crew returning with the shed's own 2-8-0 No. 3831. However, men on 'light engines' were sometimes called away to carry out other work. For example, on 25th March, 1958 one crew was removed from their rostered duties to take over what appears to have been the auto-train which ran between Stourbridge Junction (depart 2.20 pm)-Dudley (d. 3.00 pm)-Birmingham (Snow Hill) (d. 3.55 pm)-Dudley (d. 4.30 pm)-Old Hill (arrive 4.44 pm), the driver, Ray Kendrick, being relieved at 4.45 pm.

The shed was also required to provide a number of zone turns which were responsible for working 'specials' as ordered by Control. Usually these were turn Nos. 900 to 907. At Stourbridge Junction there was a zone relief cabin provided for men working these turns. Apparently, drivers were required to report their arrival immediately to Control by telephone. On 16th February, 1959 one zone turn involved class '57XX' 0-6-0T No. 9636 which was utilised on a goods from Stourbridge Junction to Round Oak. The crew reported to the yard at 9.50 pm, leaving for Round Oak with '23 on' just after 11 o'clock. After finishing at Round Oak at 12.45 am it was engine and van to Dudley where a freight train for Stourbridge was waiting. On the return run a number of wagons were exchanged at Kingswinford Junction, the only booked intermediate stop. However, whilst passing Stourbridge shed on the up main at about 3.55 am, the train was signalled into the up goods loop, presumably to allow a faster service to pass. Leaving the loop at 4.40 am, it was on to Stourbridge Junction where the crew reported completion of the job direct to Control.

The records relating to rostered turns of duty also show 'ferry' turns, whereby dmus would be moved, fuelled and routinely maintained, and 'prep' turns involving engine preparation at the shed. On this sort of job driver and fireman were required to prepare about five locomotives, for example on 'prep' turn 879 on 10th April, 1958 Nos. 2853 (a 2-8-0 heavy freight engine), 4646 (an 0-6-0PT), 6349 (a 2-6-0 mixed traffic locomotive), 7910 (a 4-6-0 'Modified Hall'), and ex-LMS '8F' No. 48448 were a day's work, followed by Nos. 2882, 6439, 6393, 4902 and 8792 the next day.

A down local (probably for Wolverhampton) approaches Engine Shed Sidings signal box. On the up main a 4-6-0 heads for Stourbridge Junction 'light engine'.   *D. Bloomer Collection*

Ex-GWR railcar No. W14W waits in the bay platform at the tunnel end of Dudley station *circa* 1960. W14W is thought to be the last ex-GWR railcar allocated to Stourbridge.   *T.J. Edgington*

A '51XX' class 2-6-2T arrives at Brettell Lane with the 12.18 pm (Saturdays only) service from Birmingham (Snow Hill) on 21st January, 1961. *E.J. Dew*

'Manor' class 4-6-0 No. 7806 *Cockington Manor* at Brierley Hill with the 1.00 pm Wolverhampton-Stourbridge Junction train on 21st January, 1961. *E.J. Dew*

'Hall' class 4-6-0 No. 5942 *Doldowlod Hall* at Blowers Green with the 2.15 pm Wolverhampton-Stourbridge Junction service on 21st January, 1961.   *E.J. Dew*

'Manor' class 4-6-0 No. 7817 *Garsington Manor* waits to depart from Dudley with a Stourbridge Junction to Birmingham (Snow Hill) local train in the summer of 1962.   *G. Bennett*

Derby-built 3-car Western Region Suburban dmu (later class '116') works the 2.30 pm Bewdley-Birmingham (Snow Hill) service between Lye and Cradley Heath on 14th June, 1958.

Michael Mensing

Three-car (Swindon) Cross-Country dmu (later class '120') and one bogie van form the 9.40 am Cardiff (General)-Birmingham (Snow Hill) via Hereford service on 30th August, 1962. It is seen here climbing towards Old Hill tunnel.   *Michael Mensing*

'64XX' class 0-6-0PT No. 6418 passes Hagley signal box as it propels the 4.10 pm Kidderminster to Stourbridge auto-train on 10th September, 1962. *Brian Moone/Kidderminster Railway Museum*

An unidentified '64XX' class 0-6-0PT leaves Hagley station with auto coach *Wren* with the same train as above, but just over a year later, 11th September, 1963. In this view the engine is leading the auto-coach. *Brian Moone/Kidderminster Railway Museum*

'51XX' class 2-6-2T No. 4179 pilots 'Grange' class 4-6-0 No. 6827 *Llanfrechfra Grange* on a Stourbridge Junction to Rhyl excursion near Stourbridge shed on 3rd June, 1963. The train has just passed under the Good Friday bridge and is heading towards Brettell Lane.

Brian Moone/Kidderminster Railway Museum

Another view of a double-headed train at the same location. No. 4155 runs bunker-first as it pilots No. 6834 *Dummer Grange* on a Smethwick-Rhyl excursion on 8th August, 1963.

Brian Moone/Kidderminster Railway Museum

The last week of auto-working over the Bumble Hole (Old Hill to Dudley) saw '64XX' class No. 6434 work the service until Friday 12th June, 1964. However, on the last day, Saturday 13th, neither No. 6434 or 6424 were available, so non-auto-fitted No. 7418 worked the service instead. During the last week the train crew comprised driver Jack Walton, fireman Mike Noke and guard Bishop. On 13th June Mike Noke was replaced by G. Walters, Jack Walton may have been replaced by Joe Garden.   *M. Noke Collection*

No. 6434 propels auto-coach No. W254 towards Dudley from Old Hill in 1964.   *G. Bennett*

The last Dudley-Old Hill local passenger service about to leave Dudley with No. 7418 in charge of auto-coach No. W254 on 13th June, 1964.   *G. Bennett*

Signalman Bill Hart looks towards the camera as Ivatt class '2' 2-6-0 No. 46490 hauls parcels vans into Dudley station *circa* 1964.   *G. Bennett*

Routes Available For Stourbridge Train Crews November 1970

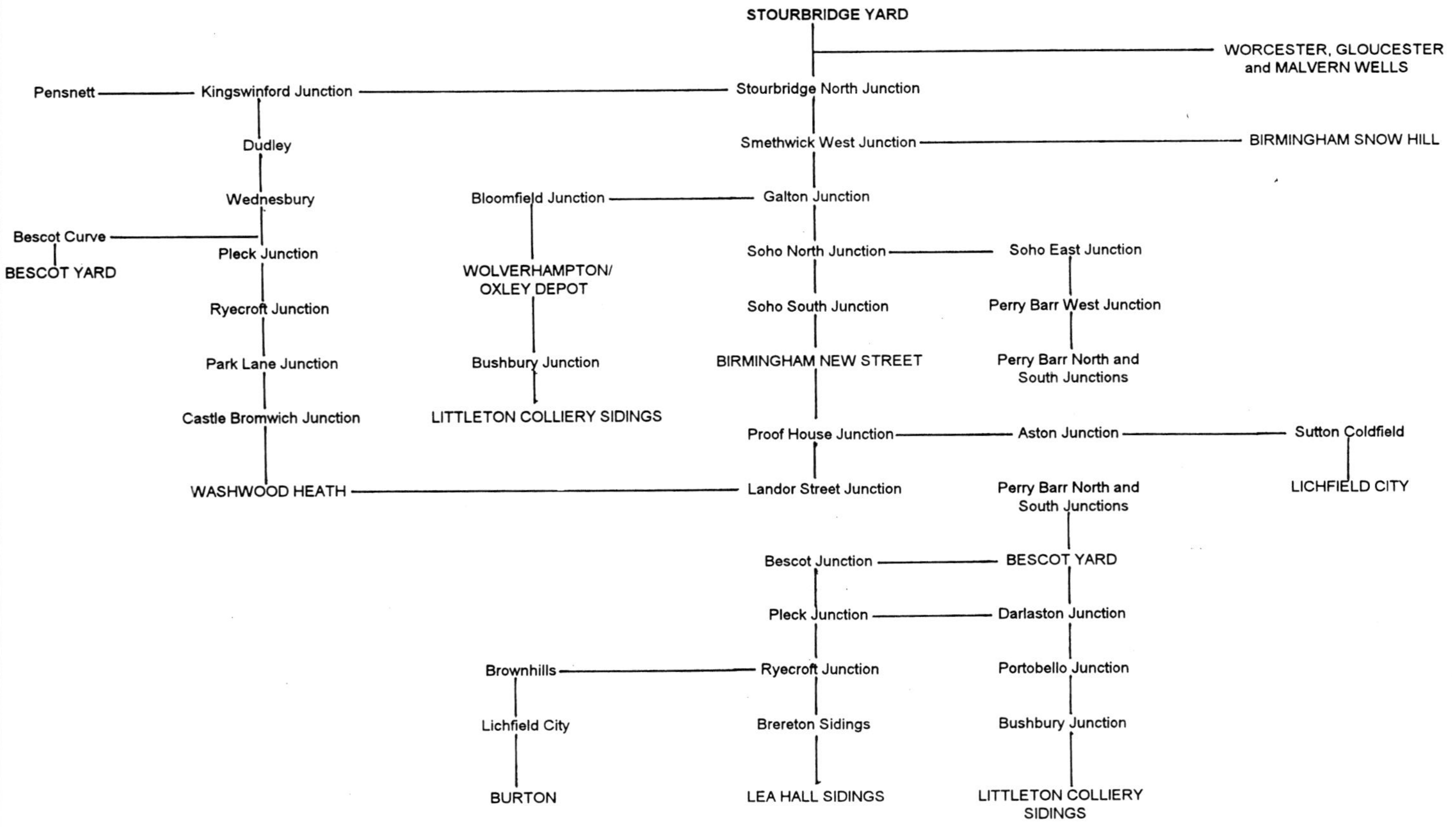

Pensnett — Kingswinford Junction — STOURBRIDGE YARD — Stourbridge North Junction — WORCESTER, GLOUCESTER and MALVERN WELLS

Dudley

Wednesbury

Smethwick West Junction — BIRMINGHAM SNOW HILL

Bescot Curve

BESCOT YARD

Pleck Junction — Bloomfield Junction — Galton Junction

Ryecroft Junction — WOLVERHAMPTON/OXLEY DEPOT — Soho North Junction — Soho East Junction

Park Lane Junction — Bushbury Junction — Soho South Junction — Perry Barr West Junction

Castle Bromwich Junction — LITTLETON COLLIERY SIDINGS — BIRMINGHAM NEW STREET — Perry Barr North and South Junctions

WASHWOOD HEATH — Proof House Junction — Aston Junction — Sutton Coldfield

Landor Street Junction — Perry Barr North and South Junctions — LICHFIELD CITY

Bescot Junction — BESCOT YARD

Pleck Junction — Darlaston Junction

Brownhills — Ryecroft Junction — Portobello Junction

Lichfield City — Brereton Sidings — Bushbury Junction

BURTON — LEA HALL SIDINGS — LITTLETON COLLIERY SIDINGS

Post-steam turns of duty

By the early 1970s, with the change from steam to diesel traction complete and the rail network and the traffic carried upon it contracting, Stourbridge depot was rapidly becoming a mere a shadow of its former self. There had been a substantial loss of local non-footplate railway jobs when the yards closed and steam was withdrawn from the engine sheds, whilst on the footplate, staff numbers had more than halved. Furthermore, by November 1970, the number of route miles worked by Stourbridge-based train crews had been severely curtailed. For example footplatemen working south of Stourbridge Junction would now only cover the lines to Worcester (Shrub Hill) and Gloucester via Abbotswood Junction and Barnwood Junction; also the Worcester (Foregate Street) to Malvern Wells route. Disappointed with the new restrictions, the men requested, through the LDC, that Hereford, Severn Tunnel Junction, Wolverhampton to Shrewsbury, Bescot to Crewe, and Worcester (Shrub Hill)-Norton Junction-Honeybourne-Cheltenham (Malvern Road)-Gloucester all be added, as some staff possessed route knowledge gained from GWR/Western Region days. Unfortunately, this request appears not to have been conceded. A chart showing Stourbridge's sphere of operation has been shown opposite.

In 1974, there were just four driving links: 1, 2, 3 and 4. Link No. 1 was made up of 11 turns, plus one spare turn and two rest day relief. This link was a dmu passenger link working between Kidderminster-Birmingham (New Street)-Four Oaks-Lichfield City; it also included the Town car, and a Worcester service. The two 'rest day relief' drivers covered the following turns:

Driver One	Turn
Monday	657 - Lichfield City (book on at 12.14)
Tuesday	665 - Town shuttle and 21.30 Birmingham N.S. (book on 15.03)
Wednesday	650 - Kidderminster-Lichfield City (book on 12.14)
Thursday	658 - Four Oaks (book on 15.02)
Friday	675 - Town shuttle and Worcester passenger service (book on 16.55)
Saturday	Rest day

Driver Two	
Monday	601 - Four Oaks (book on 05.25)
Tuesday	602 - Kidderminster-Birmingham N.S. (book on 05.25)
Wednesday	620 - Kidderminster-Birmingham N.S. (book on 06.45)
Thursday	Spare (book on 05.30; turn may have covered No. 610 Town car)
Friday	611 Lichfield City (book on 06.10)
Saturday	Rest day

The one remaining turn, No. 600, which began with the 07.03 Kidderminster to Birmingham (New Street) was not covered by the 'rdr' drivers.

Link No. 2 appeared to comprise 14 turns, plus six or seven spare turns and a rest day relief. Of the 14 turns, seven covered four trip workings, Nos. 50, 55, 58, and 60. These mainly worked over the Stourbridge-Brierley Hill-Bescot-Washwood Heath circuit. There was also a Longport freight (turn No. 200); the Pensnett to Burton coal empties (turn No. 250); a Bescot to Worcester freight (turn No. 20); and a Nottingham to Gloucester freight (turn No. 131). There also

Link Number 1 Drivers Circa 1973

Number	Booking On Time	Turn	Turn No.	Effective Mon.Only	Monday	Tuesday	Wednesday	Thursday	Friday	Saturday	Sunday
1	15:00	Spare								Rest Day	Rest Day
2	05:25	06:13 Kidderminster - Birmingham			Rest Day						
		New Street	62		16:55 T1002	15:03 T81	12:14 T75	14:55 T79	12:25 T82	Rest Day	
3		Rest Day Relief			05:25 T62	05:25 T63	06:45 T66	05:30 Spare	06:10 T65		
4	06:45	07:53 Kidderminster - Birmingham					Rest Day				
		New Street	66								06:40
5	14:55	Empty diesel to Tyseley, 17:40 to						Rest Day		Rest Day	
		Four Oaks	79								16:59 T84
6	05:30	Town service	25		Rest Day						
7	16:55	Worcester	1002				Rest Day				
8	05:25	06:35 Kidderminster - Birmingham				Rest Day					
		New Street - Four Oaks	63								
9	12:14	13:03 Kidderminster - Lichfield City	75							Rest Day	
10		Rest Day Relief									
11	12:25	15:03 Kidderminster - Lichfield City	82						Rest Day		
12	05:00	07:03 Kidderminster - Birmingham									
		New Street	60	04:40						Rest Day	
13	15:03	Town service and 21:20 Kidderminster	81		Rest Day	Rest Day			Rest Day		15:50
14	06:10	07:27 Kidderminster - Lichfield City	65	05:50							

Notes

The Link was divided into two groups of men. Each group worked early and late turns on alternate weeks.

The late turns were numbers 1, 3, 5, 7, 9, 11 and 13.

The early turns were numbers 2, 4, 6, 8, 10, 12 and 14.

seems to have been two passenger turns on the Stourbridge Town shuttle and a ferry job. No. 3 link had 11 turns, all of which were trip workings including No. 51 which has been detailed below:

Turn No.		Driver	Secondman		Time
6500	Start	04.55	04.55MO	Prepare locomotive	
				Stourbridge Jn Yard	05.40
		05.05	05.05 MSX	Banking Stourbridge North	05.45 MO
					05.30 MSX
				Relieved by Turn 6501	13.30
	Finish	13.55	13.45		
6501	Start	13.05	13.05	Relieve Turn 6500	13.30
				Banking at Stourbridge North end	13.30
				Relieved by Turn 6502	21.30
	Finish	21.55	21.45		
6502	Start	21.05	21.05	Relieve Turn 6501	21.30
				Banking at Stourbridge North end	21.30
				Leaving Stourbridge Jn at	23.40
				Arrive Langley Green at	00.01 MSX
				Leave Langley Green at	00.11 MSX
				Arrive Stourbridge Jn at	00.35*
				Continue banking duties	05.30
				Relieved by turns 6500 (MSX), 7500 (SO)	05.30
	Finish	05.55	05.45		

* Conveys driver of Turn 6308 to TCD.
MO - Mondays only. MSX - Mondays & Saturdays excepted. SO - Saturdays only.

Finally there was link No. 4, the yard shunting link, which was made up of nine turns. At this time (in the early 1970s), Kidderminster, Brierley Hill, Round Oak, and Langley Green were all allocated permanent class '08' diesel shunters. From the above it would seem that Turn 6308 was the Langley Green shunting engine. This turn was the late shift of Trip 54, booking on at 17.02 hours, Monday to Friday, whilst the early shift, Turn 6306, booked on at 05.50 Tuesday to Friday; 05.05 Mondays Only, and on Saturday 06.14 as Turn 7306. Trip 54 also included Turn 6307, a shunting job at Fellows' yard which was booked to commence at 11.02. The other turns have not been positively identified but it is thought that the Brierley Hill steel terminal shunting turns were 6301/6302/ 6303 (Trip 52), which booked on at 06.00, 14.25 and 21.40 respectively. On Saturday this job was Turn 7307 booking on at 06.00. At this time, the steel terminal was classed as an outstation, men reporting there, not to Stourbridge Junction.

The remaining turns, 6304 and 6305 (Trip 53), and 6321 and 6322 (Trip 57) were possibly the Round Oak and the Kidderminster shunting turns, but it is not known which ones were which. In August 1977 shunting at Round Oak was reduced from two shifts to one, i.e. 10.00 to 16.00 hours, although the Kidderminster shunting engine was increased to three turns.

In 1974 there also existed an 'E' link which covered secondmen (or drivers' assistants). At Stourbridge there were 12 turns which were allocated to secondmen: 6200/550 (Trip 50), 6500/6501/6502 (Trip 51), 6700 (Trip 54), 6703 (Trip 53), 6530 (Trip 59), 6252 (Trip 60) and 6250 (Trip 61). Both the Longport freight and the Pensnett-Burton coal empties were also allocated secondmen. Last, but not least, there were the goods guards which, it is thought, were known as 'M' positions. There were 15 turns covering jobs in both No. 2 link and No. 3 link (passenger guards were not part of the depot's complement but it is thought that there would be around 15 turns for this group).

In January 1980 Stourbridge depot suffered a major blow from which it was never to recover. By 16th January, 1980 the national strike of British Steel Corporation employees was having a serious effect on traffic levels in the Bescot area and a major financial impact upon British Railways as a whole. It was therefore decided that urgent action had to be taken to reduce costs. This action involved (i) curtailment of rest day working; (ii) reduction in overtime working; (iii) non essential jobs to be left, staff to be utilised to assist (i) and (ii); (iv) staff, whose regular jobs had been lost to the strike, to be redeployed upon essential work where possible; (v) any remaining staff who could not be found essential work were to stay at home and be paid in accordance with the guaranteed week arrangements. Although Stourbridge men were assured that once the steel strike had been settled normal working arrangements would resume, declining traffic in the area following the dispute soon made it clear that a return to normal was highly unlikely.

The effects of the steel dispute were felt immediately at Stourbridge with the withdrawal of Trips 61 and 62 (probably Kidderminster-Stourbridge-Brierley Hill-Bescot and/or Washwood Heath workings). These were closely followed by the loss of the night shift element of Trip 57 (Brierley Hill-Bescot-Washwood Heath-Bescot-Stourbridge), together with Trip 59, and the middle shift of Trip 56, the Kidderminster shunting engine. As a result five drivers, three from No. 2 link, one each from links 3 and 4, had to be redeployed, as were the secondmen off Trips 61 and 62. By week five of the strike, a second shunting turn, the middle shift of Trip 54 working Brierley Hill steel terminal, was also cancelled. It is thought that this was the last turn cancellation generated by the steel strike, the amended roster continuing until the dispute was resolved in March. However, further losses were on the way.

Although it had been hoped to revert to normal working following the end of the strike, the developments during the ensuing six months were soon to show that this belief had been far too optimistic. At a Consultation Meeting held at Stourbridge Junction on 5th September, 1980 the staff representatives were dismayed to learn that due to a fall off in local traffic it had been necessary to review shunting arrangements at Kidderminster goods yard. The main problem had been the ending of received coal traffic at Stourport power station and the downturn in the number of incoming wagons to the British Sugar Corporation's processing plant at Foley Park. The upshot of these changes was that the hours of the shunting locomotive (Trip No. 56) were to be reduced to two turns of duty covering the hours between 07.45 and 18.15 Saturdays Excepted; unfortunately, it did not end there.

Also at the above meeting it was proposed to review the shunting arrangements at Brierley Hill steel terminal which had been badly affected by the reduction in the flow of steel products into the West Midlands following the national steel strike. The new working arrangements for Trip 54 saw the hours reduced to 07.15 to 12.40 and 16.20 to 21.50 Saturdays Excepted; furthermore, train crews would now sign on and off at Stourbridge Junction Booking-On Point (BOP), travelling out and back within the times of duty (this meant the end of the steel terminal as an out-station). Once again, the men's representatives had no alternative but to reluctantly agree to the proposals. At Stourbridge Junction itself, existing banking duties were also subject to review. Trip 61's work was now to be included within Trip 53's schedule (the latter was the Stourbridge banking locomotive) thereby allowing the former to be withdrawn (in effect train banking and a local freight working were combined). Trip 53's Saturday Only turn was also withdrawn. However, the plan met with strong opposition from the men who argued that the unreliability of the existing diesel multiple units in particular had led to unpredictable demands being made upon the banker which could only be met by the locomotive's permanent presence at Stourbridge Junction. If the engine was required to work elsewhere, its absence could cause serious disruption to services on the main line. Despite these protests the plan went ahead, although it was agreed that a driver and driver's assistant would be on duty on Saturdays between the hours of 06.00 and 14.00 for the purpose of banking ailing dmus. By December 1981 the Brierley Hill steel terminal shunting locomotive had been withdrawn, all duties being carried out by the Stourbridge banker.

The loss of work led to further reductions in the staffing levels at Stourbridge TCD and by the early 1980s the number of links had been reduced to three. No. 1 link still continued to man the bulk of the passenger work whilst No. 2 link had a mixture of passenger and local trip workings. What was left of the shunting work was combined with Trip No. 52, a local freight job that also involved shunting at Langley Green, to form No. 3 link as follows:

Trip 52 Stourbridge-Langley Green-Bescot and return	04.45 and 13.00 hours
Trip 56 Kidderminster shunting engine	06.00 and 12.30 hours
Round Oak shunting engine	08.15 hours

No. 3 link was manned by drivers who were prevented from carrying out main line work due to ill health and therefore had to be accompanied by a secondman when required to carry out trip workings such as Trip 52. This job comprised two turns of duty, at 04.45 the early shift booked on at Stourbridge Junction and worked light engine to Bescot yard where traffic for Langley Green was picked up. After depositing the wagons at Langley Green the yard and sidings would be shunted before a loaded return was made to Bescot. Engine and crew would then return to Stourbridge Junction dropping off traffic at Langley Green on the way. The late turn booked on at 13.00 hours and would run up to Langley Green light engine to carry out shunting duties. Later, it was over to Handsworth to shunt the Blue Circle Cement Terminal and the nearby Cooper's scrap yard sidings, before returning to Langley Green to pick-up a load for Bescot. The crew would then return light engine to Stourbridge Junction where the locomotive would be stabled until the beginning of its next turn of duty. Bescot

Class '45' No. 45022 *Lytham St Annes* crosses the viaduct just north of Stourbridge Junction with the 6V70 on 11th September, 1985. The rear eight wagons are empty china clay wagons from Cliffe Vale, Stoke, the other wagons being attached at Wednesbury/Brierley Hill.

David J. Hayes

Class '25' No. 25190 heads a chemical train for Albright & Wilson's along the Oldbury branch from Langley Green. The chlorine tanks are separated from the locomotive by two barrier wagons. The train arrived at Langley Green yard as 7T48, the Bescot-Langley 'Speedlink' trip on 28th May, 1986.   *David J. Hayes*

Approaching Langley Green on 30th August, 1985 is class '116' No. 53062 leading the 16.51 Birmingham (New Street) to Stourbridge Junction. In the foreground class '31' No. 31144 waits to leave with a trip freight to Bescot.   *David J. Hayes*

depot had had their eye on this job for some time, however, it was not until Stourbridge TCD closed that they took the job over.

In the early 1980s No. 2 link would have comprised the following turns:

Trip 53 Stourbridge banking and Brierley Hill shunting engine	05.30 and 14.30 hours
Stourbridge Town passenger service	05.30, 11.59, 15.59 hours
Trip 57 Stourbridge-Brierley Hill-Pensnett-Round Oak-Kidderminster-Bescot-Washwood Heath-Stourbridge	09.00 and 17.15 hours
Spare turns booking on at	05.00, 09.00, 13.00, 21.00 hours
Ferry turn	22.00 hours

The spare turns covered holidays, sickness, LDC and consultation meetings, road learning etc. All were moveable turns, there being a two hour limit either side of the rostered booking-on time to achieve greater flexibility.

By the 1980s, Ray Kendrick was in No. 2 link and he has recalled below some of the jobs that this link carried out:

The two turns which comprised Trip 57 were both very busy. The late turn began with the crew running light engine to Brierley Hill steel terminal where a load for Bescot was attached. After exchanging traffic at Bescot yard it was on to Washwood Heath via Walsall, Sutton Park and Castle Bromwich. During winter the road through Sutton Park could be very treacherous and the less experienced driver could easily be caught out when cold frosty conditions were combined with a heavy leaf fall and there was a heavy load on the drawbar. This stretch of line had a dip in it, so running down hill had to be taken at just the right speed; not too fast as to make braking difficult, and not too slow that the train would loose momentum and stall on the climb. The principal danger was wheel slip, so there was a great deal of skill in preventing this through the use of regulator, sand and brake in just the right amounts. However, sometimes mistakes were made causing the train to come to a halt. When this happened it was out of the cab and a brisk walk to the nearest signal where a phone call to the signalman would lead to an assisting engine being sent out.

Brierley Hill was also worked by Trip No. 28, a Bescot job. Trip 28 was required to collect traffic from Pensnett, but if it was late arriving, Trip 57 would go instead and the Stourbridge banker (T53) would be summoned to Brierley Hill to carry out shunting. This mix of duties led to many disagreements between management and men for it was very annoying for a crew to run up to Brierley Hill from Stourbridge Junction after assisting a heavy freight over Old Hill bank and up to Rowley Regis, to return, almost immediately, to Stourbridge Junction to give assistance to a struggling dmu. In theory, the plan to combine shunting and banking was fine, but in practice it rarely worked as intended.

During a lull in activity at Brierley Hill, we would take the opportunity to have a break. A 20 minutes meal break was allowed between the third and fifth hour of each shift, unfortunately, this was not always appreciated at the terminal. Any lack of movement by the shunting engine soon attracted the attention of Sid Hodgson, the yard supervisor and former Stourbridge driver. Often there would be a frank exchange of views between us with the result that our TCI would be awaiting our arrival back at the depot to find out what had happened. This in turn could involve John Smout, the Area Train Crew Manager who would have a few words; still, it was all in a day's work. Occasionally, we might have to go to Round Oak to take over the shunting duties whilst the usual locomotive went off to Bescot to refuel. This meant even further to travel if we were summoned back to Stourbridge Junction in an emergency. Trip 53 was booked for class '45' haulage but often a class '46', or later a class '47' would be substituted. All our other turns tended to be confined to class '25s' or even a class '20' depending what was available at Bescot.

All our trip workings conveyed mixed loads, although the evening train from Brierley Hill to Burton was made up of empty coke wagons brought up from the fuel depot on the Pensnett Trading Estate either by Trip 28 or Trip 57. These wagons would then be reversed into the loop adjacent the main running line to await collection. This service ran to Burton via Dudley, Walsall and Ryecroft Junction where we took the centre road (now removed) to Brownhills and on to Lichfield City and Burton-on-Trent. The return working was a loaded train and was worked as far as Stourbridge Junction where the crew would be relieved by another set of Stourbridge men who would then take the train on to Gloucester. These men would then work a parcels train back to Worcester.

The reduction in available work at Stourbridge train crew depot led to a number of drivers being 'put back'. Without regular turns these men would be booked out to driving jobs when needed, the senior man being first in line. Otherwise, it was secondman duties. In the early 1980s the 'put back' link would have had the following non-driving turns:

Trip 53 booking on at 05.30 and 14.30 hours.
Ferry turn booking on at 22.00 hours
Trip 52 booking on at 04.45 and 13.00 hours.
Spare turns booking on at 05.50, 13.00, and 21.00 hours.

To finish off this chapter a quick look will be taken at No. 1 link which in the 1980s comprised 12 turns working local passenger services. After booking on, drivers would have 10 minutes to read their route notices and five minutes to walk from the booking-on point to the station. This led to some odd booking-on times, e.g. 11.33 hours, 08.37 hours and 14.31 hours, to name but three. These times reflected the departure of the trains which were, in effect, 15 minutes after booking on. Drivers booking-off were allowed 10 minutes disposal time for a locomotive or dmu, five minutes walking time to the BOP, and 10 minutes 'ticket time', i.e. completing the daily records.

On a gloomy afternoon in December 2004 class '66' No. 66168 eases its train of hooded steel carriers towards Kingswinford Junction. On this occasion the train takes precedence over the empty steel carriers waiting to leave Brierely Hill steel terminal headed by class '66' No. 66004.   *Author*

0-6-0 '2301' class 'Dean Goods' No. 2383 on a down Birmingham passenger train at Stourbridge.

0-6-0PT '645' class No. 646 on a Birmingham local passenger train.

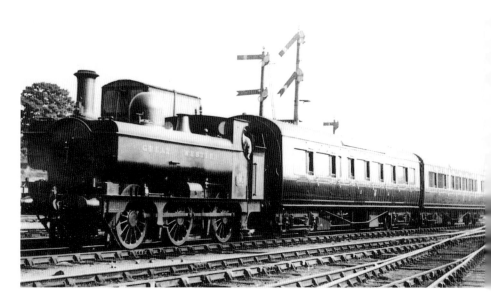

Chapter Four

Locomotives

Although the locomotives allocated to Stourbridge shed have been well documented in *The Railways of Stourbridge*, further data can now be added which should be of value to those with a particular interest in the subject. Unfortunately, the shed's pre-1901 engine allocation remains almost a complete mystery, although two locomotives known to be at Stourbridge on 18th December, 1898 were No. 1802, a class '1501' 0-6-0 saddle tank, and No. 663, a class '388' 'Standard Goods' 0-6-0 tender engine. These two locomotives were involved in a fatal accident on shed when railwayman John Alder was crushed between them. In contrast, from 1901 there is a considerable amount of data available and to illustrate this complete listings of all locomotives allocated to Stourbridge during both 1902 and 1952 have been shown below.

Stourbridge Shed Engine Allocation 1902

Class '517' 0-4-2T
Nos. 521, 557, 842, 848, 1154, 1162, 1424, 1469, 1478, 1479, 1480, 1481, 1483, 1485,1487

Class '645'/'1501' 0-6-0ST
Nos. 1504, 1506, 1507, 1508, 1513, 1519, 1520, 1521, 1523, 1526, 1533, 1535, 1537, 1538, 1539, 1545, 1553, 1559, 1801, 1805, 1806, 1809, 1811

Class '655' 0-6-0ST
Nos. 1771, 1777, 1786, 1788, 2706, 2707, 2713, 2720

Class '2021' 0-6-0ST
Nos. 2030, 2051, 2052, 2054, 2055, 2056, 2095, 2096

Class '57' 0-6-0
No. 58

Class '131' 0-6-0
No. 313

Class '388' Standard Goods 0-6-0
Nos. 434, 1103, 1105

'Sir Daniel' Class 0-6-0
No. 582

Class '3201' 'Stella' 2-4-0
No. 3517

Class '3521' 4-4-0
No. 3544

'3901' class 2-6-2T No. 3904 at Stourbridge Junction.

Steam railmotor No. 40 at Stourbridge on 24th April, 1932.   *H.C. Casserley*

Stourbridge Shed Engine Allocation 1952

Class '14XX' 0-4-2T
Nos. 1401, 1414, 1438, 1458

Class '16XX' 0-6-0PT
No. 1621

Class '2021' 0-6-0PT
No. 2107

Class '2181' 0-6-0PT
No. 2187

Class '2251' 0-6-0
Nos. 2209, 2232, 2246, 2270, 2279

Class '28XX' 2-8-0
Nos. 2804, 2852, 2856, 2865, 2868, 3827

ROD 2-8-0
No. 3028

Class '57XX' 0-6-0PT
Nos. 3649, 3658, 3667, 3710, 3740, 3743, 3751, 4638, 4646, 4687, 4696, 5719, 5726, 5754, 5794, 5795, 7705, 8704, 8742, 8791, 8792, 8797, 9613, 9636, 9719, 9741, 9767, 9782

Class '5100' 2-6-2T
Nos. 4104, 4146, 4150, 4172, 4173, 5101, 5105, 5107, 5147, 5155, 5160, 5165, 5167, 5170, 5180, 5189, 5191, 5193, 5196, 5197, 5199

Class '43XX' 2-6-0
Nos. 4375, 5309, 5313, 5371, 5379, 6327, 6332, 6354, 6391

Class '56XX' 0-6-2T
Nos. 5606, 5642, 5651, 5658, 6609, 6630, 6646, 6667, 6674, 6677, 6678

'Grange' class 4-6-0
Nos. 6803, 6828, 6857

Class '74XX' 0-6-0PT
Nos. 7402, 7428, 7429, 7430, 7432, 7435, 7441, 7442, 7448, 7449

Class '94XX' 0-6-0PT
Nos. 8419, 9427, 9450, 9477

At this time there would also have been at least three ex-GWR diesel railcars, including, it is thought, Nos. 8 and 14.

The vast majority of engine and labour resources employed at Stourbridge were utilised on freight or freight related activities, a situation underlined by the fact that during the 1950s this work represented between 60 and 70 per cent

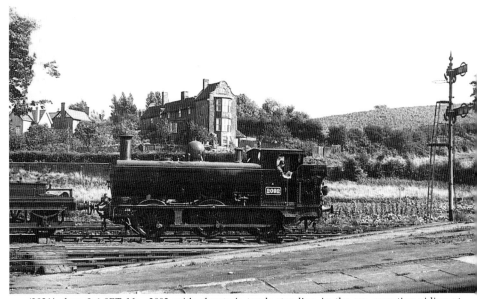

'2021' class 0-6-0PT No. 2092 with shunter's truck standing in the up reception siding at Stourbridge Junction on 10th September, 1949. Chawn Hill House is in the background.

H.C. Casserley

'57XX' class 0-6-0PT No. 8797 shunts mineral wagons near Stourbridge shed in 1960. Locomotives of this type would have seen regular use as train banking engines.

P. Coutanche Collection

'57XX' class 0-6-0PT No. 3745 outside Stourbridge shed *circa* 1960.   *D.K. Jones Collection*

'57XX' class 0-6-0PT No. 4687 at Round Oak sidings *circa* 1962.   *V. Morgan*

Diverted via Dudley and Old Hill on 23rd September, 1956 due to engineering works near Priestfield, the 11.45 am Birkenhead (Woodside) to Paddington is double-headed by '51XX' class No. 4140 and 'Castle' class 4-6-0 No. 5088 *Llanthony Abbey* and is seen near Baptist End.

Michael Mensing

'Castle' class 4-6-0 No. 7012 *Barry Castle* on the 5.29 pm Wolverhampton (Low Level) to Worcester (Shrub Hill) leaves Brierley Hill on 26th August, 1961.   *Michael Mensing*

of the shed's duties. Most of the jobs involved shunting the local yards; operating the Bank Trains (these were local freight jobs, although No. 7 ran as far as Hartlebury; No. 8 to Handsworth, and Queens Head; whilst *circa* 1955 Bank Train No. 9 was reintroduced as a trip to Cannock Road Junction, a destination not normally associated with Stourbridge Bank Trains); and working trips/pick-up freights to and from the yards at Bordesley Junction, Dudley, and the Kingswinford/Wombourn branch either as far as the exchange sidings at Baggeridge Junction, or through to Oxley Sidings in Wolverhampton. However, the double home link had several jobs which took engines and men further afield. Yard shunting, short distance trip workings and the shed's Bank Trains, were normally the province of the 0-6-0 pannier tank, the longer distance pick-up freights usually employing one of the larger tank engines, a class '56XX' or '51XX' for example. By the early 1950s much of the local work was in the hands of the ubiquitous class '57XX' engines, although these were not the only pannier tanks to be allocated to Stourbridge at this time. Working alongside these locomotives were the small, and not always popular, class '16XXs' beavering away at Brettell Lane and Round Oak yards, whilst numerous class '74XXs' were also employed on a range of jobs throughout the district. One area often associated with the latter is Halesowen* where Western Region freight services to and from Longbridge, and the workmen's trains between Old Hill and Longbridge, were always in the hands of these engines after the withdrawal of the class '27XXs' from the line. Weight restrictions imposed upon Dowery Dell viaduct effectively precluded the use of class '57XXs' south of Halesowen although the yard was regularly visited by ex-Midland Railway class '2F' 0-6-0s arriving from the direction of Halesowen Junction on the London Midland main line. Halesowen was quite an interesting area in terms of Great Western engine workings so it is probably worth taking a closer look at these often complex arrangements.

In 1958/59, Halesowen yards were worked by no less than six Bank Trains: No. 2 - Halesowen morning service; No. 8 - Halesowen evening service; No. 10 - Halesowen to Rowley Regis, and Oldbury & Langley Green; No. 14 - Halesowen and Canal Basin afternoon engine; No. 16 - Halesowen assistant engine; and No. 17 - Halesowen to Longbridge (the last mentioned may have been worked by an engine off one of the other Bank Trains?). Bank trains working out of Halesowen would usually be assisted as far as Old Hill, or Rowley Regis if continuing in the direction of Birmingham. These banking duties were undertaken by one of the other Halesowen engines. Another aspect of Bank Train working was that they also provided the local shunting engines and in 1957/58 the engines off Bank Train Nos. 2, 14, and 8 doubled up as Halesowen shunting engines 1, 2, and 3 respectively. No. 2 shunting engine was normally a job for a class '74XX' engine, however, during the day not only were the crews relieved but the engine would be changed as well. This shunting job began at 5.30 am when the engine set out from Stourbridge shed arriving at Halesowen at 6.05 am. It then continued for nearly 18 hours on Monday; 21 hours Tuesday to Friday; and 15½ hours on Saturday. Apparently such long stints may have required more coal than a single tank engine bunker could

* Halesowen was located at the meeting point of the GWR branch from Old Hill, and the Halesowen & Northfield Railway - the Joint Line - from Longbridge - *see also Volume One, Chapter Five.*

hold; they also might have led to a deterioration in the quality of the fire. To avoid these potential problems it was arranged that during the early afternoon footplatemen working the middle shift on shunting engine No. 2 would exchange locomotives with men arriving around 2.10 pm with No. 8 Bank headed by a class '57XX' locomotive. As No. 8 Bank engine had left the shed at 12.55 pm it would arrive at Halesowen with a relatively clean fire and a good supply of coal making it the ideal candidate to take over from the class '74XX'. After the exchange had been made the '74XX' would continue as shunting engine No. 3 working the yards from 2.30 pm until 9.00 pm. At the end of the stint the engine would leave Halesowen in charge of No. 8 Bank Train which involved working a trip to Queens Head, picking up London and West Country traffic at Old Hill, Rowley Regis, Oldbury & Langley Green and Handsworth. No. 8 was scheduled to arrive at its destination at around 10.30 pm and would be assisted as far as Rowley Regis by No. 16 Bank Train engine (SX), and No. 14 (SO). At Rowley Regis the crew were relieved. The engine returned to Stourbridge Junction with a load from Handsworth at 12.03 am.

At the northern end of the Halesowen branch was Old Hill on the main line between Stourbridge Junction and Birmingham (Snow Hill). Old Hill was also the southern terminus of the Windmill End branch that ran from Old Hill to Dudley via Blowers Green Junction. This branch saw both regular freight and passenger train workings, the former employing a wide variety of engines whilst in later years the latter was shared by auto-fitted class '64XX' pannier tanks and ex-GWR railcars introduced into the area during World War II (these were later replaced by BR single diesel units). Initially, the class '64XXs' were supplied by Stafford Road these being Nos. 6418 and 6422 which had been transferred to the shed from Banbury (c.June 1951) and Croes Newydd (c.May 1950) respectively. On 30th July, 1962 No. 6418 was reallocated to Stourbridge, the shed having become responsible for all Dudley-Old Hill passenger trains. One of the most interesting passenger services to run over the Windmill End branch was in the 1930s when the 8.07 am departure from Wolverhampton (Low Level) to Carmarthen was routed via Dudley and Old Hill before heading back into Snow Hill. From Birmingham it continued through Stratford and Gloucester to Cardiff, Swansea, and Carmarthen. The Windmill End branch would also be used as a diversionary route if the main line between Priestfield Junction and Handsworth Junction was affected by engineering work. Occasionally, problems between Stourbridge North Junction and Blowers Green Junction would also force Stourbridge Junction-Wolverhampton (Low Level) services to be diverted over the branch even though this necessitated a reversal at Old Hill. Diversions from off the Wolverhampton-Birmingham main line enabled the branch temporarily to experience express passenger traffic headed by a range of Great Western 4-6-0s with the exception of 'Kings' which were banned (as were the heavy freight '47XX' class 2-8-0s) from the line as it was badly affected by subsidence. Many of these passenger trains would be assisted by a pilot engine.

Both the Windmill End branch and the Halesowen branch* opened on 1st March, 1878 each section running into Old Hill station in the direction of Birmingham. Consequently, there was no direct access from one branch to the

* Originally, the two branches were known jointly as the 'Netherton and Halesowen branch'.

other, trains having to reverse in Old Hill station. Originally, plans had been drawn up which would have provided a direct route from Dudley to Halesowen, authority for construction being vested in the West Midland Railway Act, 1862. The line was to have passed under the Stourbridge Extension about 200 yards west of Old Hill station and would have had two connections to the main line. The first, from the Dudley direction, would have swung westwards to join the main line facing Stourbridge, whilst the second, from the Halesowen direction, would connect with the Stourbridge Extension Railway at Old Hill facing towards Birmingham. In the event the Great Western Railway decided not to build the through route and instead turned the connection from Dudley eastwards where it joined the main line at Old Hill (this later became known as the Windmill End branch). The connection from Halesowen was of course completed as planned. Had the GWR continued with the plan to build the through route, even after changing the direction of the Dudley connection, it would have commenced at a junction with the Dudley-Old Hill section near the 'Old Lion' colliery and joined the Halesowen branch at a junction just to the north of Haden Hill tunnel. The decision to abandon the line appears to have been taken quite late in the day as land had been purchased and some of the earthworks completed both to the north of the Extension railway, and to the south. In fact, where the latter was concerned, a bridge had been built to carry the tramway from Haden Hill Pit No. 2 across the line.

The closure of the Windmill End branch to passenger traffic occurred on 15th June, 1964 something which did not come as any surprise to local railwaymen, driver Ben Hall of Stourbridge shed stating: 'It's a wonder they didn't close it four years ago'. The section was closed completely on 1st January, 1968 whilst the branch from Old Hill to Halesowen soldiered on until 1st October, 1969 as a 'freight only' line, the workmen's trains, i.e. services between Old Hill and Longbridge, having ceased running on 1st September, 1958. This was not quite the end for passenger traffic as the branch was later visited by a number of railtours, the last steam-hauled being on 11th September, 1966 when Nos. 9610 and 9630 did the honours, although the final passenger train to visit Halesowen was a diesel multiple unit on 2nd March, 1968.

Before World War II Stourbridge shed had a number of double home workings, although these had been withdrawn by about 1945. With the loss of the long distance jobs the double home link existed in name only as the men no longer had to lodge away from home, crews being relieved at such places as Hereford, Gloucester, Worcester and Oxley. However, before the war the men in the double home link had worked as far as Crewe, London and Pontypool Road, although the engines that they were given were not always to their liking. The first recorded complaint was made in February 1938 and concerned the heavy mineral trains from Pontypool Road to Stourbridge which were normally in the hands of 2-8-0 freight engines.

It would appear that on occasion, when one of these locomotives was not available, a class '56XX' 0-6-2 tank engine would be used instead. Stourbridge men saw these engines as being totally unsuitable for the job complaining that they had insufficient braking power to enable such trains to be handled safely. A few months later in June, ROD 2-8-0 No. 3001 fell out of favour with

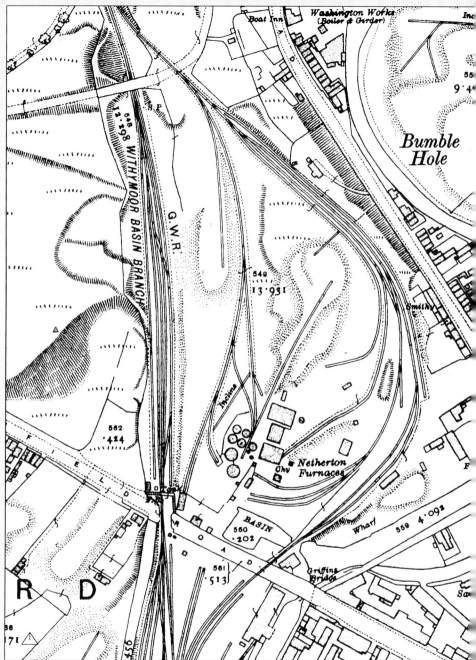

Withymoor Basin branch 1919 (later Netherton goods branch). The sidings on the branch line between the road bridge and the level crossing were ballast sidings, as were the two immediately to the right of the 'GWR'. The lines on the far right served Netherton Furnaces, there was also a line which ran through to the goods depot. The right-hand sidings were accessed by a ground frame (Rounds Siding Ground Frame) located on the branch to the north of the road bridge.

Reproduced from the 25" Ordnance Survey Map

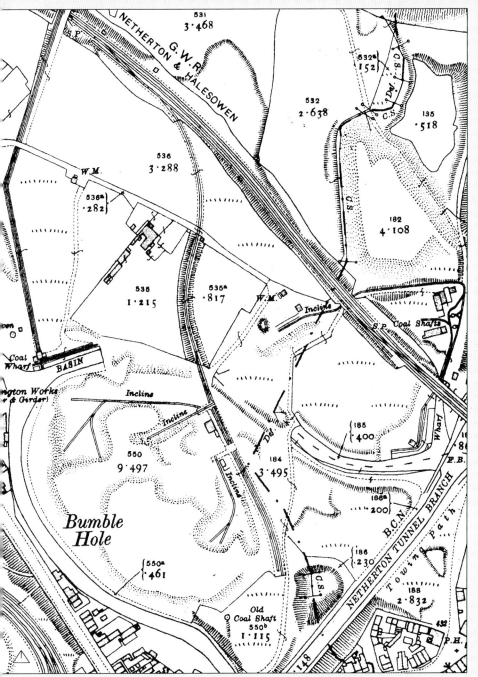

Netherton and Halesowen branch 1919. The sidings on the west side of the main line were added *circa* April 1906. The long s-shaped siding was Messrs Pearson's Bumble Hole ballast siding accessed by a ground frame on the up side. The ballast siding had been removed by 1938. The ground frame and siding were taken out of use in February 1946.

Reproduced from the 25″ Ordnance Survey Map

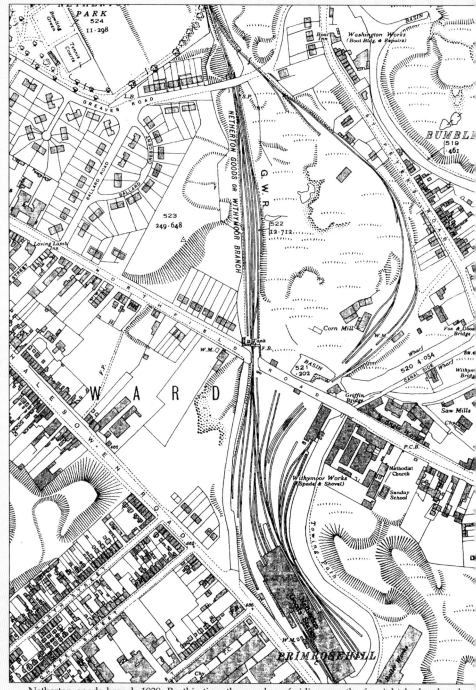

Netherton goods branch 1939. By this time the number of sidings on the far right had reduced considerably. The former through line now terminated at the Canal Basin, the other line serves a corn mill (C.F. Bush?). The ballast sidings formerly located approximately half way between the main line and the right-hand siding have been removed.

Reproduced from the 25" Ordnance Survey Map

Stourbridge crews who asked through the Local Departmental Committee for its removal from Pontypool Road jobs. Unfortunately, records do not show how these complaints were resolved. Although by the end of the war Stourbridge engine crews had stopped working double home turns the shed still had to provide locomotives for some of the long distance freights which started in the district. These would be manned by Stourbridge footplatemen who would be relieved *en route*, the engine continuing in the hands of a crew from another shed, e.g. Worcester, Hereford or Cardiff. Later the engine would normally return to the home shed by way of a similar working back into the area, the incoming crew being relieved at the appropriate yard. Identifying the class of engine booked to work a particular train is not easy, however, the task is made simpler by reference to the appropriate 'Freight Marshalling Instructions', but what this publication does not show is the shed to which the engine belonged. Luckily, some records have survived that both give the train and the Stourbridge engines which worked it. These have been shown below.

In the early 1950s Stourbridge possessed as many as four 4-6-0 'Granges': No 6803 *Bucklebury Grange* (1951-1960); No. 6823 *Oakley Grange* (1953-1955); No. 6828 *Trellech Grange* (1948-1957); and No. 6857 *Tudor Grange* (1948-1955). This type of engine would have been employed on services such as the class 'D', MX Stourbridge Junction to Cardiff which in the autumn of 1951 departed at 1.15 am. It is thought that this service would have utilised two 'Granges' working alternate days Tuesday to Saturday. After being serviced at Cardiff the shed would try and return the engines back to Stourbridge Junction as soon as possible. Interestingly, by the end of the same year, South Wales services to and from Stourbridge Junction via Hereford had been temporarily suspended due to major repairs having to be carried out on Ledbury tunnel. As a result Stourbridge shed was having difficulty finding appropriate work for the two 'Granges' normally employed on the Cardiff freight. It was therefore decided in January 1952 to use these machines in place of the shed's two 2-6-0 engines Nos. 4375 and 6327 on what was probably the 7.30 pm class 'H' service from Priestfield to Swindon (this service would also sometimes use a class '28XX' or a 'Hall'). The 4MT class '43XX' 2-6-0s were well represented at the shed, for example at various times during 1958 Nos. 5371, 5381, 6317, 6332, 6340, 6342, 6349, 6357, 6367, and 6393 had all spent some time there. One of these engines would have been scheduled for the 10.50 pm, class 'F' service from Stourbridge Junction to Crewe, returning on the 12 noon, class 'F' from Crewe to Stourbridge Junction arriving at 3.45 pm, both trains running over the Wombourn line. These useful engines were also employed as necessary on local passenger services, or filling in for a class '28XX' if the shed was thrown short by a couple of locomotive failures, or a breakdown coinciding with a planned visit to the works.

Unfortunately, apart from those few examples mentioned above, it has been difficult to be precise as to which other freight services Stourbridge engines would have been allocated as even trains starting from the Junction might not necessarily employ a local engine, especially if they were balancing workings returning locomotives to their home depots. A look at the 'Freight Marshalling

Dudley station was used by both Western Region and the London Midland Region and in this view Ivatt 2-6-2T No. 41223 shunts carriage stock probably for a local train to Walsall on 15th September, 1956.   *H.C. Casserley*

'Grange' class 4-6-0 No. 6833 *Calcot Grange* heads the lightweight 4.55 pm Stourbridge Junction to Worcester service near Kidderminster on 26th July, 1963.   *D.K. Jones Collection*

Instructions' for January 1958 illustrates this point. The 3.00 am, class 'H' (MX) from Stourbridge Junction to Little Mill Junction (located just to the north of Pontypool Road) was booked for a WD 2-8-0, as was the 'Mondays Only' service to Pontypool Road. Stourbridge at this time had no WDs in its allocation but Pontypool Road had several, so in all likelihood these two trains used engines returning to the latter. Several trains were booked for class '28XX' working, especially interesting was the 8.38 am Stourbridge Junction to Pontypool Road class 'H' which was booked for a '28XX' Monday, Wednesday, and Friday, and an ex-LMS engine on Tuesday, Thursday and Saturday. Also booked for class '28XX' haulage was the 11.10 am, class 'H' to Cardiff, and the 1.50 pm (SX)/1.30 pm (SO) class 'H' to Pontypool Road, although the 11.45 pm (SO) class 'H' to Pontypool Road was booked for a 'Grange'. From 15th September, 1958 this 'Saturdays Only' service departed Stourbridge Junction at 6.45 pm arriving Pontypool Road sometime after midnight. If this was booked for a Stourbridge 'Grange' it might have returned via the 3 am (MO) class 'H' Pontypool Road to Oxley Sidings, arriving Stourbridge Junction at 11.49 am. Another class '28XX' job in January 1958 was the 9.05 pm (SX) Stourbridge Junction to Oxley Sidings which was a class 'E' train, comprising both vacuum and non-vacuum wagons, calling at Round Oak and Dudley. Services feeding into this train were, at Stourbridge Junction, the 8.05 pm (SX), class 'H' from Cradley Heath & Cradley, and Nos. 3 and 11 Bank Trains (Amblecote goods yard, and Old Hill goods yard respectively), whilst at Dudley the 6.40 pm (SX) class 'K' ex-Tipton (Five Ways); the 7.45pm (SX) class 'K' Kingswinford Junction to Tipton (Five Ways); the 8.05 pm (SX) ex-Netherton (No. 31 Bank); and the 8.05 pm (SX) class 'H' Oldbury & Langley Green to Oxley Sidings, fulfilled a similar function. The Rowley Regis oil tank trains also provided regular work for the class '28XX' and in the winter of 1957/58 there were two such jobs. The first of these was the 2.20 pm, class 'F', empty tank train from Rowley Regis to Saltney, the engine returning to the West Midlands the next day by way of the 6.30 am, class 'F', Stanlow to Rowley Regis fuel oil service. The second working was the 9.05 pm (SX), class 'E', Stourbridge Junction to Oxley Sidings. After arrival at Oxley at 11.36 pm the engine continued north with the 12.45 am (MX), class 'F' to Saltney. At 3.40 pm the same day the '28XX' would return at the head of the class 'F', Stanlow to Rowley Regis fuel oil. With the exception of the 9.05 pm departure which ran via Dudley, these trains were routed over the Wombourn line.

Stourbridge shed also provided motive power for passenger services, although these too were largely local including trains to Dudley and Wolverhampton; over the Stourbridge Extension to Birmingham (Snow Hill) (some continuing to Leamington Spa or Stratford-upon-Avon); Birmingham (Snow Hill) via Great Bridge; the Windmill End branch between Dudley and Old Hill, and the unadvertised workmen's trains between Old Hill and Longbridge. However, the most local of them all was the Stourbridge Town branch; the shortest passenger journey in the country. Over the years the Town shuttle services were worked by steam railmotors, diesel railcars (including ex-GWR streamlined units, British Rail first generation diesel units, and today class '153s'), and auto-fitted steam engines. The last mentioned included the 0-4-2T

Tipton Basin showing the Basin branch (junction bottom left).

Reproduced from the 25″, 1919 Ordnance Survey Map

class '48XX' (later renumbered to the '14XX' series) the earliest known examples allocated to Stourbridge being Nos. 4853, 4857, and 4858 in 1936. The last 0-4-2T to work at Stourbridge was No. 1458 which was transferred to Southall on 27th December, 1957. By 1956 the ex-GWR diesel railcars had been introduced on to the branch, although by the late 1950s these had been replaced by new BR diesel units.

Dieselization of the Town services did not totally lead to the displacement of steam from the branch, the 0-4-2 tank engine's successor at Stourbridge, the auto-fitted class '64XX' 0-6-0 pannier tank, often being called upon to take over the services if a diesel railcar failed. As a result locomotives such as Nos. 6424 or 6434 for example, coupled to the standby auto-trailer, continued to do sterling work over the branch until the early to middle 1960s when steam was finally eliminated by diesel traction. Due to the nature of the Town branch the auto-trailer always had to be propelled from the Town to the Junction station; it was also subject to excessive flange wear to the wheel sets on one side (occasionally, the auto-trailer was pulled to the Junction - *see Volume One, Chapter 3, p.86*). To overcome this problem, vehicles were routinely exchanged between Town branch duties and those on the Dudley-Old Hill line. The most well known auto-trailer at Stourbridge was of course *Wren*, although records indicate that No. 44 was there in 1956; No. 45 in 1942; No. 76 in 1949; and No. 111 in 1925. On the Old Hill to Dudley line No. W254 was the trailer used for the last passenger service.

Prior to the introduction of the class '48XX' 0-4-2T the Town service was often worked by class '2021' 0-6-0 pannier tanks. A number of these engines had been auto-fitted between 1915 and 1930 including three of Stourbridge's allocation, i.e. Nos. 2102, 2152, and 2158. Two of these engines, Nos. 2102 and 2158, arrived *circa* 1925 remaining until the mid-1930s. However, No. 2152 had a far longer residency being at the shed from around 1905 to at least the outbreak of World War II. A fourth Stourbridge class '2021', No. 2106, was auto-fitted during the early 1930s, but this was only a short term modification and by September 1936 the equipment had been removed.

On the Stourbridge Junction-Wolverhampton (Low Level) services class '57XX' pannier tanks were a common sight and on 2nd May, 1958 it was the turn of No. 9719 to work the 6.10 am 'all stations' from the Junction to Wolverhampton, the three-coach train loading to 91 tons. Arriving at 6.53 am the engine was detached and after running round its train prepared to leave with the 7.35 am (SX) back to Stourbridge. After arrival at the Junction the engine was removed from passenger duties and after running light to Blowers Green sidings spent the rest of the shift shunting the yard (according to the WTT, this shunting duty was normally carried out by the engine off the 6.15 am Old Hill to Longbridge passenger which would have run light from Old Hill to Blowers Green after returning the empty stock). Class '51XX' 2-6-2 tank engines were also regulars on the line and it was No. 4173 which worked the last 'local' between Stourbridge Junction and Wolverhampton (Low Level) on 30th July, 1962. These engines also worked passenger services over the Stourbridge-Birmingham (Snow Hill) line until steam-hauled trains were ousted by the arrival of dmus (even with the introduction of dmus some passenger services remained steam-hauled for a time).

A diesel parcels unit from the W55991 series works through Old Hill towards Stourbridge Junction on 14th May, 1964. *Michael Mensing*

'Manor' class 4-6-0 No. 7806 *Cockington Manor* with the 4.35 pm Stourbridge Junction-Dudley-Birmingham (Snow Hill) restarts from Brettell Lane on 26th August, 1961. *Michael Mensing*

Whilst the Stourbridge-Wolverhampton line lost its local passenger services in 1962 it did retain one important inter-regional working; 1V73, the 1.40 am Sundays Only, Crewe to Plymouth express. The line also saw continuing use by freight traffic and when the Wombourn branch was closed on 1st March, 1965 trains formerly using this line were rerouted through Dudley and Wolverhampton. Also working over the route were a small number of parcels trains, for example during week beginning 16th September, 1962 there were five down trains between Stourbridge Junction and Wolverhampton (Low Level) including the 2.10 pm (MX) Penzance to Crewe and the 3.50 pm from Hartlebury. There were also five trains in the opposite direction including the 10.45 pm (MX) Crewe to Bristol and the 1.25 pm to Hartlebury. One of these trains, the 12.02 pm from Dudley to Stourbridge, probably utilised the Diesel Parcels Unit (DPU) that had earlier terminated at Dudley after arriving with the 10.20 am from Wolverhampton. There was also a 'Mondays Only' parcels train leaving Low Level at 9.55 am. The two long distance trains were loco-hauled whilst the local services were worked by DPUs with the exception of the 3.20 pm from Wolverhampton (Low Level) to Stourbridge Junction (train reporting number 3H29) and the 9.00 pm departure from Stourbridge Junction (3H65) which were both steam hauled. Surviving records show that 3H65 at this time was often worked by 2-6-2 tank locomotives and during one week in October both No. 4168 and No. 5192 (as well as 'Grange' No. 6816 *Frankton Grange*) were so employed. Nos. 4168 and 5192 were examples of the many Collett class '51XX' 2-6-2T locomotives to be allocated to Stourbridge, the first examples arriving at the shed *c*.1929. However, between 1930 and 1935/36 these engines shared duties with two other, smaller, 2-6-2T types: the class '4575', and the lighter class '4500'. By 18th January, 1930 the shed possessed two of the latter, Nos. 4546 and 4559.

In February 1930 a '45XX' was diagrammed to work the 5.40 am ex-Snow Hill 'local' from Stourbridge Junction to Kidderminster, departing at 6.30 am. From Kidderminster it was probably light engine to Bewdley where it took over the 7.33 am passenger service to Snow Hill arriving at Stourbridge Junction at 8.00 am. From here the engine went forward on the 8.36 am from the Junction (ex-Colwall) to Lapworth. It was then employed on the 9.48 am Lapworth to Snow Hill; the 12.15 pm Snow Hill to Solihull; and the 12.52 pm Solihull to Kidderminster (SX)/Stourport (SO). The engine may have come off at Stourbridge as the diagram continued with the 3.07 pm from Stourbridge Junction to Wolverhampton (Low Level), this being the 11.35 am ex-Oxford. The above does seem to imply several engine changes so perhaps the '45XX' was being tested over a number of different routes?

Apart from the locomotives mentioned above there were a number of other classes of engine allocated to the shed, one or two for just a short period of time. For example between 1963 and 1965 two class '61XX' 2-6-2T engines Nos. 6129 and 6137 were transferred from Banbury and Tyseley respectively. However, within 12 months of arrival both had been withdrawn from the shed. In 1961 four 'Manor' 4-6-0s, Nos. 7806 *Cockington Manor*, 7816 *Frilsham Manor*, 7817 *Garsington Manor* and 7824 *Iford Manor* arrived at Stourbridge, three in the same month, January. Almost as soon as it arrived No. 7816 was earmarked for Royal

No. 4974 *Talgarth* Hall on the 6.05 pm Wolverhampton (Low Level) to Stourbridge Junction at Brierley Hill on 26th August, 1961.   *Michael Mensing*

'Hall' class 4-6-0 No. 5977 *Beckford Hall* at the north end of Stourbridge Junction on 9th February, 1957.   *J.W. Gibbs*

Train duties and many hours were spent getting the engine into tiptop condition. Disappointingly, for the men concerned, its services were not called upon as it was one of the standby engines in case of failure. All four 'Manors' had left by September 1962. At the end of the 1950s and during the early 1960s a number of 'Halls' and 'Modified Halls' found their way into the area, although once again their stay was usually less than two years and by 1962 all examples had been reallocated.

In the early 1960s more and more 'foreign' locomotives were transferred in from the London Midland Region (LMR), a process assisted by the realignment of operational boundaries in 1963 which saw Stourbridge absorbed by the LMR. By far the most numerous of these 'new' engines were the Stanier '8F' 2-8-0 heavy freight engine, a locomotive which was already familiar to many local railwaymen. Between 1961 and 1966 twenty-three examples of the class found their way to Stourbridge including Nos. 48402, 48417, 48450, 48459 and 48460. These engines were amongst the first '8Fs' to arrive in 1961 and were also some of the last to leave in 1966. Also in 1966 four Stanier '5MT' 'Black Fives' were allocated to the shed, these were Nos. 44766, 44875, 45048, and 45064. All these engines recorded a very short stay, arriving in March and leaving around the end of May. Another LMS class at Stourbridge was the Ivatt '2MT' 2-6-0 the last of these being No. 46427 which was transferred to Tyseley on 10th July, 1966. The engine had formerly been shedded at Bescot having come to Stourbridge at the end of March 1966. In the last few years of steam at Stourbridge a number of British Railways' Standard designs were allocated to the shed: four '4MT' 2-6-0s, and three WD '8F' 2-8-0s.

Probably the unlikeliest of engines to be found at Stourbridge shed was the LNER 0-6-0 'J25'. These locomotives were transferred to the Great Western during 1939 to replace a number of 'Dean Goods' which had been requisitioned by the War Department. The 'J25s' soon became known to local railwaymen as 'Spitfires' a nickname based upon the spectacular pyrotechnics that invariably erupted from the chimney when working hard on train banking duties; and they did have to work very hard indeed, even just to keep up with some of the trains they were supposed to be assisting! Needless to say they were none too popular with Stourbridge enginemen especially firemen who often encountered great difficulty in raising a good head of steam, a problem recalled by one time fireman Albert Homer: 'I tried all ways to fire the LNER engines; round the side; over the 'tump'; nothing seemed to work!' These difficulties inevitably led to a flood of complaints and in November 1941 a formal request was made for their removal from all Bank Train work. However, even employment on station pilot and train banking duties was unsuccessful and by April 1942, after a series of problems with a 'J25' working Banking Target No. 18 which once more brought things to a head, the matter was again raised at the Local Departmental Committee where the employees' side requested that the engines should only be used on this duty if there were no other engines available.

Another unusual visitor to the area was the American-built 'S160' 2-8-0, a large number arriving in the country during 1942 prior to the invasion of Europe in 1944. Of the 174 which were employed on the GWR several found themselves allocated to Stourbridge including Nos. 1605, 1611, 1618, 1621, 1622,

Stourbridge's 'Hall' class 4-6-0 No. 5944 *Ickenham Hall* at Leamington Spa on 9th September, 1961. This may be a South Coast express working, with Stourbridge engine and men going to the edge of Western Region territory. On 11th September, 1961 the engine was re-allocated to Worcester shed.   *G. Bennett*

No. 5901 *Hazel Hall* leaves Kidderminster with the 4.55 pm Stourbridge Junction to Worcester on 25th July, 1963. Notice the Palethorpes van next to the engine.   *D.K. Jones Collection*

Light engine movements at Dudley station with a pair of ex-LMS '8F' class 2-8-0s Nos. 48474 and 48521. A Palethorpes van can be seen in the background.

G.E.S. Parker/Kidderminster Railway Museum

Ex-LMS Stanier '8F' class No. 48757 leads an unidentified 2-6-0 past Round Oak South signal box towards Round Oak station *circa* 1965.

V. Morgan

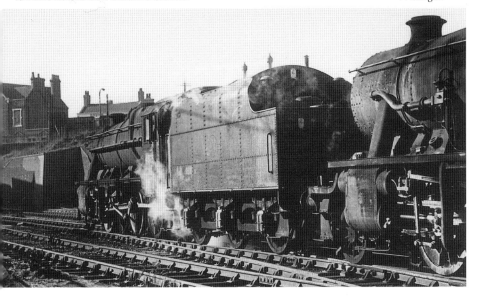

Ex-LMS '8F' class 2-8-0 No. 48766 passes Stourbridge Junction on the up main line at the head of a through freight in 1959.   *P. Coutanche*

WD 2-8-0 No. 90572 enters Stourbridge Junction with an up class 'K' freight in 1962. *G. Bennett*

and 1646. Three of these engines, Nos. 1605, 1611, and 1621, remained at the shed for the duration of their stay in England, that is from January/February 1942 until September 1944. Filling the gap created by the departure of these locomotives from Stourbridge was the arrival of four WD 2-8-0s on loan to the GWR between 1944 and 1945. Other WD 2-8-0s were also loaned to the company during 1946-47 and although it is thought that none were actually allocated to Stourbridge, local crews would surely have had a turn or two on the footplate. Albert Homer (by now a driver) and fireman Morris certainly had a memorable trip on one 2-8-0 (whether this was a 'Yank' or a WD is not absolutely clear) which the driver now recalls:

We were coming back to Stourbridge over the Wombourn branch with a heavy freight from Crewe when we were held at the signal outside Baggeridge Junction. Eventually the signal cleared and I opened the regulator,* and what a fright I had! Instead of moving away the wheels began to spin like fury. I couldn't shut the regulator so with a worried fireman looking on I grabbed hold of the hand brake and applied it with all my strength; I had to try and stop the wheels from spinning. Thankfully the wheels began to slow down and this time I was able to slam the regulator shut cutting off the flow of steam. We both breathed a huge sigh of relief and stood for a while to catch our breath. Having regained my composure I returned to the regulator dreading that the same thing would happen again; it didn't and we moved forward, no trace of wheel slip this time!

To conclude this look at steam at the shed, a summary has been given of all the engine types to have been allocated to Stourbridge between 1st January, 1948 and 16th July, 1966 when the last steam locomotives were withdrawn. Altogether, over the period analysed, a total of 313 individual engines were assigned to the depot. This figure can be broken down as follows:

Type	Total and class
0-4-2T	Seven class '14XX'
0-6-0PT	Four class '16XX'; four class '655'; one class '1813'; three class '2021'; four class '2181'; one class '2721'; fifty-three class '57XX'; six class '64XX'; eighteen class '7400'; and seven class '94XX'
0-6-2T	Twenty-six class '56XX'
2-6-2T	Forty-seven class '51XX'; two class '61XX'
0-6-0	Ten class '2251'
2-6-0	Two class '26XX' 'Aberdare'; twenty-six class '43XX'; five ex-LMS '2MT'; and four BR '4MT'
4-4-0	One class '33XX' 'Bulldog'; one class '3252' 'Duke'
4-6-0	Ten 'Grange' class; nine 'Hall' class; three 'Modified Hall' class; four 'Manor' class; and four ex-LMS '5MT'
2-8-0	Twenty-four class '28XX'; one 'ROD' class; twenty-three ex-LMS '8F'; and three WD '8F'

Of the above, 87 engines were withdrawn from traffic whilst allocated to Stourbridge. These were - class '14XX' No. 1414; class '655' Nos. 1745/49, 2706/12; class '1813' No. 1835; class '2181' Nos. 2187/89; 'Aberdare' Nos. 2620/55; class '2721' No. 2771; class '28XX' Nos. 2804/23; 'Bulldog' No. 3450; class '57XX' Nos. 3601/49/58, 3743, 4665, 5754/95, 7722/62/72/88, 8704/42/

* The regulator valve on a GWR engine was opened by lifting the handle, however, on a 'Yank' the handle was pulled outwards. If the driver was a little heavy handed with the regulator on a 'Yank' he subsequently could find it very difficult to shut the valve.

BR Standard class '4' 4-6-0 No. 75025 emerges from the tunnel at Blowers Green with a return excursion from Dudley (1Z10) on Whit Monday, 11th June, 1962.   *Michael Mensing*

BR Standard class '5' 4-6-0 No. 73028 in a sorry state at Stourbridge shed *circa* 1966.
                                                                                                    C.R. Kendrick

92/97, 9608/13/14/24/46, 9719/24/33/67/82; class '51XX' Nos. 4140/51/53/
72/73/75, 5107/09/22/31/34/36/46/76/87/89/92; class '43XX' Nos. 4326/
37/75, 5371, 6332/64/95; class '56XX' Nos. 5679, 6656/78/79/92; class '61XX'
Nos. 6129/37; class '64XX' Nos. 6403/18/24/28/34; class '74XX' Nos.
7413/14/18/24/29/30/32/41/43/47/49; and ex-LMS '8F' No. 48330.

Finally the diesels. Although the first diesel-engined machines to arrive at
Stourbridge were the GWR streamlined railcars in the early part of World War
II (J.W.P. Rowledge in *GWR Locomotive Allocations - First and Last Sheds 1922 -
1967* does mention that No. 8's first shed was Stourbridge in March 1936), it is
thought that the first real step towards dieselisation came in the mid-1950s with
the introduction of the 0-6-0 diesel-electric shunting locomotives. Initially it was
proposed to allocate four of these machines to Stourbridge shed (including one
spare) where they would replace steam shunting at Stourbridge Junction
marshalling yards. As far as it is known three machines, Nos. 13112/113/115,
were delivered during 1955 although only two, Nos. 13112/113, were possibly
at the shed at the time the scheme was set to begin, i.e. on 16th May, 1955. So
what happened to the fourth shunter? It is fairly certain that this was No. 13116
(by now renumbered to D3116) which joined the original three machines during
the four-week period ending 13th June, 1959 as existing records do not indicate
the arrival of any other shunting locomotive prior to this date. After the arrival
of this engine the number of diesel shunters allocated to Stourbridge increased
noticeably and by December 1960 an additional 11 were at work in the area,
these being Nos. D3004/3025/3029/3192/3980/3981/3982/3995/3996/3997/
3998. During 1964/65 three of the older build of diesel shunters arrived at the
shed in the shape of Nos. 12091, 12094, and 12095 presumably replacing an
equal number of existing machines. Diesel shunters driven by men barred from
main line working due to health problems were double manned, the fireman
taking the machine from the shed to the point where shunting would
commence. At this point the driver would take over. A 30 minutes preparation
time was given including an allowance for signing on and taking the machine
up to the shed signal. If the locomotive was required to give assistance to a
steam locomotive the diesel would be restricted to a maximum speed of 20 mph.
Although the introduction of diesel shunters in 1955 did cause local railwaymen
to begin to consider what sort of future lay ahead of them, it was the wider
implications contained within the Birmingham Area Dieselisation Scheme as a
whole that probably created the greatest concern as these clearly threatened a
large number of jobs over a wide range of grades.

The Birmingham Suburban Area Dieselisation Scheme comprised three phases.
Phase 1 was the introduction and expansion of local diesel shunting; Phase 2
involved the introduction of diesel multiple units to local passenger services; and
Phase 3 was the dieselisation of main line passenger and freight trains. By 1955
Phase 1 was of course well under way, although it was not until early in 1957 that
Phase 2 began to impact on the shed's working arrangements. The year before, on
1st August 1956, the allocation of diesel units to sheds in the Birmingham Division
was published (*see chart for full allocation*). This showed that Stourbridge shed was
to receive three of the new British Railways (BR) diesel railcars and five, three-car
suburban sets each comprising two power cars and a trailer, one or more of the

BIRMINGHAM SUBURBAN AREA DIESELISATION SCHEME

REPORT	Turn No.	Type of Unit	Power Cars	Trls	Fuelling	Stabling	Day to Day Maintenance	Periodical Maintenance	REMARKS.
Birmingham Suburban Scheme	Leam 1	3 Car Cross Ctry	2	1	Leam	Leam	Leam	Tyseley	
	Leam 2	Single	1	—	"	"	"	"	
	Leam 3	3 Car Suburban	2	1	"	"	"	"	
	Leam 4	"	2	1	"	"	"	"	
	Leam 5	Single & D.E.Trailer	1	1	"	"	"	"	
	S/Avon 1	3 Car Suburban	2	1	TYS	S'PRAT	TYS	T YS	
	" 2	"	2	1	"	"	"	"	
	" 3	"	2	1	"	"	"	"	
	Tys 1	"	2	1	TYS	TYS	TYS	T YS	
	" 2	"	2	1	"	"	"	"	
	" 3	"	2	1	"	"	"	"	
	" 4	"	2	1	"	"	"	"	
	" 5	"	2	1	"	"	"	"	
	" 6	"	2	1	"	"	"	"	
	W'ton 1	"	2	1	Cannock Rd	Cannock Rd	Cannock Rd	Tyseley	
	" 2	"	2	1	"	"	"	"	
	" 3	"	2	1	"	"	"	"	
	" 4	"	1	—	"	"	"	"	
	S'bridge 1	Single	1	—	S'bridge M.P.	S'bridge M.P.	S'bridge M.P.	Tyseley	
	" 2	3 Car Suburban	2	1	S'bridge Shed	S'bridge Jcn	S'bridge Shed	Tyseley	
	" 3	"	2	1	"	"	"	"	
	" 4	"	2	1	"	"	"	"	
	" 5	"	2	1	"	"	"	"	
	" 6	"	2	1	"	"	"	"	
	" 7	Single	1	—	"	"	"	"	
	" 8	"	1	—	"	"	"	"	
	Didcot 1	6 Car Cross Ctry.	4	2	Cannock Rd	Didcot	Cannock Rd.	Tyseley	

latter probably arriving at Stourbridge as early as 17th June, 1957. As mentioned above, examples of the ex-GWR streamlined diesel railcars had been around since at least 1940 and possibly throughout the war Nos. 3 and 4 had been allocated to Stourbridge; they were certainly there in January 1945 having been joined by Nos. 25, 26, and 29. By June 1947 the only railcars known to have been at Stourbridge were Nos. 8, 14 and 33. At various times between 1948 and 1958 a number of different cars were recorded in the Stourbridge area including Nos. 7, 8, 13, 14, 15, 17, 22, 26, 29, and 33, with at least Nos. 8, 13, 14, and 17 being at the shed on 29th June, 1958 along with three of BR's new Gloucester & RC&W Company's motor-brake second single units Nos. W55002/003/009. This is a clear indication that by now branch line services were being shared by the two types (a BR railcar had been employed on the Town branch at least a month earlier).

The arrival of the new units signalled the beginning of the end for the elderly ex-Great Western cars and it is thought that by the summer of 1960 all had been transferred, the last one to leave possibly being W14W. On the Stourbridge Town branch the diesel car was worked by three turns and on Monday 19th November, 1962 driver Lawrence was on the early turn which began at the diesel shed between 4.00 am and 5.00 am. After carrying out the required checks on No. W55026, the car left the shed at 5.25 am for Stourbridge Junction before leaving empty for the Town at 5.30 am. The first revenue earning duty was the 5.38 am, and altogether the driver made 26 journeys backwards and forwards before being relieved at 8.30 am for a 35 minute break after which he carried out a further 16 round trips before being relieved at 12.10 pm. The middle turn driver took over the railcar (on 12th November, 1962 this was No. W55006) at Stourbridge Town, the first departure being at 12.50 pm. Forty round trips later the turn ended at the Town at 7.45 pm. Mention of the break time relief takes the story for a moment back to the days of steam when, in the winter of 1939, both the Stourbridge branch and the Old Hill branch were worked by auto-train. To enable the Stourbridge Town crew to take their meal, relief was provided by the men off the carriage sidings shunting engine whilst Old Hill No. 1 auto crew would be relieved by the 4.30 am carriage warming turn. On Old Hill No. 2 auto the driver and fireman would have their meal break at Stourbridge shed having first prepared the engine prior to it being taken over by the relief.*

As far as it is known main line diesel locomotives were never allocated to Stourbridge shed, nevertheless a few did turn up during the months leading up to closure e.g. Brush type '4' (later class '47') No. D1683 on 7th February, 1965. However, after closure diesel locomotives assigned to local trip workings and train banking duties up the hill to Rowley Regis, and over the former OWWR to Brierley Hill and Dudley, could be found at a major stabling point located on the west side of the down main line just to the north of Stourbridge Junction station. By the late 1980s trains arriving at the Brierley Hill Steel Terminal from South Wales (continuing to Wednesbury Exchange Terminal) were hauled by class '37s'. These trains often required banking assistance from Stourbridge Junction, a job usually given to another Cardiff '37' which had been retained in the area by Bescot. When the banking engine was due for maintenance the crew of the incoming '37' would swap locomotives with the Bescot men to enable the assisting '37' to return to its home depot at the head of a train of empties, its role

* The crew off No. 1 auto would possibly take over No. 2 auto. The crew off No. 2 would later relieve the carriage warming turn on No. 1 auto.

Class '60' No. 60018 at Brierley Hill aggregates terminal on 27th October, 2001. The train was 6Z50, the Saturday only departure from Dove Holes. *David J. Hayes*

Class '66' No. 66067 at Brierley Hill aggregates terminal on 18th October, 2001. The train has arrived as 6Z50, the 10.00 Tuesdays and Thursdays only from Dove Holes, loaded to 16 MBA box wagons with a gross weight of 1,120 tonnes. *David J. Hayes*

as area banking engine being taken over by the new arrival. This change over normally took place at Wednesbury. In the 1990s the class '37s' were replaced by class '56' locomotives and to avoid the need for a banking engine to be attached at Stourbridge Junction these heavily loaded trains would be divided at Worcester and forwarded as two separate services. At the time of writing Stourbridge Junction still regularly saw class '56s' on the Scunthorpe-Brierley Hill steel trains, class '66s' on the Dove Holes-Brierley Hill aggregates service, and class '60s' and '66s' at the head of South Wales-Round Oak steel trains, one of these being in the hands of No. 66008 on 17th December, 2002. However, it was super power on the Stourbridge line on 25th November, 2003 when five brand new DRS class '66/4s' Nos 66406-10, trundled through the Junction station at around 3 pm on their way from Newport docks to their new home at Carlisle Kingmoor.

Before leaving the chapter the story returns briefly to the days of steam and two episodes recalled by Keith Tilbrook concerning the 'ups and downs' of life at Birmingham (Snow Hill) Control Office. Both stories involve Stourbridge's freight banking engines which in the late 1950s worked Bank Target Nos. 18, 19, 20 and 23. Altogether, five engines were employed on this work as two different engines were utilised on Target No. 18, the second engine being turned out to cover the night shift thereby replacing the 'day' engine which returned to Stourbridge shed if not required to work elsewhere. Through the night there were four 'bankers' available, although with two engines overlapping on No. 18, there were, for a short time, five. In fact it is Banking Target No. 18 which is central to Keith's first story, an incident that took place very early on in his career at Snow Hill Control:

I was a new and fairly 'green' recruit to the West Midlands traffic table in Birmingham (Snow Hill) Control Office. This table was in charge of Stourbridge Junction to Handsworth Junction (exclusive) and Priestfield Junction (exclusive); the Windmill End branch; Kingswinford Junction to Oxley Middle and North junctions (both exclusive), and all branches leading off those lines. It could be quite busy on the night shift, especially at the start. As was the custom, if the crew were in the mood to earn a few extra 'bob' (and they usually were) on overtime, I would have the 'day' No. 18 pilot* on hand at Blowers Green waiting to assist the Bilston-Banbury stone empties over the Windmill End branch (the 'Bumble Hole' to local railwaymen). However, as I busied myself keeping abreast (or trying to!) of the various movements on my 'patch', disaster struck. It was reported that the engine on the stone empties, a class '72XX' 2-8-2T, was 'off the road' in the sidings at Bilston. So, in addition to following the normal goings on, I was trying to ascertain (i) how things were going at Bilston, and (ii) when the engine was back on the rails would it be OK to carry on? Then, in the early hours, yet another light came up on the panel; it was the driver of the 'day' No. 18 pilot asking, 'Do you still want me to wait at Blowers Green?' I nearly had a fit. With all the other distractions he had totally slipped my mind. Consequently, he had been standing idle for two to three hours! I therefore urged him to return to Stourbridge shed with all possible speed and then waited for the rockets that I would no doubt receive. One came very quickly; a mother and father of a rollicking from the shed running foreman. Whatever else this telling-off achieved it certainly served to ensure that I didn't make that sort of mistake again! A favourite 'put-down' used by the more experienced Control staff when one of the juniors dropped a clanger was that there were 'too many little boys trying to do men's jobs'. This was probably given a good airing that night.

---

* For 'pilot' also read 'banker'.

Keith's second story concerns the oil tank trains from Ellesmere Port to Rowley Regis:

> Sometime in the very late 1950s, or maybe 1960, the powers-that-be decided to speed up these trains by upgrading them to 'E' class headlights with a short fitted 'head'. Also, at least some of them were rostered for 'Hall' class engines rather than '28XX' 2-8-0s. One week I was on the night shift and on the first night I received a call from the guard of such a train, which was at Oxley, wanting to know what sort of pilot we had available for the 'Bumble Hole'. I was pretty certain that all four were '57XX' class panniers, but I checked to make sure and then rang him back. 'OK mate', he said, and that was that. The same thing happened on Tuesday night, and again on the Wednesday. So, somewhat intrigued, I asked him what it was all about. He explained that since they had started using 'Halls' the standard load was one or two tanks too many with just a '57XX' pilot, and it could take anything up to an hour to knock them off. Having mused over this, I (still relatively junior) decided to try and persuade the shed running foreman at Stourbridge to provide a '56XX' or maybe a '51XX' on one of the pilot turns. Much to my amazement he said he would see what he could do. Early on the Thursday night shift I checked and sure enough we had a '56XX' as one of the pilots, so when the guard rang I told him, 'Bring the lot, mate', and explained about the engine. 'Good for you, mate!', he shouted down the phone and went off to get things moving. It would seem that whoever in the Freight Train Office had introduced the new working arrangements hadn't taken into account the pilot working. When this sort of thing happened it was usually the Control Office which took all the criticism. Many railwaymen did not, by and large, rate Control personnel very highly and probably the guard's euphoria at my solving his immediate problem would have evaporated after about 10 minutes.

BR Standard '9F' class 2-10-0 No. 92220 *Evening Star*, the last steam locomotive to be built at Swindon works, is seen at Stourbridge shed *circa* 1962.   T. *Lawrence*

Chapter Five

Firing Days at Stourbridge

Ray Kendrick joined the Great Western Railway as a cleaner on 2nd February, 1942 at the age of 15. After almost two years Ray was ready to take his first step up the 'ladder' and at the end of 1943, and just gone 17, it was down to Cardiff to take the obligatory medical and examination for promotion to fireman. Ray was successful and was immediately sent to Oxley shed in Wolverhampton. Oxley supplied the shunting engines for Wednesbury goods yard located about 4½ miles from Wolverhampton (Low Level) station on the main line to Birmingham (Snow Hill) and this was the job to which he found himself assigned. His firing days had begun and who best to relate his time on the shovel but the man himself:

My first firing job was on the yard shunting engine at Wednesbury goods yard under the watchful eye of driver Ted Luxberry whose expert tuition improved my firing technique enormously. I also learnt something else: who was boss on the footplate, and it certainly wasn't me for I soon realised that it was most unwise to disregard my driver's instructions. All firemen develop their craft in the shunting link often firing to experienced men whose best years were behind them. These men possessed great skill and knowledge gained from many years working in a senior link; a shrewd fireman would always pay very close attention to what they had to say or demonstrate. Ted was a good teacher; he certainly helped me out of some sticky situations. One duty where my driver's skill and experience came to my aid was on a Sunday ballast train relaying track in the goods yard at Wednesbury. On the front was a huge class '47XX' 2-8-0 which I don't think I had even seen before let alone fire, so when I stepped onto the footplate I was really entering the unknown. As a cleaner at Stourbridge I had heard some of the senior drivers talk about these engines which had been employed on the return leg of double home turns between Acton goods yard and Hockley goods yard before the war. Consequently I approached the firebox with a certain amount of apprehension and looked in, unfortunately the sight which greeted me confirmed my worst fears; it was enormous! It was so long that I imagined that I would need a wheelbarrow to get the coal to the front of the fire. Luckily my mate had worked on these engines before and he soon put me right. It was still a daunting task but with Ted's help I coped and was a better fireman for it.

Although I accepted that travelling to Wednesbury from my home in Stourbridge was part and parcel of the job I was anxious to move back to Stourbridge shed and so when a vacancy arose I quickly put in an application. Happily, I was successful the first time of asking, although there was a certain amount of sadness in my departure from Wednesbury as I had learnt a lot from Ted and in some ways I was sorry to leave. However, it was back to Stourbridge and into the shunting link where my first job was at Halesowen yard. Halesowen was an out-station of Stourbridge so I reported directly to the yard. There were two shunting turns for the out-station men: 11.00 am Monday to Saturday and 12.15 pm Monday to Friday with an 8.30 am turn Saturday each turn representing a 48 hour working week. Shortly after World War II, the working week was reduced to 44 hours. For enginemen this meant an 88 hour fortnight; one week of 48 hours (a six day working week), the next 40 hours (a five day working week). This arrangement gave us one rest day every two weeks, plus Sundays of course. The out-station drivers and firemen, myself included, would relieve the two crews on No. 2 and

'43XX' class 2-6-0 No. 8359 at Stourbridge shed on 13th September, 1936.
F.K. Davies/Kiddermister Railway Museum

'655' class 0-6-0PT No. 1777 at Stourbridge shed. This locomotive was built in 1893, fitted with panniers in 1923 and withdrawal came in 1941.   *L.B. Lapper/Kidderminster Railway Museum*

No. 14 Bank Trains.The Halesowen men who took over the engine off No. 2 Bank would later change engines with the crew off No. 8 Bank which arrived at Halesowen just after 2 pm. This exchange provided us with an engine well stocked with coal and water. At the end of the shift it was light engine to Old Hill for relief. On the other turn (No. 14 Bank engine) we would be relieved at Halesowen by men who had arrived by bus from Stourbridge. I was only based at Halesowen for three months and throughout this period my mate was Joe Floyd, a smashing man who taught me a lot about two-cylinder shunting engines and the rules and regulations. On the down side, cycling back from Halesowen or Old Hill after a hard day on the shovel was pretty tiring to say the least. Over the years Halesowen had developed something of a reputation for being a little too susceptible to accidents and it did seem that the Stourbridge breakdown gang did get called out to the area quite frequently. The falling gradient of 1 in 38 from the canal basin to Canal Basin Junction (on the main line) was often the source of problems and one incident in particular always springs to mind. At the time the engine off No. 14 Bank was bringing a train of loaded tube wagons from the basin to the main line sidings (the basin served as a transhipment centre where steel tubes, amongst other commodities, would arrive by barge from the manufacturer Stewart & Lloyds). On the falling gradient engine crews had to exercise extreme care with heavily laden trains and well judged use of the sanders was the order of the day, especially if the rails were greasy or frosty. Unfortunately, despite all the normal precautions having been taken, the crew lost control and the train ran away. Unable to bring it to a halt driver and fireman jumped clear. Near the main line was a dead-end siding and the train was turned into this where it hit the stop-block with tremendous force. As a result wagons literally piled up behind the engine and pipes were scattered in all directions; what a mess! Luckily no one was seriously injured. Steel pipes were just one of the many items handled at Halesowen and records show that in 1936 a total of 94,112 tons passed through Canal Basin. This comprised 56,182 tons of general merchandise, 28,764 tons of coal and coke, and 9,166 tons 'other' minerals, all totals being aggregates of the amounts dispatched and received. On the main line Halesowen goods yard handled far less traffic, 32,089 tons in fact, of which 20,599 tons was general merchandise, 6,208 tons was 'other' minerals, plus 5,208 tons of coal and coke.

The shunting link possessed some real characters; Bob Brown knew his engines inside out; a great theoretician but often seemed to lack the confidence to put theory into practice. At Round Oak 'Nipper' Smith insisted that his firemen kept the cab very clean and tidy. One job involved blacking the surface each side and above the firebox door with engine oil, whilst all the brasses and windows had to sparkle. Only when 'Nipper' was satisfied would his mate be able to sit down to a sandwich and a well earned mug of tea. Incidentally many of 'Nipper's' former firemen carried on these cleaning practices long after they had moved on; they had learned to take a pride in their engines. 'Nipper' was one of many local railwaymen with nicknames, and although some of these were predictable, for example Jack 'Doc' Holiday, and Ray 'Copper Top' Williams, others were derived from the way a man worked, 'Top Um Up' Ted Roberts for instance liked to fill his engine's water tank at every opportunity, although the 'Bromley Diver' obtained his nickname from attempting a most bizarre athletic feat. Apparently Sam Broadhurst during his time as signalman at Bromley Basin bet someone that he could jump the width of the nearby canal. He tried, failed, and got a good soaking for his trouble, hence the name. There was another driver who went by the name of Monday Smith, a great snuff taker and so rumour had it, one of seven children all named after the days of the week.

My stay at Halesowen lasted for just three months as in those days wartime labour shortages led to faster promotion so I soon found myself on the next rung of the ladder firing in the bottom bank link. The railway's system of seniority helped as this was calculated by length of service and not age, therefore, with a couple of years experience

Right: Fireman Barry Shillingsford *circa* 1952.   *M. Noke Collection*

Below: On the footplate of '43XX' class 2-6-0 is Graham Borsberry in 1960.   *C.R. Kendrick*

under my belt, I had a head start over some of the other, older lads in the shunting link.The bank link provided a broad mix of work taking me to all of the yards and branches worked by the shed. An interesting job was the Kingswinford branch engine which took traffic to and from the exchange sidings at Baggeridge Junction, the location where the GWR met the Earl of Dudley's Pensnett Railway. Here coal mined at Baggeridge colliery would be transferred to Great Western metals to be tripped down to Kingswinford Junction. Other jobs were not quite so interesting; shunting the coal stage for example where we would take full wagons up the incline and pull empty ones out. However, one of the worst turns was engine preparation. This job saw both fireman and driver preparing five engines during an eight hour shift, hard work especially in the winter when sometimes snow and ice had to be cleared from the frames. A bad winter could mean injectors freezing up and the lubricating oil becoming so thick that it was like treacle. Once, the turntable was out of action and engines stabled outside had to be prepared in the yard. Very unpleasant if it was raining or snowing, especially when working underneath the engine. As a young fireman I would sometimes be allocated a shed turn firing to former top link drivers such as Fred Bailey, Oscar Moisey, or Joe Plant. These men could no longer drive on the main line due to ill health and were therefore confined to positioning engines in the shed or outside in the yard. Engines had to be moved to the ash-pit road where grates, smokeboxes, and ashpans were cleaned out, and then it was over to the coal-stage for coaling. If there was no available footplate work I might be assigned to the coal stage emptying 10 cwt tubs of coal into bunkers or tenders. After replenishing up to 30 engines in a shift the muscles really ached and I looked forward to returning to the footplate; any footplate! But this was all part of the job and accepted as such.

Firing in the bank link meant working shifts usually on a rotating basis, but once again I was lucky with my mate for Joe Brickwell was a solid and good-natured man who for 3½ years taught me everything he knew. Nothing was too much trouble for Joe who was always willing to right my wrongs in a professional and understanding manner. We regularly exchanged places, Joe showing me the best way to fire certain engines, or allowing me to take a turn on the regulator. I soon found out that each train had to be handled differently, the engine fired and driven in accordance with the track conditions, the nature of the area and the load on the draw bar. Joe's advice on such matters was absolutely invaluable and held me in good stead later on in my career. In all the time I was his mate I don't think a bad word passed between us, remarkable really considering the hours we worked together, in all weathers, often in the close confines of the cab of an 0-6-0PT, and sometimes under very tricky operational conditions.

My first couple of years firing were of course during the war and at this time Stourbridge Junction was even more heavily used than usual, especially by Government stores trains taking vital supplies to the South Coast to support the invasion of Europe. This increased traffic led to Stourbridge shed having to provide many more relief turns to take over freight trains and both drivers and firemen were required to report to specially appointed Zone inspectors such as Jack Jones and Bill 'Buck' Shale who were stationed at the yard and were responsible for seeing that the correct trains were relieved by the right crews. With so many trains trying to get through the district Stourbridge Junction yard was sometimes in real danger of grinding to a halt as trains piled up behind each other and all the local loops and sidings became packed with war supplies. These Zone relief turns showed no mercy with delay after delay and 12 hour shifts commonplace. As well as the frustration of having to stand for what seemed an eternity before being given the right of way, the delays played havoc with the fires which quickly became dirty and clinkered. It was then out with the pricker (a long, pointed, metal rod) which was used to break through the clinker to allow air to reach the fire, however, what made things worse was the quality of the coal. Good Welsh steam coal was hard to come by and firemen had to make do with some pretty poor stuff: slack, and sometimes even coke was mixed in, but worst of all were the 'eggs', compressed coal dust and cement. These tended to burn quite well but the ash! This would turn to clinker in almost the blink of an eye if the fireman was not careful and after a long tiring shift, he had his work cut out to keep the fire clean and bright. The other major problem was operational. The high volume of southbound traffic and the corresponding lack of return workings tended to leave many engines stranded far away from their home shed. To get engines back to Stourbridge, crews would have to travel out during Sunday 'on the cushions' to such places as Banbury, Oxford, or Old Oak Common, to bring an engine back 'light'. One Sunday night I came back on a 2-8-0 'Austerity' from Old Oak Common : what a journey! The engine rolled one way, the tender the other, and was it noisy! By the time we reached Stourbridge not only were we tired and dirty but almost stone deaf! In war-time we enginemen worked all the hours God sent, often in appalling conditions.

The subject of appalling conditions brings to mind a job involving ROD 2-8-0 No. 3010. I was firing to Charlie Lawrence at the time and I think it was a Saturday night at the end of the shift. We were walking through the shed when we passed this engine which had been subject to some pretty major repair work to its valves and pistons. The engine was in a right state, filthy dirty and rust everywhere. Charlie turned to me and said 'God help the crew who have to take that engine out for the first time'. Well, when we booked-on the following Monday night for the Bumble Hole banking turn what machine did we have: that's right, No. 3010. By the time we had finished the shift after a very wet and busy night, and with no storm sheet to speak of to give us at least some protection from the elements, neither of us were too keen upon life on the railway and if we never saw 3010 again it would have been too soon. That engine made a lasting impression on the pair of us and whenever I saw Charlie afterwards he would always say, 'Remember 3010!', Indeed I do!

By 1947 another fast promotion had seen me move into the senior bank link where I fired to a number of different drivers including Bob Owen, H. Surrell, H. Mullis, F. Saunders, and then eventually my old mate Joe Brickwell. This link dealt with a wide variety of work; it also gave me the opportunity to fire on some weekend excursions to such places as Windsor and Cardiff, where on both occasions my driver was Tom Worrall. However, my abiding memory of 1947 was the winter which was absolutely horrendous with heavy snows and continuous bitterly cold temperatures leading to many cancellations of regular turns and the substitution of snow clearing duties. One day my booked turn fell victim to the weather and I retired to the enginemen's cabin on the side of the shed where over a hot cup of tea and a sandwich I waited for developments; I did not have to wait long. Dai Williams, the duty running foremen, had received a message from Control that some men were required to carry out snow clearing over the Halesowen branch. Three sets of men were required and I would be one of the firemen. At the front of the shed three class '27XX' 0-6-0 tank engines had to be coupled to the breakdown vans; one at the front, two at the back, the leading engine having been fitted with the large snow plough. This done everyone clambered on board their respective engines and prepared to depart. I had often fired a class '27XX' and still had the bruises to prove it! Unfortunately both sand boxes were on the footplate in just the right position to catch the hands and knuckles of the fireman who might for a split second forget that they were there. The pain though soon reminded him. I had also fired these engines on the workmen's trains over the same line we were now heading towards. Some of these trips could be quite unforgettable especially if you had as your mate Charlie Pearson, a quite unpredictable man and someone who kept the fireman on his toes. It was Charlie who enlisted the assistance of an outside fitter to repair the steps of 'his' engine after they had been slightly damaged in a shunting incident. No one at the shed gave Charlie the authority to get the work done; he just went ahead and did it. This was the sort of character he was. Yes Charlie was a bit of an oddball but I preferred his company to one or two other drivers I could mention, especially on a tedious shunting job at a yard like Round Oak in the dead of winter cooped up in the cab of a '2021' 0-6-0PT. But I digress, so back to the snow clearing episode. With all crews aboard and the shed signal in our favour the ensemble moved down to the signal box where the signalman was informed of the details of the job, the destination, and the engines involved. This done it was onto the down main line, the train accelerating up the hill towards Blowers Green Junction. It was the first time I had worked on the snow plough and things seemed to being going smoothly; far too smoothly in fact.

At Blowers Green we came to a halt outside Dudley tunnel and after reversing onto the up main line we were signalled left at Blowers Green Junction where we continued along the Windmill End branch. No problems were encountered on this stretch of line and we soon reached Old Hill South Junction. The signal was in our favour and having run slowly through the station the train pulled up just beyond the crossover, at the Birmingham end of the station, which led to the Halesowen branch. The dummy came off and we crossed over to the down main line before taking the Halesowen branch. Things had gone according to plan up to now and there was a feeling amongst the three crews that the job would soon be over; how wrong we were! The run to Halesowen station was quite easy, however, doubts began to creep into our minds when we were ordered by Control to continue over the Joint line as far as Rubery where an engine was stuck in deep snow. Just to the south of Hunnington rail conditions dramatically worsened and our engines had to work very hard to force the plough through the snow which had formed a 20 foot high drift in the cutting on the approach to Dowery Dell viaduct. Eventually we got through, the men on the footplate being assisted by the fitters who had to dismount from their van and work away with shovels. Dowery Dell viaduct was a flimsy looking structure and was subject to a severe weight restriction that meant that only one engine in steam at a time was allowed across. So it was off the footplate for the firemen and into the knee high snow to uncouple the engines. Even with the engines buffered up close frozen fingers made hard work of dropping the couplings but eventually the job was done and one by one the engines crossed the viaduct where they were once more coupled together. Forcing our way through the rest of the snow we arrived at Rubery where we set about releasing the engine whose crew had long departed, heading home on one of the few buses still running. Having got the engine out it was coupled up inside and we towed it back to Stourbridge, but not before staggering into Halesowen for a welcome cup of tea in the shunters' hut. What a sight we must have been; soaking wet, frozen stiff, and dead tired. We eventually arrived back at the shed at 8.30 in the morning over 20 hours after we had first set out around midday the previous day. But there was still no end to our misery for we were told that we were required to report back in nine hours time; just about enough time to get a change of clothes, a hot bath, a good meal and a short sleep. It was then back into freezing temperatures once more.

After six years in the bank links a vacancy arose in the double home link, although by now the lodging turns associated with the job were a thing of the past, at least at Stourbridge. I had heard some pretty off-putting stories about lodging turns from some of the men who had been in the link before the war. Charlie Lawrence once told me that after booking-off in London after working the class 'C' express freight from Kidderminster he and his mate would take some coal to the lodging house for as sure as night followed day there would have been none in the grate. This way they were certain of a fire that morning and the means to cook some bacon and eggs for breakfast. The bed though was warm; it had just been vacated by another crew who were reporting back for their return working! There was no change of sheets and it was into bed in the clothes they stood up in. Now, changes in train working arrangements meant that Stourbridge engine crews would usually be relieved at places such as Hereford, Gloucester, Worcester, or Oxley North Junction returning to Stourbridge either on a booked working or 'on the cushions'; or sometimes bringing back a 'light' engine. The link still had an occasional job through to Crewe and I remember firing a mineral train

'27XX' class 0-6-0PT No. 2718 near Rubery with an Old Hill-Longbridge train on 12th July, 1939.
H.C. Casserley

'2182' class 0-6-0PT No. 2186 at Stourbridge shed on 12th November, 1950.   *T.J. Edgington*

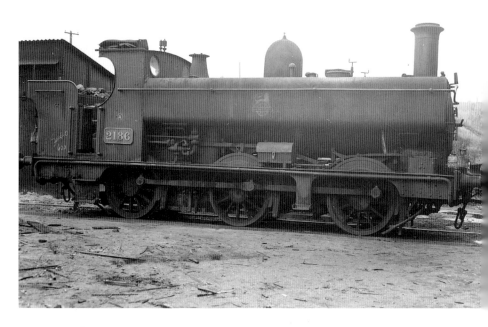

from Kingswinford Junction via the Wombourn branch (this may have been the 1.55 am, class 'F' service which ran MX the Stourbridge crew normally being relieved at Oxley Branch Junction). At Crewe the engine would be stabled at Gresty Lane and we came back on a passenger train either to Wolverhampton (High Level) or Birmingham (New Street), before catching a local to Stourbridge Junction.

One of the fastest services I ever fired on was a fully fitted class 'C' express freight from Bordesley Junction to Llanelly which departed Stourbridge Junction around 12.45 am. The train required an engine change at Stourbridge Junction so driver Fred Lamb and myself would probably have booked-on just after 11 o'clock to prepare our engine before the short run to Stourbridge Junction where our train would be waiting in the up sidings. We were booked to work the service as far as Hereford (Barton) where a crew from '85C' would take over. This was a double home turn for the Hereford men who would return with what was probably the 9.15 pm, class 'D', Llandilo Junction to Stourbridge Junction freight. We would relieve the crew at Hereford (Barr's Court) for the last leg of the journey. Coming back to the outward journey, it was common practice to try and gain a few minutes before reaching Worcester's Rainbow Hill Junction thereby providing the driver with a bit of slack for the climb over the Malverns. After Ledbury the regulator on what would normally be a 'Grange' would be opened wide and every attempt was made to get to Hereford on time. On this night our task was made easier by the fact that we were quite lightly loaded and Fred, an excellent driver and a good mate, was undoubtedly in a hurry as we reached Shelwick Junction on the West to North route in record time. For me it was quite an exhilarating experience but not so for our guard, Percy Inch. Poor old Percy, he certainly had a rough ride having to hang on like grim death for much of the journey.

Having been relieved at Barton we made our way to Barr's Court to take over from the Hereford men on the freight from South Wales. Heavy trains working back to the West Midlands through Ledbury tunnel usually required assistance from the resident banker, and when this was needed the driver would sound two crows on his engine's whistle at Stoke Edith, the signalman there phoning through to Ledbury to alert the crew. On this trip assistance was not needed and we simply acknowledged them when we passed through Ledbury station. Immediately beyond was the tunnel where the bore was so narrow that we had to ensure that the fire irons were stowed well within the width of the tender. Little ventilation meant that the atmosphere was so heavy and dank that it could almost be cut with a knife, the sulphur fumes making it sometimes almost unbearable on the footplate. Usually the only means of relief was to hold a damp handkerchief over mouth and nostrils, and if on a tender engine to lift the plate between cab and tender to try and create a draught. Neither remedies were that effective but certainly better than nothing. It was certainly a relief to emerge into the clean air of the Malvern countryside especially in the spring and summer when flowers in the adjoining fields were in full bloom. Not that we had much time to admire these natural beauties of course.

I had learnt my craft over many years and in the double home link the fireman had to be adept at firing anything from an 0-6-0PT to a 4-6-0 mixed traffic engine or 2-8-0 heavy freight loco. There was no standard method of firing as different engine types had contrasting firebox shapes which dictated the way the fire was formed and maintained. However, even amongst engines with similar fireboxes the firing technique required to get the best out of each could vary from locomotive to locomotive. Having said that, the key to efficient engine operation was the footplate crew working as a team, and certainly in my experience the fireman benefited enormously from listening to and heeding the advice of his driver who had done it all before. Good team work influenced the amount of coal consumed in the production of steam, unfortunately, despite the crew's best efforts, sometimes things went wrong and boiler pressure would drop and engine power lost. A drop in boiler pressure could occur for several reasons, for example, poor quality coal; or perhaps the engine was one that simply did not steam well; sometimes, if the engine had been out on the road for a long time, the fire would clinker up. When this happened the fireman had to work hard with bar and pricker to break up the deposits to enable air to get into the fire. Occasionally the fault lay with individual crew members themselves, a situation which could generate much ill-feeling on the footplate with both driver and fireman blaming each other for the misfortune which had befallen them. But in the main most crews worked together to get themselves out of their difficulties whether they were self-inflicted or otherwise. The immediate aim was to raise boiler pressure, so the train had to be stopped somewhere safe for a 'blow-up'. This was usually off the main line near a signal box or station so that the crew could easily inform a signalman or station master of their difficulties. Once boiler pressure was regained, and the line was clear, the train would be on its way.

Another factor the skilled fireman had to take account off was the quality of the coal. Swindon engines thrived on a diet of soft Welsh steam coal, however at times we had to make do with what was available. As stated earlier it was team work on the footplate that counted and no matter how good the fireman was if he was with a heavy-handed driver then coal consumption could soar and firing became harder than it was already. Bad driving would cause unburnt coal to be sucked through the flues and discharged into the atmosphere via the blast. The type of train and whether it was running over a rising gradient rather than on the level also influenced coal consumption and certainly a mile up Old Hill bank would consume far more than a mile from Stourbridge Junction to Hagley. Oddly, engines of the same type would also have differing characteristics and an experienced fireman soon remembered which engines were going to give him a hard time and those which were not. Firing was indeed a strenuous task made harder by adopting the incorrect stance. The trick was shovelling with the minimum amount of leg movement. This was very important on a rough riding engine if the fireman wanted to put more coal into the fire-box than over his driver's boots! It was not a glamorous job firing, and at the end of some shifts I was sometimes so exhausted that after getting down off the footplate I was hardly able to walk.

A further skill that the fireman had to learn was taking water when the engine was on the move. If he got this wrong it would usually mean an unscheduled stop at a yard or station water column, the guard highlighting any time lost in his report. On the approach to the water troughs the fireman would be on the look out for the white board, nicknamed the 'white cow', positioned at the side of the track. Having taken into account the train's speed he then had to judge the precise time to drop the scoop into the water. As the tank filled he would keep a close eye on the tender water gauge and at the right moment wind the scoop up, much harder than lowering as the force of the water in the troughs had to be overcome. The big danger was to raise the scoop too late thereby overfilling the tender causing it to overflow sending gallons of water over the following wagons or carriages, in the latter event drenching anyone unlucky enough to be sitting near an open window. The water might also flush coal onto the footplate making working conditions dangerous and earning an even sharper rebuke from the driver. Intimate knowledge of the road was of course very important as this enabled him to prepare well in advance for the troughs without having to rely on actually catching sight of the board. Knowing the road also meant that the fireman was aware of the precise location of signals especially those awkwardly positioned and difficult to see by the driver.

Producing the right amount of steam at the right time was very important, however, what the fireman did not want to do is to produce too much especially when standing in the station, this was a practice that was always frowned upon and would usually attract a caustic remark from the driver. An engine 'blowing off' whilst standing could also have unwelcome repercussions especially when the steam condensed causing a mini shower to descend upon the platform. This was not only an example of poor firing, but it could also lead to a ticking-off for the crew if reported to the shedmaster by the station master or an accompanying locomotive inspector. On the road the driver and fireman might engage in some friendly competition, testing each other's ability to get the best out of their engine, each man taking turns to drive. The principle behind good driving was to get from A to B on time; using the minimum of coal and water; and avoiding unnecessary delays especially those caused by misjudgements of line conditions.

Returning to my firing days, after working in the double home link I was promoted into the auto link firing on the auto-trains which worked local services between Stourbridge Junction, Dudley, Old Hill, and Birmingham (Snow Hill). Some of these ran via the quaintly named 'Bumble Hole' on the Windmill End branch; others over the main line from the Junction to Dudley or Snow Hill, or over the Swan Village line; and of course on the shortest branch line in the country between Stourbridge Junction and the Town station. One job I remember well was on a return working from Birmingham (Snow Hill) to Dudley which ran via Swan Village and Great Bridge. We left Snow Hill on the relief line (the Stourbridge line) with our diminutive 0-4-2T at the head of a single auto-trailer at the same time as an ex-Paddington express, headed by one of the former GWR's mighty 'Kings', which occupied the main line to Wolverhampton. This uneven contest presented us with a challenge that was impossible to resist and as far as Handsworth Junction we kept neck and neck. At Handsworth Junction our tussle ended as we were brought to a halt outside the station, the express having the right of way as the quadruple section reduced to double track. Now the 'King' pulled away, the driver giving us a scornful glance accompanied by a long blast on the whistle. As the express disappeared from sight the signal came off and we left the down relief to continue our journey on the down main as far as Swan Village where we branched off for Dudley. This little contest certainly brightened up the day! Firing the auto-train meant that the fireman had a lot more responsibility as for part of the shift he would be working alone on the footplate, the driver being at the other end of the train in the driving compartment of the trailer. In this situation the fireman was in total charge of the footplate, working without the benefit of the driver's knowledge and experience; he also had to react promptly to signals from the driver who although having control of the train brake and the regulator, the latter connected to the engine via a linkage which ran beneath the frames of the trailer, it was the fireman who operated the reversing lever and the handbrake.

Another job for the auto-engine was the Stourbridge Town shuttle service. On the afternoon turn there was always a brief lull in activity to enable the engine to be coaled up and the gas tanks on the auto-trailer refilled (lighting on the trailer at this time was gas lit). After the last passenger had disembarked a telephone call would be made to the shed running foreman requesting the dispatch of a tender engine to the Junction station. This engine was the source of our fresh supply of coal. A few minutes later a 'Dean Goods' or a '2251' class would be spotted on the up main. However, before we could refill the bunker the auto-train would first leave the branch platform line and reverse into the platform avoiding line, or as it was also known, the down goods running loop, pulling up at the water column so that we could also fill the tanks. In the meantime the 0-6-0 would have come to a halt just beyond Middle box before reversing onto the down main. It was then a simple task for the crew of the 0-6-0 to access the branch platform line and draw level with the bunker of our tank engine so that coal could be transferred directly from the tender, the fireman on the assisting engine usually lending me a hand. Once sufficient coal had been taken on, the Middle box signalman would be informed that the 0-6-0 was ready to depart and as soon as the line was clear, off it would go back to the shed. Having filled the water tanks and topped up the bunker we crossed back to the branch platform line before swinging left onto the Town goods as far as the carriage siding. Here a colleague from the Carriage & Wagon Examiner's Department would be waiting to connect the trailer to the gas supply. As the gas tanks were being filled I cleaned the fire which had been allowed to die down to make the job that bit easier. After about 15 minutes all the jobs had been completed and after disconnecting the gas supply to the trailer it was back to the branch platform in time to begin the next round of trips to and from the two stations.

'14XX' class 0-4-2T No. 1414 at Stourbridge Town on 10th September, 1949. The locomotive still carries the legend GWR.   *H.C. Casserley*

A Stourbridge Junction to Stourbridge Town auto-train stands at Stourbridge Town station in October 1963. The locomotive is '64XX' 0-6-0PT No. 6424. By now the bridge has been reconstructed and the moveable stop block removed.

Brian Moone/Kidderminster Railway Museum

One of the senior firing turns was on the passenger service to Birmingham (Snow Hill) which usually meant a day on a class '51XX' 2-6-2 Prairie tank. I remember that one of these jobs was the 5.15 am 'stopper' which entailed booking-on a good hour before our scheduled departure time from the shed. Four in the morning is quite a depressing time of the day and I must confess that like most people I was never at my best at this unearthly hour. On arriving at the booking-on point, a little bleary-eyed but ready for the day's labours the walk and the chill of the early morning air bringing me quickly to life, I went through the usual routine of calling out my number to the time-clerk who resided in the timekeeper's office behind the small hatch in the shed wall. My arrival duly recorded I read the notices and then made my way over to the roster sheet to see who my driver was today and which engine we had. The driver was someone who I had fired to many times before and I got on well with, 'Gentleman' Joe Wilkinson, a man who never swore and who frowned upon anyone who did, although it was sometimes difficult not to when things went wrong on the footplate. No. 4104, our engine, was not a bad machine either. All-in-all it had the makings of a pretty good day. Having obtained the keys to the engine's tool boxes from the storeman I walked into the roundhouse and, surrounded by the dark outlines of the engines, I made my way towards the central turntable. At this time of the morning the shed was quite eerie and less than welcoming, the lack of good lighting hardly improving matters. The location of our engine was to be found on the notice fixed near the turntable and having established which road 4104 was on I walked over and climbed aboard. I then began the fireman's mandatory checks. The first and very important duty was to ensure that the handbrake was firmly on. Next check the boiler pressure, and also the water level in the gauge glass to ensure that there was sufficient water in the boiler. I would usually flush the water out of the glass and after closing the valve, check the level again thereby ensuring that I had a true reading. A fireman normally carried a spare glass and rubber washers and I was no exception. If one broke on the road the fireman had to change it, not an easy matter dismantling hot parts and refitting new ones when the engine was travelling at a good speed. Having rechecked the glass I opened the firebox door; good, the fireraiser had left me with a decent fire so there was little work for me to do. Now over to the reverser, yes this was in midgear. Unlocking the toolboxes (it was sad but true, if these were left unlocked essential tools would usually have 'walked') I took out the tools of the trade. From the large box came the shovel; coal pick; two head lamps; bucket; hand brush; a box of detonators, and a couple of red flags. From the smaller one out came the oil-filler cans for the lamps; the water-gauge lamp, and two flare lamps; an adjustable spanner; a long and a short oil-feeder; two bottles of oil (one thick for the lubricator, one containing engine oil for the motion and slide bar assembly); a bottle of paraffin, and finally the damping down pipe for the coal. I now filled the oil feeder for my driver who was due any minute (it was usual for the fireman to be on the engine before the driver booked-on) and the thick oil feeder. To make the thick oil easier to apply I would place the feeder by the fire-box door, the heat thinning the substance. These tasks completed I was now ready to start on the outside of the engine. However, before leaving the footplate I opened both dampers so that I could later check the contents of the ash pan from below, and put the blower on a touch to keep any smoke off the footplate. Then, after checking that the sand box operating handles were in good working order, it was down the cab steps and to the first outside job: checking the sanders.

The sanders were a vital piece of equipment for these deposited the sand onto the rails to improve adhesion and it was amazing just how effective even a small quantity of the material could be when trying to start a train on a greasy or icy track. Having first obtained a couple of buckets of dry sand from the sand drying furnace at the end of road fourteen, I filled the sand boxes and ensured that the sanding mechanism was clear and working properly. Happy with the performance of this equipment I then walked round to the front of the engine and climbed up onto the platform over the buffer beam so that I could open the smokebox door to check and clean any accumulations from around the

'2301' class 'Dean Goods' 0-6-0 No. 2360 at Stourbridge shed in the 1940s. Notice the ATC shoe beneath the front buffer beam.   *Camwell Collection/Kidderminster Railway Museum*

'51XX' class 2-6-2T No. 5185 arrives at Great Bridge South on the 20th August, 1957 with the 5.08 pm Dudley-Birmingham (Snow Hill).   *T.J. Edgington*

jumper ring (when the engine is working hard this moveable metal ring would lift by exhaust steam pressure thereby providing an additional outlet for the exhaust. This in turn reduces the blast so tending to prevent the fire from being lifted). When closed the smokebox door should be airtight as any air leaking into the smokebox will reduce the vacuum and bad steaming will result. Having swept a small amount of ash from off the frames with the hand brush I dropped down into the inspection pit to carry out the under-engine check of the ash-pan. This was clear so it was back into the cab to make sure the fire-hole ring and the deflector plate were in good condition and using the pricker I spread the coals evenly over the fire-bed. Closing the front damper the blower is put on hard to bring the fire up to get near a full head of steam. I wanted to raise the steam pressure so that the injectors could be tested as early as possible. The bunker was well filled with coal and after breaking up a few lumps I added a shovelful or two to the fire to keep it going. The firebox on 4104 was long and sloping and the fireman worked off the 'tump' at the back of the fire. Breaking up the coal had created quite a bit of dust on the footplate so I gave the area a good sweep before washing it down with the hose. The two headlamps were then cleaned, filled and placed on the lamp irons. If we were running bunker first from Stourbridge Junction to Birmingham, the journey from the shed to Stourbridge Junction would be made with one lamp showing a white light placed at the smokebox end (to denote a light engine movement). At Stourbridge Junction the lamp on the smokebox would be removed whilst the lamp on the bunker would be repositioned to show that the train was a local passenger service. If our return working was a freight from Bordesley Junction enginemen preferred to work bunker first to Snow Hill as this meant that the engine would return smoke-box leading, infinitely preferable to running bunker first especially over the uphill section through Snow Hill tunnel. I think on this turn we did have a return freight so 4104 would have worked bunker first from the Junction. After giving the controls one last wipe down with cotton waste and making sure that the windows were clean, all that remained for me to do was to fill the cylinder and valve lubricators with oil. This done, I checked the water level in the boiler and the steam pressure, and with my driver having now finished his preparations we were ready for the off.

Our first task was to summon the turntable man to align the turntable with our road. As the turntable is pushed into place I release the handbrake enabling Joe to ease the 2-6-2T into the centre of the turntable. Handbrake back on, mid-gear selected, and the cylinder drain cocks wide open, the turntable man now re-positions the table in line with the shed exit road. Moving slowly off the turntable we run up to the water column to replenish the tanks. It was my job to fill-up so it was onto the running plate to open the tank cover and drop the bag into the side tank. After filling-up we rolled to the shed signal to await the right of way, Joe giving two blasts on the whistle to attract the signalman's attention. Almost immediately the board came off. At the box the signalman was waiting at the window to take the details of engine and train for his register, then it was onto the up main line for the short run into Stourbridge Junction carriage sidings to pick up the stock. After the shunter has coupled up and joined the heating and brake pipes, the vacuum brake is tested and the steam heating turned on. Our guard comes up to confirm our load; four on = 128 tons. The train then eases out of the sidings into the down main line platform ready for departure up the bank to Snow Hill. There was still a few minutes before departure so I nip over to the shunters' cabin to brew up. There was nothing like a good hot mug of tea to prepare a fireman and driver for the long haul up to Rowley over Old Hill bank.

On the footplate the steam heating gauge indicated a good supply of steam to the carriages whilst the steam pressure gauge showed that pressure in the boiler was spot on and the boiler water gauge indicated that the water level was just right for the steep climb to Rowley Regis. One of the problems of working bunker first on a Snow Hill train with a 2-6-2T was that the water floods to the smoke-box end of the boiler and

An up local prepares to depart Rowley Regis with an unidentified '51XX' class 2-6-2T in charge on 1st May, 1957. *T.J. Edgington*

'51XX' class 2-6-2T No. 4173 pauses at Smethwick West with a local passenger train *circa* 1955. *T.J. Edgington*

consequently there was always a danger of priming, that is water entering the cylinder chest instead of steam. If this happened power would be lost as the cylinder drain cocks would have to be opened to enable the scalding hot water to escape otherwise serious damage could take place. I would not be very popular with my driver if on Old Hill bank the engine was not in perfect fettle for the climb ahead so I always kept a very close eye on the gauge glass and only used the injector to keep the boiler at three-quarters full. Satisfied that all was well I looked out of the driver's side of the cab in the direction of the rear of the train to catch the guard's signal as latecomers rushed to get on board; and there it was, a green lamp and a sharp blast of his whistle. The guard quickly disappeared into his van, the last carriage door slamming shut. Having received the signal I told Jim we were clear to go and we both slipped easily into our well rehearsed routine. I made sure that the fire would not need attention until Lye, our first stop, and dropped the coal bunker plate to close off the shovelling hole and wound the handbrake off. A long blast of the whistle startled some sleepy commuters on platform 3 as we began to accelerate out of the station, past Stourbridge Middle box and on towards Stourbridge North Junction where signalman Bill Tilbrook, leaning out of the window of North box, gave us a cheery wave as we crossed from the down main line of the former OWWR to the up main line of the Stourbridge Extension. On the way to Lye we pass Timmis' siding which at one time had been controlled by a signal box, but that had been replaced some years ago by a ground frame. The run to Lye was usually uneventful, the falling gradient allowing for an easy run, and today was no exception, the train coasting into the platforms as steam was shut off. I put on the blower for a moment to clear some smoke off the footplate, a small problem when working with just the front damper open. When firing on engines with sliding fire hole doors I sometimes found it necessary to position a fishplate nut on the door runners to stop the doors from closing completely after coal had been added to the fire. This aided combustion in certain circumstances by allowing additional air to enter the firebox.

Having taken on board a few more passengers the guard gives us the signal to proceed. The fire now needs some attention so it's two shovels each side of the firebox and a couple on the 'tump'. Incidentally the 'tump' was a shallow mound of coal stretching half-way down the centre of the fire-box from the firehole doors. Adjacent Lye station was the goods yard and to the right the Lye shunting engine was going about its business. We soon leave Lye behind and within four minutes we were passing Cradley goods yard on our left and the down staggered platform of Cradley Heath & Cradley which was separated from the up by a level crossing. I put on the injector and bring the water level in the boiler to the desired level; just enough to avoid priming. After a brief stop we prepare for the first part of our assault upon the incline to Rowley Regis. Firing on this stretch of line with a 2-6-2 Prairie requires coal to be added to the 'tump' under the firebox doors, two shovelfuls of coal down each side of the fire, and one or two at the front of the firebox. Care had to be taken with the engine working hard not to allow the fire to be drawn to the front of the firebox where it could mound up against the brick arch and reduce steaming. The jumper in the smokebox helped avoid this but if it did happen I would use the pricker to break up any accumulation before pulling the fire back evenly over the grate. I also had to keep a very close eye on the water level in the boiler. Just before Old Hill the Windmill End branch trails in from the left; I had often worked on the Coxes Lane banking engine giving assistance to heavy freights either from Coxes Lane to Blowers Green, or in the opposite direction, off the branch and up the hill to Rowley. Pulling in to Old Hill we came to a halt almost opposite the Halesowen branch now only used by goods traffic and a couple of workmen's trains to Longbridge in the morning and two in the opposite direction early evening. On the other platform Joe Gibbs, the station foreman, was busily preparing packages and parcels for loading onto the next train to Stourbridge. However, he still had time to glance up on our arrival and exchange a few early morning pleasantries.

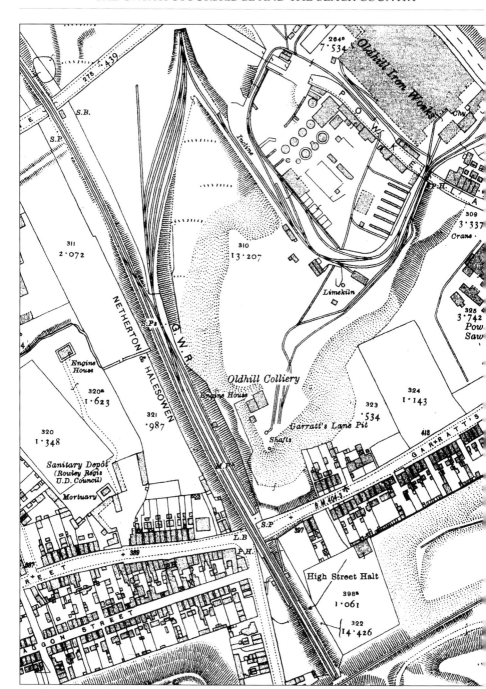

Coxes Lane sidings.   *Reproduced from the 25", 1919 Ordnance Survey Map*

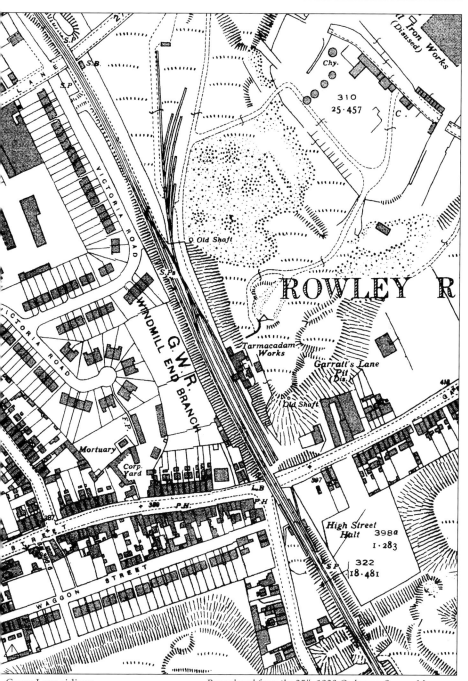

Coxes Lane sidings.

Reproduced from the 25", 1939 Ordnance Survey Map

'51XX' class 2-6-2T No. 5180 with a local passenger train at Lye on 1st May, 1957.

T.J. Edgington

A view along the platform at Oldbury & Langley Green.   *Lens of Sutton Collection*

Our friendly banter is interrupted by the platform starter coming off; 5.26, time to go. The next ¾ of a mile is up the 1 in 51 gradient and into the 896 yard Old Hill tunnel. I have to look sharp for there is only about two minutes to make sure that the fire is right before we enter the tunnel as it was not good practice to have to attend to it whilst passing through. Bursting out of the heavy atmosphere of the tunnel came as a relief for, although I was not claustrophobic, I was always glad to be clear of the smoke and the smell.

Arriving at Rowley station I open the firehole doors and note the fire's condition. It was still in good shape so I decide to leave it alone for the time being. The boiler pressure gauge reading was quite high and I didn't want the engine blowing off whilst still in the station. Allowing the engine to blow off whilst stationary could earn the engine crew a good ticking off as it was a sign of the fireman failing to pay special attention to his fire and poor use of the injectors. I looked out to my left and noticed the Rowley shunting engine working the coal sidings, his task made easier by the presence of the yard's ace shunter Joe Franklin. I had to smile to myself at the thought of Joe spinning one of his famous yarns to the engine crew over a mug of tea in the shunters' cabin.Then back to it and once past Rowley it was through the yards at Langley Green. Here there would often be an oil train being shunted into position before the shunting engine nipped off to perform work in Hughes & Johnson's siding. It was also possible to look down the Oldbury branch towards the chemical sidings where another shunting engine could sometimes be seen pushing empty phosphorous wagons into the yard. Langley Green is the last yard where Stourbridge men are employed on shunting duties; all the others passed are Tyseley turns including Hockley where the numerous sidings and two goods sheds are on our right as we pull into the station. We are now only three minutes away from our destination; just three-quarters of a mile to go. With the station in sight I shut off the steam heating and the driver begins to slow the train down before gently coming to a halt at the platform.

Firing in No. 2 passenger link often meant a return from Birmingham with a freight from Bordesley Junction to Stourbridge Junction and on one occasion it was a mid-morning class 'K' goods. However, first we had to dispose of the carriage stock at Tyseley carriage sidings before running light engine to Bordesley Junction yard for a shovel-cooked breakfast and the engineman's friend, the piping hot mug of tea. Now that we had been fed and watered the driver and I get down to the serious business of checking over our engine for the trip back. Whilst the driver does his rounds I trim the bunker and change the headlamps, the one at the smokebox end now showing a white light and placed on top of the buffer beam to indicate the train class. The fire is checked and levelled, removing any hollows or dead patches and ensuring the fire is evenly burnt through all over the grate, adding coal as necessary. The water tank gauge is checked, as is the water level in the boiler. All is well so we are now ready to move and the yard shunter directs us to our train which is standing at the north end of the sidings. Our guard comes to the cab and informs the driver of our load: the number of wagons; the weight; and where traffic has to be dropped off. The wagons are marshalled in the order that they are to be detached, the first drop next to the engine. I partly close the firehole doors to help raise the temperature in the firebox when the yard foreman calls us forward. Easing out of the yard and onto the main line the driver notches up prompting me to start to fire, paying attention to where the fire is thinnest. I take a look out of the cab at the chimney and see a light smoke; the fire is just right. Soon we will pass Moor Street and enter the forbidding gloom of Snow Hill tunnel.

In the tunnel we make slow progress, our load of 25 heavily laden wagons proving a stern test for our 2-6-2 Prairie and I have to open the front sanders to drop sand ahead of the leading driving wheels to gain extra grip. The driver manages the regulator and cut-off accordingly. Working up hill with a full load is always a difficult job; the beat of the exhaust blasting back from the tunnel roof; the roar of the engine struggling to

Diverted via Old Hill and Dudley on account of engineering work near Priestfield the 2.10 pm Birmingham (Snow Hill) to Wolverhampton (Low Level) makes progress up the incline to Baptist End on 23rd September, 1956 headed by the last surviving Churchward 'Star' class 4-6-0 No. 4061 *Glastonbury Abbey*.   *Michael Mensing*

Ex-LMS Stanier class '8F' 2-8-0 No. 48514 trundles through Dudley Port (Low Level) with a freight on 25th July, 1959.   *Michael Mensing*

master its load on the incline; the glow from the firebox reflecting in the face of the fireman, and the flashing lights as carriages rush past on a passenger train. Progress is sometimes so slow that it becomes difficult to judge just how fast we are travelling so it is imperative that a close eye is kept upon the lights embedded in the tunnel wall. These lights are set at a fixed distance apart enabling crews to roughly calculate the speed of their train. As a fireman I always had a fear that the engine might stall, especially if in the hands of an inexperienced driver, although the tunnel is a severe test for any freight crew. Drivers had to carry a 'wrong line' order and if the train did stall it was my job as fireman to take the order to the appropriate signalman who would then summon the station pilot, the order authorising the assistant engine to work wrong line in order to reach us. It would then be hooked up so that it could pull the train up the hill into Snow Hill station. Thankfully I never had cause to use the order, my drivers always knowing exactly how to coax the last bit of power from their engines in a sure-footed and professional manner. Despite this I was glad to pass the 'clappers' as these instruments told us that the end of the tunnel was near. A driver once turned to me and said, as we ran slowly through the platforms, 'You looked a little worried for a while back there, mate'. He was probably right.

Having emerged from the gloom of the tunnel, steam is shut off and I open the cold water injector replenishing the boiler with water taken directly from the engine's tanks. The signals are clear through to Hockley and from there it is up Soho bank to Handsworth Junction where we are routed onto the Stourbridge line. The first drop is at Langley Green and as we approach, the signal comes off for the down goods loop and we slowly leave the main line and come to a halt adjacent to the water column. The journey from Bordesley is always heavy on water so my driver decides to top up while we wait for the yard shunter to arrive. We don't have long to wait and the wagons for the yard are soon uncoupled, the shunter then joining us on the footplate. We draw forward leaving the rest of the train in the loop. The signal clears and we accelerate onto the main line before coming to a halt beyond the crossover. The dummy grinds to the off position and following the signals and commands of the shunter we reverse over the up main line into the yard and pull up in the loop where our wagons are detached. There is an express due so we take this opportunity to have a quick mug of tea as we have to wait for it to pass before we can cross back over the main line and re-enter the down loop to pick-up the rest of our train. After the express clears the section we cross the main line and reverse into the loop where we are reunited with the remaining wagons. We are now signalled back onto the main line and I wind the hand brake off, the driver opens the regulator and with the engine in full forward gear we head towards Old Hill.

All loose coupled or partially fitted freight trains have to come to a halt at the stop-board at the summit of Old Hill bank, the board itself being adorned with the names of those who, over the years, have stopped there before us. I prepare a shallow fire spreading the coals evenly over the coal bars, forsaking the usual 'tump'. Meanwhile the guard, with brake pole in hand, has dismounted from his van and begins to pin down the brakes in readiness for the descent. The driver gives me the nod and I release the handbrake, my mate easing the engine forward, the guard continuing to pin down the brakes as we go. When my mate is satisfied that there is sufficient braking power available he gives two sharp blasts on the whistle and the guard jumps aboard his van, signalling to the driver that he is safely on the platform. The guard will now stand at the van's handbrake all the way to the bottom of the bank ready to give emergency assistance if required. However, there is no need, for the driver has judged it to perfection. Slowly we continue our downward path, through Old Hill tunnel and into Cradley Heath & Cradley. There is no down goods loop here so we come to a halt opposite the up platform. The wagons for the yard are uncoupled and we move forward over the level crossing into the down platform pulling up beyond the trailing crossover from the up main. The train is then reversed into the up platform where the drop is to

'Hall' class 4-6-0 No. 4905 *Barton Hall* races through Lye at the head of the 5.00 pm Birmingham (Snow Hill) to Cardiff express on 27th March, 1954.   *W.F. Deebank*

'Grange' class 4-6-0 No. 6857 *Tudor Grange* on a Tavistock Junction to Crewe freight passing Bromley Basin sidings just to the north of Kingswinsford Junction.
Brian Moone/Kidderminster Railway Museum

be made. Throughout this manoeuvre I am advising the driver with a series of practised hand signals whilst at the same time keeping a close eye on the shunter as he directs us to where he wants the train to stop. After detaching the wagons it's back onto the down main where we reattach the remaining wagons. Our final call is at Stourbridge Junction where the rest of the load will be deposited in the south (or up) yard.

After passing the outer home signal we approach the home just before Junction Road overbridge. The latter is a bracket holding the main line board and two goods running loop signals. Through North Junction and another bracket with a similar signal arrangement but this one has a distant below the home. The signal is set for No. 1 up goods running loop in the Middle yard. As we slow down for the loop we are met by the train meeter who takes us to the south end where we draw to a halt. Having detached the remaining wagons the shunter gives the all clear and we move up to the bracket signal opposite Middle box. A wave to the signalman who pulls off the calling-on arm and we accelerate over the points into platform 3 on the up main line. I look towards the Middle box as the first and second dummies clear giving us access to the down main. The driver puts the engine into full reverse gear and with the regulator at the first valve setting we change from the up to the down main and hurry past the Middle box. Under clear signals we head for Stourbridge shed. As we approach Engine Shed sidings the shed signal is against us so the driver gives a sharp blast on the whistle to alert the signalman who obligingly gives us the road. Branching off the main line we pass Engine Shed box on our left and head for the ash-pit road where we are met by one of the firedroppers who climbs onto the footplate to take a look in the firebox to see how much work is left for him to do. He seemed quite happy as I had levelled the fire down low so there was little in the grate. Clearing the footplate I lock the tools away, if not they would be on the footplate of another engine the following day. Before leaving the cab I take one last look at the firebox and check that the water levels are satisfactory and that there is enough steam to enable the shed driver to stable the engine in the roundhouse. With the hand brake on, regulator fully closed and the engine in mid-gear, the engine is safe to leave although before we go the driver takes a good look round the engine, lifting the trimmings from the oil cups which lubricate the slide bars on the motion so as to avoid waste. There are no defects to report so a repair card need not be filled out. Having reported our arrival to the time clerk and deposited the keys in the stores it's time to say goodbye to my mate and it was off home for a well earned rest.

By now it was 1957 and after 13 years on the shovel I was soon to take my driver's examination at Swindon. I had spent many a Sunday morning in the Mutual Improvement Class listening to and learning from the old and the wise who used models and drawings to explain the mysteries of that complex piece of machinery known as the steam engine. On top of that was a thorough grounding in the rules and regulations. There seemed so much to learn but with the help of sympathetic mates on the footplate it had all begun to gel and I felt confident that I now had the right mix of theory and practice to impress the examiner. However, two years earlier I had seen British Railways' modernisation plan and suddenly life as a railwayman was no longer as certain as it had seemed way back in the 1940s. I was as realistic about the future as any other railwayman for we all recognised that the end of steam was not far away and the change to diesel traction could only mean one thing: loss of jobs. Drivers in the passenger links were already undertaking main line diesel training at Derby, it was then four weeks driving under supervision before being passed as a qualified diesel driver. Some drivers in the top passenger link with less than two years to retirement were not put forward for training on dmus and therefore remained on steam until they left the service. Many drivers welcomed the change; no more dirty overalls; no more freezing cabs; yes, they were happy to see the back of steam so when their dmu failed and it was back onto the footplate, it came as quite a shock to the system. The first dmus began to arrive during 1957 and very unreliable machines they were too. As a result passenger jobs continued for some time to be a mix of

'Grange' class 4-6-0 No. 6844 *Penrhydd Grange* heads a train of empties out of the goods yard at Kidderminster on 25th May, 1963. Unusually this locomotive has a straight-sided Hawksworth tender. *Brian Moone/Kidderminster Railway Museum*

'Grange' class No. 6845 *Paviland Grange* waits at Dudley to return to Great Malvern with the return leg of an excursion to Dudley Zoo on 3rd August, 1964. *G. Bennett*

both steam and diesel traction although the diesel shunters had by the late 1950s early/1960s taken charge at virtually all of the yards. Other drivers were not too sure about the changes. Life on the footplate was not glamorous, in fact at times it was downright awful, but being a railwayman meant something and many, myself included, felt that this 'something' might not survive the transition into the diesel era.

Despite the wind of change that had begun to blow through the industry my view at the time was that the best course of action was to remain with my chosen career and to pass as a driver. So on Tuesday 22nd December, 1957 it was down to Swindon to face my biggest test yet. On the previous Sunday morning I had spent two hours with Eric Webb, as good an instructor as any budding engine driver could wish to have. If I failed now it would be my own fault and certainly no reflection on the quality of our MIC. On the Monday I had overcome a more practical challenge having been rostered to drive a freight to Worcester and returning with a local passenger service. On the footplate with the regular driver was the locomotive inspector who closely watched every move I made and asked a number of pertinent questions. At the end of the shift I felt that I had handled the situation well, a belief confirmed by my acting fireman for the day; but could I impress the Swindon inspector? And so came Tuesday and with the best wishes of my wife I left for Stourbridge Junction hoping that I could do myself and my instructors justice when I came face to face with the man from Swindon. During the journey I could not relax as I tried to recall everything that Eric had said just two days earlier. I knew that if I did not pass I would be allowed just one more attempt and if unsuccessful it was shed duties for the rest of my time in the service. Enough of this I thought, I am going to pass, however, by the time I walked up the steps of Park House my arguments supporting such a belief seemed less and less convincing, but I was here and I was determined to do my best. The medical and eyesight test proved to be a formality, but the stiffest test was yet to come. In the waiting room another fireman sat nervously awaiting his fate and all attempts to start a conversation were strangled at birth, both of us having more important things on our minds. I was to be the first in and then the door opened . . !

Without doubt this man knew his stuff; Swindon inspectors had railways in their blood and they had the knack of extracting that same substance from the men they were testing. Questions came thick and fast, testing my knowledge and understanding of two- and four-cylinder engines; the workings of the piston and slide valves; faults and failures; standard and Stephenson's link motion; Walschaerts valve gear; would the questions never end! More questions on the rules and regulations; what to do if working the main line, or a branch line, or single line. How did the slip coach operate; what would I do if the engine failed in the Severn tunnel; what did this signal mean; what did that sign indicate; this man was a torturer! At last my interrogation ended and with my palms damp with sweat and my mouth dry I walked back to the waiting-room; what an ordeal! I sat down, my mind churning over trying to remember the questions asked and the answers given when the door opened and my tormentor stood before me. 'Congratulations', he said, and smiling he held out his hand. At first I was taken aback, the implications of that one word not immediately registering. Then the truth dawned and I rose. Taking his outstretched hand, and shaking it a little too vigorously, I thanked him for his fairness. I left the building with totally different feelings from those that I had when I first entered several hours earlier and I almost ran all the way back to Swindon station. All of a sudden Christmas had taken on a far brighter hue. I was now a driver; well a passed fireman for that was my position until I could get myself a permanent position in the links. Fifteen years of working in all weathers, at all times of the day and night, in the shed, on the coal stage, under the engine, on the engine, being shouted at, sometimes ridiculed, but in fairness mainly encouraged, it all seemed worthwhile. Although I may have had a more prestigious title, in reality I now found myself on the bottom of a different ladder. The trials and tribulations of the climb up that ladder are recounted in the following chapter.

'57XX' class 0-6-0PTs were regularly employed on Dudley shunting turns and in this view No. 9636 waits for its next duty on 15th September, 1956.   *H.C. Casserley*

'16XX' class 0-6-0PT No. 1619 at Stourbridge shed in 1959.   *P. Coutanche Collection*

Chapter Six

In Control: Driving at Last

During 1958 Ray Kendrick, now a passed fireman at Stourbridge, would search the vacancy list for a suitable driving position, one that would preferably be local. He knew that it was highly unlikely that a position would arise at Stourbridge as the men now in driving posts were either recent arrivals, many of whom were from South Wales and keen to settle in the area, or had plenty of years in front of them. He was therefore looking for a post at Wolverhampton or Kidderminster. As a passed fireman his first driving 'milestone' was the achievement of 100 driving turns, the 100th being on Stourbridge's class '57XX' No. 4696 shunting the goods yard at Langley Green. Surviving records show that most of Ray's driving jobs as a passed fireman were on shunting engines, often standing in for the regular driver who would have a main line turn, in fact of the 174 driving turns identified, the majority were on the Langley Green shunting engine, driving such locomotives as Nos. 3658, 4646, 4687, 5754, 8792 and 9767. He also spent a considerable time on the Halesowen and Dudley shunting engines driving both class '57XX' panniers and class '74XX' panniers, although he also had turns on class '51XX' 2-6-2 tanks and class '56XX' 0-6-2 tanks. At Round Oak and Brettell Lane 0-6-0PTs Nos. 1621 and 1619 were his regular steeds, whilst a week on Bank Train No. 15 saw him at the controls of 0-6-2T No. 6698. Although over 50 per cent of known driving turns were on shunting duties, he also obtained experience on other types of engines working a range of different trains. On a number of occasions he drove long distance freights, usually on ex-GWR 2-8-0s but also on 4-6-0 'Granges' and on at least one occasion a WD 2-8-0. At the end of 1959 a vacancy arose at Kidderminster and with well over 200 driving turns to his credit Ray successfully applied for the job moving there on 30th November. His time at Kidderminster was unexpectedly short for in the middle of 1960 a vacancy arose at Stourbridge and Ray grabbed the opportunity with both hands. Unfortunately things at Stourbridge were not quite the same as when he had left, and with the change to diesel traction now picking up momentum life at the shed was never to be the same. From now on Ray's career underwent a series of ups and downs as the available work for Stourbridge men was steadily eaten away creating a climate of uncertainty which hung over the depot like a black cloud. Ray remained at Stourbridge until closure when he was by then also serving as an ASLEF shop steward working with colleagues to secure the best deal for the remaining men. With the final closure of Stourbridge TCD, Ray Kendrick retired after 46½ years in the service, however, it's now back to the beginning as Ray recalls his driving career from his days as a passed fireman to his final years in the cab of diesel locomotives and multiple units:

Above: '51XX' class 2-6-2T No. 4149 takes on water at the south end of Stourbridge Junction station. South signal box can just be seen on the right.   *H.C. Casserley*

Right: Driver Ray Kendrick (right) and fireman Cliff Totney on the footplate of '57XX' class 0-6-0PT No. 4646 at Halesowen sidings *c*.1960. *C.R. Kendrick Collection*

'3521' class 4-4-0 No. 3557 at Kidderminster shed on 19th July, 1932. This locomotive was the last member of the class to be withdrawn in May 1934.   *W. Potter/R.S. Carpenter*

Locomotive Allocation - Kidderminster

1st January, 1948

Ex-Cleobury Motimer & Ditton Priors Light Railway 0-6-0PT
28, 29

'2021' 0-6-0PT
2093

'51XX' class 2-6-2T
4153, 5110

'43XX' class 2-6-0
5303

'4575' class 2-6-2T
4584, 4586, 4594, 5518, 5573

'57XX' class 0-6-0PT
4625, 7700, 8718, 8727

'81XX' class 2-6-2T
8101

1st January, 1960

'43XX' 2-6-0
5333, 6314, 6382, 6388

'4575' 2-6-2T
5518

'51XX' class 2-6-2T
4114, 4153, 4175

'56XX' class 0-6-2T
6679

'57XX' class 0-6-0PT
3601, 4629, 4641, 5791, 8718

'81XX' class 2-6-2T
8101

South Bound Train Services Calling/Starting at Hartlebury and/or Kidderminster
26th September, 1949

Kidderminster Arr.	Kidderminster Dep.	Hartlebury Arr.	Hartlebury Dep.	Head Code	Train Time	Service
		0251	0304	F(MX)	2320	Priestfield-Pontypool Road
0257	0307	0319	0329	F(MX)	2340	Bordesley Junction-Pontypool Road
		0330	0338	H(MXRR)	0300	Stourbridge Junction-Pontypool Road
0335	0416			E(MX)	2135	Crewe-Worcester Goods Yard
	0553			B		Alveley Halt
0628				B	0535	Ex-Wolverhampton
		0654		B	0640	Ex-Bewdley
0649	0700			B	0540	Birmingham Snow Hill-Bewdley
	0705	0711		B		
	0722	0728	0729	B		Henwick
0717	0739			B	0612	Birmingham Snow Hill-Bewdley
0727	0742	0753	0820	F(MX)	0515	Oxley Sidings-Worcester goods Yard
	0757			B	0742	Ex-Bewdley
0756	0802	0808	0811	B	0650	Wolverhampton-Paddington
0834	0837			A	0800	Birmingham Snow Hill-Cardiff
	0850			B		Woofferton
		0855		B	0840	Ex-Bewdley
	0855	0901	0902	B(SX)		Worcester Foregate Street
0857	0901			H(RRMO)	0836	Stourbridge Junction-Severn Tunnel Junction
0929	0933	0939	0942	B	0815	Wolverhampton-Oxford
0958				B	0855	Ex-Birmingham Snow Hill
	1018			B		Woofferton
1018	1028			B	0815	Shrewsbury-Birmingham Snow Hill
1025	1027			A	0945	Birmingham Snow Hill-Cardiff
		1050		K(RRSX)		Newnham Bridge
1038	1115			F	0450	Crewe-Worcester Goods Yard
		1126		B	1110	Ex-Bewdley
	1130			K		Woofferton
1124	1131	1137	1140	B	1110	Stourbridge Junction-Worcester Shrub Hill
1155	1157	1203	1204	A	1120	Birmingham Snow Hill-Hereford
		1210		K	1045	Ex-Alveley sidings
	1240			B(SO)		Highley
1244				B	1145	Ex-Birmingham Snow Hill
		1251		G(SO)	1241	Ex-Stourport
		1306	1320	K	0940	Dudley-Elmley Lovett sidings
		1317		B	1120	Ex-Shrewsbury
1314	1325	1331	1333	B	1205	Wolverhampton-Paddington
1330	1331			A(SO)	1240	Birmingham Snow Hill-Bewdley
1337	1340			A	1300	Birmingham Snow Hill-Cardiff
	1345			B(SX)		Bewdley
1359				B(SO)	1345	Ex-Stourbridge Junction
	1410			B		Woofferton
1424				B	1325	Ex-Birmingham Snow Hill
		1440		B	1425	Ex-Bewdley
1459	1502	1508	1512	B	1355	Wolverhampton-Oxford
1518	1525	1531		B	1420	Ex-Birmingham Snow Hill
1618				B	1520	Ex-Birmingham Snow Hill
		1559	1609	K(SX)	1500	Alveley sidings-Worcester Goods Yard
	1623			B		Shrewsbury
1629	1632			A	1550	Birmingham Snow Hill-Hereford
	1638			B		Woofferton
		1656		B	1642	Ex-Bewdley
		1559	1620	K(SO)	1500	Alveley sidings-Worcester Goods Yard
1654	1701	1707	1717	B	1545	Wolverhampton-Worcester Shrub Hill
1740	1743			A	1700	Birmingham Snow Hill-Cardiff
	1748			B		Bewdley
1754	1758	1804	1808	B	1650	Wolverhampton-Worcester Shrub Hill
1817	1819			A	1740	Birmingham Snow Hill-Malvern Wells
1804				B(SX)	1705	Ex-Birmingham Snow Hill
	1810			K(SO)	1800	Ex-Stourport
	1825			B		Woofferton
1828	1830	1836	1838	B	1729	Wolverhampton-Malvern Wells(SX)Ledbury (SO)
1840				B(SX)	1825	Ex-Stourbridge Junction
		1855		K(SO)	1845	Ex-Stourport
1914				B	1900	Ex-Stourbridge Junction
	1920			B(SX)		Highley
		1927		B	1912	Ex-Bewdley
		1855		K(SX)	1845	Ex-Stourport
		1956		H	1837	Ex-Great Bridge
1954	1957	2003	2006	B	1910	Birmingham Snow Hill-Worcester Shrub Hill
		2005	2017	2030	F(SX)	Worcester Goods Yard
		2012	2023	2033	F(SX)	Worcester Goods Yard
		2005	2042	2044	B	Worcester Shrub Hill via Bewdley
	2025			B(SO)		Woofferton
2052	2056			A	2010	Birmingham Snow Hill-Hereford
		2105		K(SX)	1130	Ex-Coton Hill
2124	2128	2134	2136	B	2020	Wolverhampton-Worcester Shrub Hill
2224				B	2120	Ex-Birmingham Snow Hill
	2228			B(SO)		Highley
		2205	2217	2234	F(SX)	Worcester Goods Yard
		2250	2256	2257	B	Worcester Shrub Hill
2217	2255	2307	2328	F	1930	Priestfield-Swindon
2304				B	2205	Ex-Birmingham Snow Hill
2344				B(WSO)	2245	Ex-Birmingham Snow Hill
2322	M-night	0012	0030	H(MX)	1910	Bordesley Junction-Worcester Goods Yard
2356	0028	0044	0140	F(MX)	2200	Hollinswood-Worcester Goods Yard

Key to Head Codes
A Express Passenger; B Ordinary Passenger
C, D or E Express Freight, F Fast Freight
H and J Through Freight or Mineral Train; K Branch Freight, or Ordinary Freight/Mineral Train

North Bound Train Services Calling/Starting at Hartlebury and/or Kidderminster
26th September, 1949

Hartlebury Arr.	Hartlebury Dep.	Kidderminster Arr.	Kidderminster Dep.	Head Code	Train Time	Service
0012	0035	0046	0106	F(SX)	2345	Worcester Goods Yard-Moor Street
			0405	F(RR)	0050	Hereford-Foley Park
0429	0439	0453		J(MX)	0330	Ex-Newland
0429	0439	0453	0508	F(MO)	0400	Worcester Goods Yard-Oxley Sidings
		0507	0515	F(MX)	2155	Cardiff-Oxley Sidings
			0545	B		Birmingham Snow Hill
			0553	B		Alveley Halt
		0612	0614	B	0552	Arley-Birmingham Snow Hill
			0648	B		Wellington
	0655			K		Alveley Sidings
0657	0700	0706	0710	B	0633	Worcester Shrub Hill-Birmingham Snow Hill
0717	0722			B	0655	Worcester Shrub Hill-Shrewsbury
			0732	B		Wolverhampton
		0739	0743	B	0730	Bewdley-Birmingham Snow Hill
			0800	B		Birmingham Snow Hill
		0744	0830	F	0225	Didcot-Kingswinford
0807	0809	0816	0818	A	0715	Ledbury-Birmingham Snow Hill
		0809	0824	B	0800	Bewdley-Birmingham Snow Hill
	0810			B		Buildwas
	0816			B		Bewdley
0831	0832	0838		B	0804	Ex-Henwick
		0851	0853	A	0720	Hereford-Birmingham Snow Hill
		0909		F	0725	Ex-Worcester Goods Yard
	0910			K		Stourport
		0910		B	0809	Ex-Woofferton
	0922			B		Bewdley/Kidderminster
0905	0923			F(MO)	0245	Swindon-Kingswinford Junction
0906	0923			F(MX)	0300	Pontypool Road-Oxley Sidings
0915	0917	0923	0925	A	0755	Hereford-Birmingham Snow Hill
	0930			K		Coton Hill
0959	1002	1008	1011	B	0935	Worcester Shrub Hill-Crewe
	1010			B		Bewdley
		1018	1028	B	0815	Shrewsbury-Birmingham Snow Hill
		1032	1050	H	0940	Worcester Tunnel Junction-Market Drayton
	1055			K		Stourport
		1112		B	1005	Ex-Woofferton
		1121	1123	A	0830	Cardiff-Birmingham Snow Hill
	1210			B		Bewdley/Kidderminster
		1236		B	1210	Ex-Hartlebury
		1247	1250	A	0950	Cardiff-Birmingham Snow Hill
		1300		K(SX)		Ex-Bewdley
		1311		B	1155	Ex-Woofferton
		1320	1337	H(MX)	0545	Swindon-Oxley Sidings
		1320	1337	H(MO)	0015	Tavistock Junction-Kingswinford Junction
		1330		B		Birmingham Snow Hill
1340	1344	1350	1354	B	1315	Worcester Shrub Hill-Wolverhampton
	1400			B		Shrewsbury
1455	1457	1503	1505	B	1435	Worcester Shrub Hill-Stourbridge Junction
	1505			K(SX)		Coton Hill
	1505			K(SO)		Stourport
	1516			B		Bridgnorth
		1545		B	1320	Ex-Shrewsbury
1535	1545	1559	1609	K	1530	Elmley Lovett-Stourbridge Junction
	1600			B		Bewdley
		1628	1631	A	1310	Cardiff-Birmingham Snow Hill
			1648	B		Birmingham Snow Hill
		1657		B	1547	Ex-Woofferton
		1710		B	1620	Ex-Bridgnorth
		1720		K	0820	Ex-Shrewsbury
	1715	1721	1724	B		Stourbridge Junction
1720	1725	1731	1736	A	1345	Paddington-Stourbridge Junction
	1735			B		Highley
		1738		B	1530	Ex-Shrewsbury
1745	1747	1753	1755	A	1635	Hereford-Birmingham Snow Hill
	1810			B		Shrewsbury
		1810		B	1800	Ex-Bewdley
			1820	B		Birmingham Snow Hill
		1830	1885	C(RR)	1800	Worcester Shrub Hill-Crewe
		1855		K	1600	Ex-Woofferton
1852	1857	1903	1908	B	1620	Leamington Spa-Wolverhampton
		1905	1915	E(RR)		Bridgnorth-Stourbridge Junction
		1916		B	1733	Ex-Shrewsbury
1821	1905	1919		J(SO)	1440	Ex-Worcester Goods Yard
	1930			K(SX)		Stourport
1821	1947	2001		F(SX)	1640	Ex-Worcester Tunnel Junction
2001	2004	2010	2013	B	1941	Worcester Shrub Hill-Wolverhampton
	2010			B		Buildwas
		2024		B	1955	Ex-Highley
2024	2027	2033	2036	A	1905	Hereford-Birmingham Snow Hill
		2050		B	1950	Ex-Woofferton
	2012	2024	2040	K		Stourbridge Junction
			2100	B		Birmingham Snow Hill
		2038	2108	E(RR)		Tenbury Wells-Stourbridge Junction
		2103	2128	C(SX)	2035	Worcester Goods Yard-Crewe
		2111	2130	E(SO)	2035	Worcester Goods Yard-Crewe
2204	2205	2211	2213	B	2145	Worcester Shrub Hill-Birmingham Snow Hill
		2218	2240	C(RRSX)	2150	Worcester Goods Yard-Crewe
		2245		B	2130	Ex-Buildwas
		2226	2254	E	2145	Worcester Goods Yard-Crewe
		2255		B(SO)	2145	Ex-Woofferton
		2323		B(SO)	2302	Ex-Highley
2257	2305	2315	2336	E(SXRR)	2230	Worcester Goods Yard-Crewe

Left and above: An example of trains working through Kidderminster in 1949.

0-6-0PT No. 29, formerly of the Cleobury Mortimer & Ditton Priors Light Railway and fitted with a spark arrester at Kidderminster shed on 10th September, 1949.   *H.C. Casserley*

Kidderminster shed in 1960. Praiire tanks Nos. 8105 and 4114 stand outside.   *D.K. Jones*

From Passed Fireman at Stourbridge to the end of steam

After my success at Swindon I soon informed the roster clerk and running foremen of my newly acquired status and after obtaining a copy of the Stourbridge route card, and signing those that I knew, I began to look forward to getting on the controls permanently. To do this I knew that I must leave Stourbridge, at least temporarily, so every month I scanned the vacancy list for a driving position preferably close to home. In the mean time I still had a job to do at Stourbridge and sooner rather than later a driving turn would come my way. But when it did, it came just when I least expected it. There was, though, another matter to attend to and on the first Sunday after my examination I went before the MIC for about two hours putting the questions that I had been asked to the men assembled before me. In this way firemen had a good idea of what would be in store for them on the day of their test. I had written all the questions down during my journey back from Swindon and that piece of paper survives today.

As mentioned above, my first driving duty arrived out of the blue. I was booking-off at the end of a firing turn on an early passenger duty and as usual I looked at the duty roster for the following day. To my surprise my name had been crossed out and another substituted. So I looked at the driver's duty sheet and there was my name for the first time as a booked driver on the 11 am Relief on one of the Dudley shunting engines. When I booked-on the following day I was a little nervous as it was the first time on the footplate in charge of an engine; today, I thought, there would be no-one to hold my hand if things went wrong. However, I quickly put these thoughts to the back of my mind and after meeting up with my fireman we caught the bus to Dudley and walked to the station where the crew we were to relieve were waiting on the platform. This shunting turn operated at the north end of Dudley sidings working both sides of the main line which included the ex-GWR goods shed; the coal sidings on the down side; and traffic interchange with the LMR on the up side. It certainly was a very busy job! The points controlling the up sidings were operated from North signal box, the signalman working to the directions of the head-shunter, in fact I can still visualize shunter Bridgewater standing at the box shouting out which siding he wanted wagons directed into. When the shift ended I reflected upon the day; not too bad for my first time in charge.

Another job I remember well was during the first week in May 1958 when I was called upon to relieve the regular driver on Turn 887, Bank Train No. 15. My fireman on this job was Don Smith and we had one of Stourbridge's familiar 0-6-2 tank engines No. 6698. After finishing our preparation we were ready to move out of the shed so I called over turntable man Fred Bailey to move the table round to our road. It was 11 pm precisely and with the turntable now set, it was off with the hand brake and in full reverse gear I eased the engine forward halting in the middle of the turntable. With the engine correctly balanced Fred had a much easier job rotating the turntable and lining it up with the shed exit road. Slowly we made our way to the nearby water column where Don replenished the tanks. With full tanks and a bunker already topped up with good Welsh steam coal I could see that the shed signal was 'off' so on the way towards Engine Shed signal box I sounded the whistle twice indicating to the signalman that we were heading for Stourbridge Junction. Opposite the box I pulled up so that I could inform signalman Jack Horton of the job 6698 was to be employed upon. We were scheduled to work out of Stourbridge Junction down sidings where the head-shunter directed us to our train, the usual mixed bag of open wagons and vans. Stan Watkins was the guard and after telling me the load I was all set to leave for Lye, the train comprising some 18 vehicles.

I now waited for the yard foreman Jack Chew to call the train forward. At 11.30 pm we got the all clear and slowly the train was eased out of the yard before almost immediately crossing from the down main onto the up main of the Stourbridge-

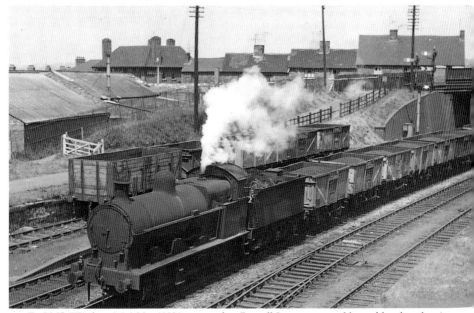

Ex-LMS '7F' class 0-8-0 No. 49021 approaches Brettell Lane on a southbound local coal train to Hartlebury, for Stourport power station, on 19th June, 1959.

Brian Moone/Kidderminster Railway Museum

An unidentified '57XX' class 0-6-0PT stands at Stourport station.

J. Tarrant/ Kidderminster Railway Museum

Birmingham line, halting at the up starting signal to wait for the Stourbridge banking engine to buffer up at the rear. There was a slight jolt and the engine moved forward against the brake and on hearing two crows on the banker's whistle I acknowledged with a similar signal. By now the signal had dropped to the 'off' position, so with a clear road in front of us I sounded the whistle and opened the regulator, the fireman releasing the handbrake at the same time. Lye was reached five minutes later at 11.35 pm, shunter John Griffiths waiting pole in hand to direct us into the yard to attach uphill traffic. At 12.05 am we were back on the main line heading towards Cradley Heath where a few more wagons would be put on. This too was uphill traffic although any wagons for Dudley and beyond would also be attached and taken to Rowley where they would then be dropped off. It was at Rowley that we said farewell to our banking engine which would cross over to the down main and return to Stourbridge. Our destination was now Oldbury & Langley Green yard (known as Langley Green & Rood End until the 1930s) which we reached at 12.55 am, and after entering the yard we were met by shunter Ron Perks who soon had things moving, cutting out wagons with a practised hand and directing them into the sidings. Our next duty was the 3.17 am inter-regional coal train from Great Bridge to Hartlebury. My driving log indicates that it was engine and van from Langley Green to Great Bridge, although sometimes we would pick-up Dudley traffic at Rowley if required. However, today there was no pick-up so it was straight down to Old Hill where we were signalled onto the Windmill End branch heading for Dudley. There was no direct access from the down main line at Dudley to the LMS lines so we had to come to a halt just outside the down platform before setting back onto the up main line from where we could then cross over to the London Midland side. Great Bridge was reached at about 3 am and having a few minutes to spare there was time for a brew and a sandwich before the coal train was due to arrive.

Having completed our refreshments a quick glance at the watch showed that the 3.17 am booked departure was not going to be met. We knew from experience that the late arrival of this train would have a considerable impact on our finishing time, as from Kidderminster in particular the heavy commuter traffic heading towards Birmingham would take precedence over an engine and van. At around 4 am we finally heard the familiar sound of the 'Super D' arriving with its train from Bescot. Pulling up in the platform the train engine was detached; with the 'Super D' out of the way, we backed our 0-6-2T on to the train to be coupled up by the shunter. Meanwhile, at the other end of the train, the Great Bridge shunting engine had removed the LMR van, putting the WR van in its place. The guard checked the load and having made sure that everything was secure gave us the signal to proceed. It was now 4.45 am and with the equivalent of 31 class one wagon loads behind the engine we summoned-up the LMR banker; the 'Super D' that had brought the train in, the engine assisting us as far as Dudley. On arrival at Dudley the banker dropped off before we crossed onto Great Western metals for the journey south. The train was scheduled to run non-stop from Great Bridge to Hartlebury where Kidderminster men would later 'trip' the wagons to Stourport power station. However, on this occasion we were stopped at Round Oak where the train was held for about five minutes. Whilst we waited a sharp lookout had to be kept as it was not unknown for lads from nearby houses to climb onto the wagons and throw out some coal to be picked up later and used on domestic fires. This time nobody tried their luck; too early probably and slack was not good for house fires anyway. At 5.25 am we got the right of way. Being a loose-coupled train the guard had pinned down a number of brakes at the stop board and continued to do so as we moved slowly down the 1 in 69 gradient. Satisfied that I had sufficient braking power I sounded the whistle twice and looked back to ensure that the guard was safely on board; he was. At Engine Shed sidings we once more had to come to a halt, this time it was to pick-up the brakes. This done it was non-stop to Hartlebury, an uneventful journey although we arrived about two hours behind schedule. In the reception sidings the wagons were detached and at

'Grange' class 4-6-0 No. 6879 *Overton Grange* departs from Kidderminster with 1W76 which is a troop train *circa* 1959.   *D.K. Jones*

Ex-LMS Fowler class '4' No. 42422 arrives at Kidderminster goods yard on a sugar beet train for the factory at Foley Park on 9th November, 1960.

Brian Moone/Kidderminster Railway Museum

8.20 am, after coupling up to the brake van which had been dropped off in the nearby loop, it was back onto the down main line to Kidderminster. Normally it was a straight run through to Stourbridge but today we were late and were soon delayed by the local passenger services. At Kidderminster itself we incurred a 35 minutes hold-up, the journey as a whole taking well over an hour. After detaching the guard's van in Stourbridge down yard it was a sharp run to the shed where we arrived on the ash-pit road at 9.35 am. Having completed my ticket and entered a couple of minor faults on the repair card, Don and I wearily made our way over to the offices where the paperwork was handed into the time-office and the keys to the storeman. It was now 10.10 am and we derived little comfort from the fact that in 12 hours time it was back on 6698 for another day.

Late in 1959 I successfully applied for a driving job at Kidderminster and on 30th November I booked-on at the shed. As a passed fireman at Stourbridge I had accumulated well in excess of 200 driving turns and on reaching 220 I had received my first pay rise. Some of my firing and driving turns had been in the Kidderminster area so I was certainly no stranger to the district, or Kidderminster shed and the men who were employed there. However, it was still a nervous new driver who met the gaffer, Percy Hodgson, that morning although the shed foreman soon put me at my ease and after meeting the duty running foreman, the clerical and the shed staff, I began to look forward to meeting this new challenge. The rest of the day was spent familiarising myself with the surroundings and finding out where everything was and who was responsible for what. I gave top priority to getting to know both the roster clerk and the running foreman, and finding out what work my link, No. 2, was responsible for. I also took a look at the condition of the engines, and found out who was to be my fireman; I also wanted to set-up a route learning programme. In the 1950s Kidderminster shed had both passenger and freight jobs. A number of passenger turns were on the main line to Wolverhampton (Low Level) and Birmingham (Snow Hill) whilst a branch line job was the steam-hauled passenger service to and from Woofferton [this was the Leominster train]. As far as I can recall steam hauled passenger services to and from Shrewsbury over the Severn Valley line were not worked by Kidderminster men; perhaps these were Salop or Worcester turns. Most passenger jobs were Top Link turns although No. 2 did have a couple of main line turns: a passenger job to Birmingham (Snow Hill) as well as the Kidderminster portion of 'The Cathedrals Express'. Many of the branch line services were worked by Worcester men in their ex-GWR diesel railcars including the one that left 'Kiddi' at around 5.50 am. This was specially laid on to take miners to Alveley Halt. The miners returned via a Shrewsbury to Kidderminster 'stopper'.

On the freight side, most of the services operated by the shed dealt with coal traffic although some served the agricultural and farming communities in the district; there was certainly a pick-up goods from Kidderminster to Woofferton and back. Both Bridgnorth and Tenbury Wells held cattle markets, usually on alternate weeks, and this provided a weekly livestock train to and from each of these towns. During the winter sugar beet season a great many loads were delivered to Kidderminster yard. These were subsequently tripped into the British Sugar Corporation's private sidings near Foley Park. However, the staple commodity was coal and slack, much of it for the nearby Stourport power station. This provided Kidderminster shed with a huge amount of work. Traffic from the Stourbridge direction arrived at Hartlebury yard behind a variety of locomotive types especially ex-LMS '8Fs', '7Fs', WD 2-8-0s and of course ex-GWR 0-6-2Ts. Wagons would then be tripped to Stourport by Kidderminster crews who would deliver the coal direct to the CEGB's sidings where the Board's own shunting engine would take over. I seem to recall that there were two or three trips per day, each train usually having a brake van at each end. After leaving the full wagons in the sidings, engines would return to Hartlebury with either the brake vans, or a train of empties. Power station coal would also be conveyed from Alveley colliery sidings.

A '43XX' class 2-6-0 at Alveley colliery *c*.1960.   *C.R. Kendrick*

'43XX' class 2-6-0 No. 6314 hauls a train load of coal from Alveley colliery near Hartlebury Castle, between Stourport and Hartlebury, on 27th May, 1963.

Brian Moone/Kidderminster Railway Museum

Kidderminster crews working these services were normally allocated one of the shed's class '63XX' 2-6-0s. Coal from Alveley was also transported by class 'K' mixed goods from Bridgnorth or Shrewsbury to either Kidderminster or Hartlebury, traffic being dropped off at intermediate stations as required. Whilst I was there the shed had two trips per day from Stourport to Alveley colliery starting with a light engine movement to the power station sidings to pick up empties for the colliery. I had a number of driving turns on this job, however, before I could take out a train, any train, I had to be sure that I had intimate knowledge of the route. I had worked over many of the local lines as a fireman at Stourbridge so I wasn't starting from scratch, but before signing the route card I had to be confident that the position of every signal and box; gradient and curve; tunnel and bridge; the arrangements at stations, sidings, and yards; in fact every element that each individual route possessed in abundance was indelibly etched in my memory. These routes though couldn't be learnt overnight and some took quite a time to master. Equally important was the local working timetable and its appendix, the latter describing the operational arrangements in force at locations in our particular section. Prior to going out with a train I also had to be aware of changes in line conditions, especially temporary speed restrictions; signalling alterations; or permanent way possessions; I had to ensure that I had read all of the relevant notices, absolutely essential as most of Kidderminster's work was over single line. Driving a steam engine was not just about getting onto the footplate and working the controls; it was a lot more complex than that!

One of my first duties at Kidderminster was the early morning turn to Alveley colliery sidings which began when I booked-on at 4.20 am, a few minutes after my regular fireman Graham Borsebury. One hour was allowed for preparation of the 2-6-0 so it was off shed by around 5.20 am normally attached to the Stourport shunting engine. The night shed turn would sometimes help enginemen out by doing the oiling and checking that everything was all right on the footplate. They would then move the engine out into the yard where we would take over. The shed roads and the inspection pits at 'Kiddi' were quite short so there was always a great demand for space especially first thing in a morning. To ease congestion the night shed turn would get the early engines out of the way thereby keeping delays to a minimum. I used to go to work on a Lambretta scooter and as it was winter, by the time I had reached the shed I was pretty cold. However, I could always count on the night turn having a pot of piping hot tea on the stove; a mug of tea certainly helped warm me up before making my way over to the engine.

Our last job before going off shed was to fill the tender tank, Graham climbing onto the top to undo the cover before placing the bag into the tank. I would then turn on the water. With the tender tank full, the water was turned off and I climbed back into the cab to be joined moments later by my mate; we were now ready to depart. I opened the regulator and with a slight touch of the whistle we set off towards Kidderminster Junction, the shed signal having cleared as we started on our way. On arrival at the junction we entered the down loop before crossing to the up main at Kidderminster Junction box where we were joined on the footplate by the guard. The journey to Stourport was via Hartlebury with the shunting engine leading. We made good time and soon we were coming to a halt outside Hartlebury Junction signal box, situated on the up side of the main line. Here the headlamp was changed over. Both engines then reversed across the down main and onto the Stourport line, the 2-6-0 leading, running tender first, a single white light above the centre of the buffer beam having now replaced the red tail light. At Stourport station the shunting engine was uncoupled and went about its business. With the line clear the signal came 'off' and with the Stourport shunter also on the footplate we headed for the CEGB branch which joined the main line from the right-hand side via a west-facing point located just before the bridge over the Staffs & Worcester canal. The single line branch ran down to the power station's reception sidings which comprised a nest of eight double-ended sidings. A loaded train

'Grange' class 4-6-0 No. 6814 *Enborne Grange* rattles through Kidderminster station on 30th August, 1962 with a down fitted freight. *Michael Mensing*

An ex-GWR diesel railcar arrives at Kidderminster on 30th August, 1962 and will form the 2.05 pm for Bridgmorth and Shrewsbury. *Michael Mensing*

for these sidings would have had a brake van attached front and rear, the guard riding in one, the shunter in the other. From the junction with the main line to Mill Road bridge the wagon brakes would have to be pinned down on the falling gradient of 1 in 56. At the bridge the brakes would be released, the engine drawing the loaded wagons into an unoccupied loop leaving the rear brake van on the Stourport side of the sidings. If there was a return load, engine and front van would set back on to the empty wagons held in No. 5 loop. After the van had been coupled-up to the wagons the engine would run round via No. 3 loop, the second van being attached to the front of the train in readiness for the return journey up the hill. Today we simply buffered up to our train of empties and prepared to leave tender first on the scheduled 45 minutes run to Alveley colliery.

Our guard has given me the load and having received the right of way, Graham unwinds the hand brake and I ease open the regulator; I wanted to judge the 'weight' of the train before starting it in earnest up the hill towards the junction. The signal is 'off' and we pull onto the single line, taking it steady past the goods yard and shed on our left and Stourport canal basin sidings and signal box on the right. We then enter the platforms of Stourport station, pulling up at the signal box just before the level crossing. There was a certain Kidderminster driver who found it quite difficult stopping at this point and on one occasion he went straight through the gates, however, I had no such problem. The signalman was already at the gates with the token for the single line section to Bewdley. Graham took hold of this and the signalman returned to his box. The gates opened and after locking into place, 'off' came the starter and we began our journey to Alveley. Over the level crossing and past the coal sidings on the left it was then into the dark confines of the 123 yds-long Mount Pleasant tunnel. Our engine is running very freely and manages its load with ease. On the other side of the tunnel I have to be careful to hold the train back on the incline to Sandbourne viaduct where the line from Kidderminster comes in from the right. From Bewdley South Junction, through Bewdley station to Bewdley viaduct, there was two way working, however, just beyond Bewdley viaduct, at Bewdley North Junction, single line working recommenced, the right-hand line continuing as the Severn Valley branch to Bridgnorth, the left-hand line becoming the Tenbury branch. At Bewdley South box Graham drops the token on to the post and prepares to collect the next token off the North box signalman who is standing outside his box at the far end of the station. The train runs slowly through the platforms towards the north end before the smack of metal against arm indicates that the token has been safely gathered in, Graham confirming that it is the correct one for Arley. The right-hand bracket is 'off' and we cross over to the single line of the Severn Valley branch leaving the line to Woofferton, with its permanent 15 mph speed restriction as far as Cleobury Mortimer, to swing away to the left. On another day it was about 6.20 am when we passed Bewdley. We were travelling tender first as usual and there was a bitterly cold wind blowing from the north and snow was falling heavily making visibility very tricky. To give us some protection the storm sheet had been pulled over the space between cab roof and tender. We had just passed Northwood Halt when we ran over three detonators that had been placed on the line. Immediately I looked out of the cab and my fireman did the same on his side. There, just about visible through the driving snow, was the dark shape of a man swinging a red light. Quickly I applied the brakes and drew up alongside the shadowy figure; it was one of the local platelayers. To our dismay we were told that there had been a land slip by Trimpley reservoir, however, the line was still passable but extreme caution had to be exercised. Landslides were quite common in the area and often the line would be blocked.

On the approach to Arley I give a long, loud blast on the whistle to remind the signalman to be ready with the token for the next section. The line from Arley to Highley rises at 1 in 145 and after Highley, where we pick up the token for Alveley colliery sidings, it steepens slightly to 1 in 135 but this presents no challenge to our engine. We now pass Alveley Halt before coming to a stop at Alveley Sidings South ground frame

'Hall' class 4-6-0 No. 5980 *Dingley Hall* on a southbound freight passing under the footbridge south of Kidderminster on 18th September, 1960.   *Brian Moone/Kidderminster Railway Museum*

'51XX' class 2-6-2T No. 5152 leaves Kidderminster with the 8.30 am through coaches to Paddington on 30th July, 1963. These carriages would be attached at Worcester to the 'Cathedrals Express'.   *D.K. Jones*

where shunter Clive King is waiting to collect the token that will unlock the frame to enable us to enter the sidings. The electric token instrument was fixed in a cabin midway between the two ground frames (Alveley Sidings North and South) and having inserted the token the points are thrown over and we draw into the loop. Once the main line was clear the points are returned and with the main line secured the signalmen at Highley and Hampton Loade are informed that the single line is clear. Having detached the brake van in the loop the empty wagons are reversed through the private siding gate and into the sidings to the south of the loading plant. Having completed this first shunt we run to the 'loaded' sidings (on the north side of the plant). As there are loaded wagons for various destinations, e.g. Bridgnorth and Shrewsbury to the north, and Highley, Arley, Stourport, Hartlebury and Kidderminster to the south, we have to do quite a lot of shunting before being able to hook up to the train in readiness for the journey back to Stourport. But first breakfast cooked on the shovel!

The return working was booked to leave Alveley at 10.45 am and it was quite a pull over the 1 in 100 gradient with a fully loaded coal train on the draw bar. We would halt at Highley where any coal wagons would be put off as required. On arrival at Bewdley at about 11.30 am we were relieved by the afternoon turn, and after handing over our train it was down to the bus stop to catch the next bus to Kidderminster, booking-off at the shed. The afternoon turn would now take the loaded train on to Stourport and Hartlebury, the crew returning to Alveley colliery with another train of empties almost immediately. However, the return working which left the sidings at about 3.00 pm ran direct to Kidderminster yard, the engine being put on shed where the crew booked-off.

As mentioned above the shed also had an express duty of sorts. This was of course the Kidderminster section of the prestigious 'Cathedrals Express' which joined the ex-Hereford portion at Worcester (Shrub Hill). The motive power provided by Kidderminster was usually a 2-6-2T, the shed being allocated, at various times during the post-war period, examples of '45XX', '51XX', '61XX', and '81XX' class locomotives. Occasionally I had a driving turn on this working and I can remember always feeling a little envious of the crew of the 'Castle' waiting to back on to the express at Worcester, it always looked in tiptop condition and dwarfed our tank engine. Still our engine did the job it was asked to do with ease. I also worked the freight traffic over the Tenbury Wells and Woofferton branch via Cleobury Mortimer, the latter being the southern terminus of the Cleobury Mortimer & Ditton Priors Light Railway (CM&DPLR) which opened in 1908. In 1922 the line was absorbed by the GWR and although passenger traffic was withdrawn in 1938 a daily goods in both directions kept the line just about alive. In 1939 the Admiralty built the Royal Naval Armament Depot (RNAD) which was supplied by goods trains worked by Kidderminster men. This arrangement lasted until 1957 when the Admiralty acquired the whole route, RNAD Ruston & Hornsby diesel locomotives taking over all the work on the branch from the ex-GWR/Western Region 0-6-0PTs. GWR/WR steam engines had only ever run as far as Cleobury North crossing where loaded trains were taken over by the Admiralty locomotives and the empty wagons returned. However, former CM&DPLR No. 29, an 0-6-0PT, had been fitted with a spark arrester just in case it was required to work into the Admiralty depot. This spark arrester was fitted to other 0-6-0 tank engines after No. 29 was withdrawn in 1954. I came too late to Kidderminster to experience any branch line work but I regularly dropped off loaded ammunition wagons in Cleobury Mortimer yard and picked up the empties when working the pick-up freight to and from Woofferton.

My stay at Kidderminster shed proved much shorter that I could have imagined and in mid-1960 a vacancy arose at Stourbridge and I grabbed the opportunity with both hands. On my last day I said my farewells to some of the good friends I had made and to this day I still meet up with some of them on our annual outing on the Severn Valley Railway. Kidderminster was an excellent shed to work at and I had no complaints at all at the way I had been treated. Percy Hodgson the shedmaster was a very fair man and fostered good working relationships with the men of whom he was in charge. I also had some good mates, Harold Shingles for one. It was he who taught me many of the local routes. There was also Walter 'Napper' Neal, Roy Davies, Eric Porter, and Howard Gillard, all good drivers and friends, as were the firemen: my regular mate Graham Borsebury, Eric Preece, Derek Lamb, Ray Golding and the inimitable Barry Cook, a bit of a lad and still is. I would also miss the little 'get-togethers', especially Christmas Eve in the 'Blount Arms' after completing shunting at Cleobury Mortimer, or the walk down to the 'Rose & Crown' in Tenbury Wells on market day for a swift half and a game of bar bagatelle to pass the time while the cattle were being loaded. Although short, I think my stay at Kidderminster was the happiest time of my whole career. Anyway, on 9th May, 1960 I once more packed my gear and headed back to Stourbridge. As I did so I wondered if I had made a mistake, but the closure of Kidderminster was being talked about so I thought that I had better move while I still had a choice. But things were changing on the railways and with the introduction of more and more diesels many jobs were soon to be under threat.

So having returned to Stourbridge, and after a couple of weeks on route refresher duties, I took my place in the bottom bank link. I had fired on many of the turns in this link and as a passed fireman I had also some driving knowledge, so I soon got into the swing of things. In the bank link I usually would drive 0-6-0PTs but sometimes I would have a 2-6-2T Prairie, a type of engine I had fired on many occasions during my first tour of duty at Stourbridge, but of course now I was not on the shovel but at the controls and therefore with a different set of responsibilities.

At the beginning of the shift I would report to the time clerk at the shed who would record my arrival time against my number (203). I would then pick up a daily record sheet which would be used to record engine details, load, and at the end of the shift any delays and the reasons for them; I also had to collect my job card which gave the day's duties, and read any notices that may contain details of line restrictions that may affect the running of the train. Having identified the day's engine a look at the repair book would indicate if any defects booked against it had been signed off by the fitter as repaired, if not the engine would have to be referred back to the fitting shop and replaced by a spare if one was available. With all outstanding repairs booked-off the engine became my responsibility. I now went quickly to my locker to change, and then, suitably dressed in my oiling coat, it was over to the engine, a 2-6-2T Prairie. As I approached I took note of how the engine was 'standing'; in other words the position of the coupling rods. This told me if the big-ends were going to be reasonably accessible for oiling. If not I would ask my fireman to move the engine a fraction, assuming of course there was sufficient steam in the boiler. Reaching the cab I saw that my mate was already on board and had prepared and filled my oil feeders. After testing the water gauges and checking that the fusible plugs and tubes were tight, I had a quick look at the fire and steam pressure and seeing that everything on the footplate was in order i.e. the hand brake was wound on hard; the reverser was in mid-gear; and the cylinder drain cocks fully open; I left the cab for the murky world beneath the frames. But first I inspected the brake blocks and having found them satisfactory I shouted to my mate that I was going underneath. At some sheds, e.g. Stafford Road, the engine inspection pits were quite shallow, however at Stourbridge they were much deeper therefore drivers had more space in which to work. To prevent hot ash falling down the back of my neck the front damper has been closed. Having checked the vacuum pipes and buffers at each end of the loco, and the springs, brake cylinders, and rodding, I climb onto the side of the pit to top up the oil in the eccentrics. There were two eccentrics connected to the driving axle, one enabled forward motion the other reverse, both being operated by the reversing rod. Whilst doing this I kept a wary eye open for any movement hoping that I would not feel the eccentric straps begin to rub over my stomach for if I did it was rapid evasive action, usually jumping immediately back into the pit. I also had to be careful that my mate did not put on the live steam injector to top up the boiler as this could lead to hot water overflowing from the top feed and running down the boiler barrel and under the engine and over me. It had happened before and I was not anxious for it to happen again. Having finished my under-engine routine it was onto the frames to check that the mud hole doors were not leaking. Then, having made sure that the trimmings that supplied oil to the slide bars were in the oil cup pipes, I checked that the washout plugs were not blowing before returning to the shed floor to inspect the axle boxes. If a box had any water in it the liquid had to be pumped out and fresh oil added. If this was not done there was a real possibility of the engine suffering a hot axle box and being failed on the road. In the cab was the automatic lubricator for the valves and pistons and this had to be checked before leaving the shed. The oil was delivered at four spots per minute and this could be confirmed via the sight glass. Last but not least I test the steam-operated vacuum brake; the ejector is opened and I watch the needles rise as the vacuum is created. I then make a test brake application keeping a close eye on the vacuum and train brake needles. As air enters the train pipe the partial vacuum on the lower side of each brake piston is destroyed, however, the vacuum on the upper side is maintained. If the valve needle on this gauge also starts to drop I know that there is a problem with the brake, often a leak on the brake cylinder caused by a defective slipping rubber band on the piston. The entry of air into the system raises the brake pistons and applies the brakes. To release the brakes the action of the ejector causes air to be drawn from below the brake pistons allowing the pistons to return to the bottom of the cylinders. Having satisfied myself that all is well on the footplate I check with my mate and it is off shed to begin our day's work.

A noticeable feature of the lines in the Stourbridge area was the severity of many of the gradients and thinking back there were two examples which really stood out. The first was on the line from Coxes (aka Cox's) Lane to Dudley, although the real tester was in the opposite direction, from Coxes Lane to Rowley Regis through Old Hill. Coxes Lane lay at the bottom of a hollow and due to the nature of the Windmill End branch a lengthy freight waiting at the up starter would be stretched over a line comprising both rising and falling gradients (often two of the former and one of the latter). As can be imagined, working loose-coupled freights in particular over such a terrain had to be developed into a fine art, especially starting off.

Usually banking assistance was required for heavy trains out of Coxes Lane so when I had the right of way two crows would be sounded on the engine's whistle and having received the same from the banking engine the handbrake would come off. Having wound the reverser to full forward gear I would open the regulator and gently ease away up the hill toward Old Hill South Junction. Moving forward I would feel the drag on the train as the driver of the banker applied the hand brake to bring the couplings tight; at the moment the assisting engine was not working. Over the hill and down into the dip the driver of the banking engine instructs his fireman to release the handbrake and he opens the regulator, buffering up to the guard's van and taking the strain out of the couplings. Both engines are now working hard on the approach to Old Hill South Junction and then onto the main line heading towards Rowley Regis. Through Old Hill North Junction and the climb stiffens. As the train engine enters Old Hill tunnel the driver of the assisting engine takes note of the distant signal. If it is 'on' then in all likelihood the Rowley Regis home signal will also be 'on'. He therefore will reduce power so as not to push the train engine past the signal at danger. An experienced driver on the banking engine could tell what was happening at the front of the train by the 'feel' as they worked through towards Rowley; but not all drivers were experienced! On the Wombourn branch there was a similar gradient problem at Pensnett but here there was no assisting engine. Instead it was a test of the team work of driver and guard, the latter applying his hand brake or releasing it when he senses the change in the way the train was working. Loose-coupled trains had a tendency to part if the braking was not carried out correctly.

As stated above the action of the reverser worked the eccentrics thereby determining which direction the engine would travel. Once, on a light engine movement with a BR Standard '9F' 2-10-0, the reverser almost caused a serious incident. Ray Silvester was my fireman and we were on a routine run to Kidderminster to pick up a northbound freight. However, on arrival at Churchill & Blakedown station we were brought to a halt at the end of the platform just before the level crossing. Wondering what was happening I asked Ray to run over to the box and see what the problem was. On his return he jumped up onto the footplate telling me that we had to get off the main line as a South Wales express was coming up behind us. The signal cleared and we moved forward past the south end of the up loop and came to a halt. The points swung to the left and the dummy cleared and we prepared to reverse into the loop, the signal behind having returned to 'danger'. The reverser on this type of engine was operated by a wheel, very much like the one on the old hand-operated mangle. Unfortunately, getting from full forward gear to full reverse often implied a great deal of effort. Gradually the wheel turned and eventually I got the engine into reverse gear. I looked back out of the cab and to my surprise the points had been returned to the main line position and the dummy to 'danger', whilst the main line signals had cleared. I immediately asked Ray to run down to the box and ask the signalman what was going on. A minute or two later a breathless fireman reported back. Apparently the signalman had assumed we had reversed into the loop and had set the signals for the express. Only one thing to do, put the engine back into forward gear, open the regulator and go like a bat out of hell to 'Kiddi'. Luckily getting into forward gear was much easier than reverse and we made a spirited departure to say the least. Behind us the signals had been returned to 'danger' and what could have been a nasty accident was avoided.

Another incident happened when I had a passenger driving turn. The engine involved was one of our own 4-6-0s, No. 6842 *Nunold Grange*. It was the summer of 1962 and we were working a Sunday local from Worcester (Shrub Hill) to Stourbridge Junction, a service that was supposed to be a diesel multiple unit. The train was a jaunt for the 'Grange' so I was not anticipating any problems especially as I had with me an experienced fireman, someone that I had worked with on a number of occasions. However, as we pulled away from Hagley past the cattle pens I heard a roaring in the firebox; this could only spell trouble! I looked at my mate and it was clear from the expression on his face that he too had similar concerns. I opened the firebox doors and my worst suspicions were immediately confirmed, for shooting down from the firebox crown onto the fire below was a jet of steam. Immediately we checked the boiler water gauge glass. After blowing it through we saw that instead of a full boiler as my fireman had thought, it was almost empty exposing the lead plug which had melted. So here we were half way between Hagley and Stourbridge with a fairly full train and an engine with a dropped plug. Immediately the injectors were put on and my thoughts turned to taking steps to either deaden the fire or dropping it. However, stopping here would have meant blocking the main line with little chance of getting an assistant engine from Stourbridge in reasonable time. What should I do; stop or try and get to Stourbridge? I had to make up my mind quickly and if things went wrong I had to be prepared to take the consequences; I therefore decided to nurse the train on to Stourbridge. Gingerly we crept forward and keeping our speed as low as possible we eventually arrived at Stourbridge Junction. A few passengers enquired as to why the late arrival, a question I answered with a convenient but vague response. Once the train was empty and the stock uncoupled I informed the station staff that I would have to leave the stock in the platform. I had no intention of pushing my luck any further as by now steam pressure had almost disappeared and it would be touch and go whether we could even make it to the shed. Reach it we did and after handing the engine over to the firedropper and explaining what had happened we quickly made for the shed pilot engine and after checking that the fire and water levels were acceptable it was back to the Junction as quickly as possible where we were able to pick-up the carriages that were so hurriedly abandoned. With a feeling of great relief the stock was shunted into the carriage sidings and after returning the engine to the shed we gratefully finished for the day, although both of us knew that the matter would not end there.

Obviously the incident had to be reported on the repair card, and when the fitters picked this up such a potentially serious failure would immediately be communicated to the foreman fitter who was obliged to pass on the details to the shedmaster. There was only minor damage inflicted upon the engine's firebox crown and 6842 was not out of traffic for long, although this did not prevent me from getting a good dressing down from Mr Gregory. This, though, was as far as it went. Afterwards, many of my colleagues were quick to point out what they would have done in similar circumstances, but, as the man on the spot, I had to take the decision and face the consequences if that decision was the wrong one.

By the early 1960s not only were many of the passenger services operated by Stourbridge being turned over to diesel traction but also we lost our Great Western identity. In 1963 the district was absorbed into the London Midland Region and as a result a number of ex-LMS engine types were drafted in, especially the Stanier '8Fs'. I was not unfamiliar with these engines as they had been regular visitors to the area certainly since the 1940s. However, driving on the left-hand side took some getting used to as did the absence of the Automatic Train Control (ATC) that was a standard fitting on the former GWR engines. With the ATC in the cab it was possible to drive at a reasonable speed even when fog made visibility very difficult. On the approach to a signal at 'caution' the system gave a loud audible warning in the cab and automatically applied the brakes. The driver now alerted to the danger would then cancel the warning returning the train to his control. Driving in fog even with the ATC on board was still a nightmare and the crew had to be constantly on the look out for landmarks to confirm their location. In those days we had some real 'pea soupers' in the Black Country, a situation that only began to improve with the Clean Air Act. Drifting smoke from the chimney and the glare of the fire didn't help matters and we were grateful to alert platelayers who were equipped with flags and detonators and strategically placed at the side of the track to help us on our way.

With the end of steam on the horizon more and more men were being trained on diesel traction and when it was my turn it was on shunters. Stourbridge shed had two excellent instructors on these machines, Sid Aimes and Vic Chapman, who ensured that trainees received a thorough grounding not only in driving techniques but also on routine maintenance and the identification and rectification of minor faults. Consequently, when it came to the examination I had little difficulty in passing. Shortly afterwards I moved on to diesel multiple unit training at Derby where, along with about 20 other drivers from different depots, I undertook five days of intensive theoretical instruction in the classroom before returning to Stourbridge to get my hands on the real thing. Once again Sid and Vic put me through my paces until they were confident that I was in good enough shape to meet the inspector; once again their instruction paid off and I was passed to drive dmus.

My last driving turn on a steam engine was on the preserved 0-6-0 No. 3205 with George Poole as my fireman. The engine had been at a steam gala in Hereford and had to be brought back to the West Midlands where it was taken to Bewdley, the then terminus of the infant Severn Valley Railway. The turn brought back many memories, although in reality driving steam engines was not a romantic or glamorous occupation at all, in fact it was usually quite the opposite. In the freight links at both Stourbridge and Kidderminster a driver and fireman had to work unsocial hours and as a young fireman in particular this meant that many of the activities enjoyed by young men in

'Grange' class 4-6-0 No. 6857 *Tudor Grange* at the south end of Stourbridge Junction station *circa* 1954. This locomotive was allocated to Stourbridge shed between 1948 and 1955. *W.F. Deebank*

An ex-LMS '8F' class 2-8-0 No. 48410 at Round Oak sidings on a freight *c.*1963.   *V. Morgan*

those days had to be forsaken. The early mornings, weekend work, nights and extended shifts played havoc with men's social lives and I have often wondered how my long suffering spouse put up with it. But these sort of hours had to be worked; railways were simply not a nine to five occupation. I didn't miss getting under an 0-6-0 tank engine on a freezing cold January morning to do the oiling either. These things enginemen learnt to live with and accepted as part and parcel of the job. But the railways were about to change, especially for Stourbridge men and working life was never to be the same again.

Steam has been withdrawn and I move on to diesels

The withdrawal of steam and the closure of the shed seemed to come suddenly, although in truth Stourbridge men had been aware of the plans for some considerable time and it was simply impossible to ignore the increasing number of diesel multiple units that were replacing the former steam-hauled services. The end came in July 1966 and although the two sheds remained in use for a time, the 'old' shed having been turned into diesel fuelling point, by 1969 they had been demolished and all trace of their existence was later submerged under a new housing estate. After closure all train crews moved to Stourbridge Junction where they now reported to a train crew supervisor. The old titles had disappeared and many of my former colleagues had left. In overall charge at the station was Henry Holloway, a station manager whose area of responsibility extended well beyond the Junction. The move to the Junction meant that some men qualified for a disturbance allowance to ensure no one was out of pocket after the move. We also saw the introduction of fine new uniforms, green at first but later blue to match the corporate image; gone were the serge jackets, the overalls, and our familiar plastic-topped caps. Diesel cabs were much cleaner, comfortable places, so our neat work-wear was not out of place, although some of the older railwaymen felt that it was they that did not belong. I had worn overalls since my cleaning days so this new uniform felt odd, and not really something I could easily associate with railway work.

After the closure of the shed to steam, freight traffic in the area, as far as I can recall, was all diesel-hauled. Stourbridge's freight turns were all double-manned; driver and secondman now. The depot also continued its shunting turns and by now virtually all of these were single-manned although some drivers with health problems would be accompanied, the driver being prohibited from driving over the main line between depot and yard. Dmus of course were all driver only. The reinstatement of the curve between Smethwick Junction and Galton Junction and the introduction of passenger trains over the Stourbridge line to Birmingham (New Street) in 1967 meant back to route learning, as did the depot's freight turns to Burton-on-Trent via Lichfield City; to Littleton colliery via Wolverhampton (High Level); and also to Lea Hall sidings; Bescot; Saltley; Washwood Heath, and Sutton Park. As a result, for the next few months, it was in the cab at the side of a driver who knew the road, or behind a desk in Birmingham (New Street) Road Learning School. After I had signed for a road I would often accompany older drivers who were not scheduled for route learning because of their age, so in effect I was acting as pilotman. Some of these drivers had taught me similar lessons on the footplate of steam engines when I was a fireman, so it felt quite odd that I was now showing them the ropes. On the whole Stourbridge men eagerly grabbed the opportunity to gain route knowledge for this meant work in what had become a rapidly shrinking industry. Unfortunately, as contraction set in, competition between depots for jobs became more and more fierce and Stourbridge TCD came under increasing pressure from the bigger Train Crew Depots elsewhere in the district. It was now becoming a fight for survival! Our Local Departmental Committee (LDC) did everything it could to get a bigger share of the available work for Stourbridge crews; one proposal was to gain an express job between New Street and Euston, the men coming

Brush type '4' (later class '47') No. 1743 at Stourbridge old shed *c.*1966.   *C.R. Kendrick*

350 hp diesel shunter (later class '08') No. D3026 at Stourbridge old shed *c.*1966.   *C.R. Kendrick*

Dmu sets occupy the roads of the old coal storage area at Stourbridge shed *c*.1966.

C.R. Kendrick

up on a local, working London there and back, and finishing the shift with a local back to Stourbridge. Additional work to and from Stratford, Leamington, and Hereford was also requested, but all to no avail. There constantly seemed to be reasons why jobs could not come to Stourbridge, the larger TCDs always seeming to win the day. Perhaps bowing to the big battalions was an easier option for these certainly had more industrial clout than Stourbridge.

Route learning was accompanied by familiarisation of the new diesel locomotives. I had driven shunters since my return to Stourbridge but the larger locomotives were all new to me. Some of the driver training was carried out at the depot under the watchful eye of our own instructors, however, this would be backed up with class work undertaken at Duddeston near Saltley depot and also 'hands on' experience at Saltley itself. In between training courses it was putting theory into practice and my first diesel locomotive driving job was on the Stourbridge banking engine which was on duty at the north end of Stourbridge Junction ready to assist heavy freights to Dudley or over Old Hill bank to Rowley. Even with diesel traction some of the trains were simply too heavy for one engine to cope with, however, it was the high failure rate of the dmus on the Stourbridge-Birmingham line that made us scratch our heads and think, 'Is this progress?' The day turn on the banking engine was particularly busy and sometimes it was necessary to provide assistance for as many as 10 trains in one shift. However, the banking job was not my only driving turn and sometimes I would have a trip working from Kingswinford Junction to Bescot via Dudley, or Washwood Heath via Sutton Park. There was also an afternoon Gloucester-bound freight that had a crew change at the Junction. The banking jobs normally utilised type '4' locos whilst the trip workings employed a wide variety of traction from type '1s' to type '4s', depending upon what was available at Bescot. I also had driving turns on the single diesel unit that worked the Town branch. I had worked over this line many times, firing on the auto-train but driving the diesel was a totally new experience, although around 40 trips per shift over the shortest branch line in the country was quite monotonous and tiring. It was quite lucrative though, with driver shortages providing considerable overtime opportunities. In addition to branch line work some main line passenger jobs came my way. These were the local dmu service to Birmingham (New Street) and Lichfield City, or in the opposite direction to Worcester.

In my link there were also the 'ferry' turns. Prior to the closure of the 'old' shed, a ferry turn involved taking an empty dmu or a light engine up to the fuelling point and then returning it to the sidings or stabling point. After closure the 'ferry' turns worked further afield; locomotives to and from Bescot, dmus to Tyseley. On the night shift the 'ferry' turn was responsible for checking over dmus stabled in the sidings on the down side to the north of the station. The first task was to consult the driver's repair book to see if there were any outstanding faults, and if I found any myself, these would be reported to the duty train crew supervisor who would arrange for a fitter to come over from Tyseley as there were no fitters now employed at Stourbridge. After satisfying myself that there were no outstanding repairs, the fuel and coolant levels would be checked and if necessary the latter would be topped up. This procedure would be repeated on all stabled units before they were shunted into position ready to be taken off the sidings first thing in the morning. Before signing off I would have to ensure that all dmu and locomotive engines were switched on and running satisfactorily. They would then be left running thereby avoiding the need for the booked drivers to have to restart them at the beginning of their turns. There was also a guard on duty and he would attend to the shunting and coupling and uncoupling of the units. I had a good working relationship with these men which came from many years working together in often very trying circumstances.

When Stourbridge shed closed there were 138 drivers and 62 firemen. However, from then on train crew numbers began to drop steadily. A number of drivers and secondmen (the position of fireman no longer existed) applied for jobs at depots elsewhere in the district, whilst some went further afield, especially secondmen whose future at Stourbridge appeared very bleak indeed; others left the industry under the redundancy arrangements. One of the conditions of redundancy was the opportunity to return into the line of promotion if a vacancy arose within two years of leaving the service. Someone who chose this option was David Beech who was made redundant from the depot in August 1968. Having first obtained a job as a lorry driver at Lye goods depot he later returned to train crew duties as a secondman at Saltley depot just before his two years were up. David went on to make driver at Birmingham (New Street) before being promoted to train crew manager at Leamington. This was one of the few examples of the redundancy arrangements working out quite well.

No matter how many men left the service or transferred elsewhere, there never seemed to be sufficient work for those that remained, consequently the threat of redundancy at Stourbridge never seemed to be too far away. However, I felt reasonably confident that I would hold on to my driving job. I was getting a good mix of driving turns especially as cover for holidays and sickness and with the retirement of a couple of elderly drivers things did not look too bad. But what was obvious was that the depot was rarely getting any new jobs; it really did seem that we were being deliberately starved of work. Surely they were not thinking of closing Stourbridge? Our Local Departmental Committee tried its hardest for the men, appealing to both management and colleagues at other depots for a more equitable share of the available work; but what the big depots had they clung on to and management seemed reluctant to upset them. Then came the bombshell! It was on one Sunday in September 1968 and there was a special meeting of the local branch of ASLEF; I feared the worst! For me it was the loss of my driver's job, perhaps not totally unexpected given the current climate but still a blow after serving the railway industry for 26 years man and boy, working up the promotion ladder from cleaner to driver; working all hours and in all conditions; what a reward! I wanted to stay at Stourbridge, as did a number of other men who found themselves in a similar position, so I opted to be 'put-back'. Other drivers moved elsewhere including Harold Attwood who elected to move to Watford and never regretted his decision, unfortunately some decided to leave the industry and British Rail lost some good men. I think we all felt let down by what was happening in the industry and it certainly left a bitter taste in the mouths of all remaining Stourbridge train crew. I still had a job of sorts, but as most services were single manned there were often little for me and other 'put-back' drivers to do. Spending hours at a time in the messroom, together with guards who had also lost their permanent jobs, was soul destroying to say the least. We were all active railwaymen and spending our time like this was simply an appalling waste. Often, after as many as six hours sitting around, the supervisor would let us book-off; he could see the look in our eyes as we said cheerio to each other; he could also see that this was no way to treat men.

I remained 'put-back' until 11th May, 1970 when for the first time in almost two years Stourbridge depot received some new work. I was reinstated as driver in the shunting link; nothing too dramatic but certainly better than twiddling my thumbs at the depot. The goods yards though were mere shadows of their former selves and were just about eking out an existence. Kingswinford yards had closed some years ago but at least the steel traffic meant that Brierley Hill Steel Terminal was continuing to provide some badly needed jobs. At Stourbridge Junction nearly all the sidings had been taken out of use and those that remained hardly saw any traffic. However, things seemed to have at least settled down and we were looking forward to some job stability. Unfortunately it only lasted for just over 12 months and on 9th August, 1971 I once again received notification that I was to lose my driver's job and that the same redundancy arrangements would apply as before. Angry and dispirited I again chose to be 'put-back'. For the next 12 months it was back into the old routine: the odd driving or secondman's turn; route refresher turns; but worst of all were the wasted days in the messroom. But then, in the week before Christmas 1972, I was again reinstated as driver and for the next three years I found myself in the bottom bank link working pilot turns, trip workings, and even some passenger work on the Town car, as well as some spare turns. I also worked 'ferry' turns moving empty dmus to and from Stourbridge Junction and Tyseley depot. On some Sundays I would come in to check over the dmus stabled in the down sidings, in fact a very similar routine to the work I had carried out back in 1968. These units had to be road worthy for the early driving turns on Monday morning. Occasionally a Sunday ballasting job would come Stourbridge's way and whilst this could mean long hours if things went wrong, the overtime always came in useful. During these three years I often wondered if I had made a mistake staying at Stourbridge, but vacancies were few and far between at the local depots and wherever I went I could never be sure that redundancy would not be just around the corner. This feeling hardly inspired loyalty and interest in the job.

In the early 1970s I joined the First Aid class at Stourbridge, an organisation that had its origins in the late 19th century. Our instructors were Jerry Young and Vic Chapman and this training was to prove invaluable when in 1986 I was called into action whilst driving the 11.45 am Birmingham to Kidderminster local. The train was approaching Langley Green when the guard burst into the driving cab. 'Quick', he shouted, 'A lad has stuck his head out of the window and is very badly injured'. Pulling up at the station I made my way back into the carriage to the scene of the accident; I was horrified by what I saw. The lad's head had obviously been struck by something, probably whilst passing under a bridge, and he was clearly in a bad way. His mate was hysterical and I had to gently but firmly move him away from the scene. It was clear to me that I could only provide the basic first aid and only emergency hospital treatment could save him. One of the station staff, Ian Tomlinson, brought me the first aid kit and having told the guard to summon an ambulance I did what I could. Thankfully the ambulance soon arrived and I moved the train up to the level crossing to the west of the station where the ambulance crew were waiting to transfer him. This done I continued the journey although I was very upset by the incident and had to be relieved at Stourbridge. There was no such thing as professional counselling for drivers involved in such incidents; it was just a case of getting on with the job, although it was a day that I never forgot. In

Class '45' No. 45068 hauls a southbound train of castings just south-west of the site of Round Oak station on 13th September, 1977.   *Michael Mensing*

On Wednesday 1st May, 1985, class '45' No. 45034 slowly approaches Stourbridge Junction with the Cliffe Vale to Severn Tunnel Junction 'Speedlink' service. At the rear of the train are empty steel carriers picked up from Brierley Hill steel terminal.   *David J. Hayes*

total I did 16 years in the First Aid service, many of which as an instructor; very useful and rewarding work it was too.

Many of Stourbridge depot's freight jobs were generated by Brierley Hill Steel Terminal located at Kingswinford Junction and the branch to the Pensnett Trading Estate. The branch was used mainly for moving coal and coke to the LCP concentration depot at the terminus where shunting was carried out by a privately-owned diesel shunter. At the steel terminal it was judged that there was enough work to keep a diesel shunting engine occupied over three shifts per day. The evenings were the busiest period with incoming loads and outgoing trains of empties. At the steel terminal yard were employed a number of men on shunting duties and one of them, Jack Caswell, had one of the heaviest Black Country accents that I have ever heard. Even I had difficulty understanding some of the things he said so I don't know how anyone from outside the area coped. The yard manager was Sid Hodgson, a former driver at Stourbridge, in fact Sid was the son of my old boss at Kidderminster, Percy Hodgson, whilst Sid's son is a driver at New Street. Clearly the family tradition of following in the father's footsteps has not completely died away. One of my driving turns was the empty coke wagon train to Burton-on-Trent that started at Kingswinford Junction after the wagons had been tripped down from the Pensnett Trading Estate. Other turns were local trips to Bescot via Dudley or Washwood Heath via Walsall and Sutton Park. This latter working could be quite tricky especially with a heavy load over a leaf strewn track at Sutton. Careful handling of the type '3' or '4' was required if the train was not to stall on the bank. Some of the trains heading out of Kingswinford Junction sidings towards Dudley were heavy enough to require assistance from the Stourbridge banking engine which was based at the Junction. One day I had a turn on this locomotive, it was a type '4' (now class '47'), No. 47100, and I had assisted a very heavy oil train as far as Rowley Regis where I was photographed by an enthusiast just after dropping off and making ready to return to Stourbridge. As stated above, this turn could be very busy and it was certainly not unknown for the engine to have to run light over to Bescot to refuel. Yes, Stourbridge depot had at last some worthwhile jobs but sadly uncertainty was never too far below the surface.

The threat to jobs continued throughout the 1970s and as men retired or left, driving turns went with them. New staff were not recruited so as employee numbers reduced so did the number of turns. When three turns were lost, a spare turn and a rest day relief turn were also withdrawn. Then in 1975 came my third redundancy; on 15th December; what a Christmas present! Once more I chose to be 'put-back'. So it was back to secondman's duties and the odd driving turn. This work provided me with two turns on the Stourbridge banking engine, early mornings and afternoons, and two turns on the Langley Green to Bescot trip working. The usual driver on the latter was by railway standards in poor health so a secondman was compulsory. There was also a night ferry turn; a night parcels train relief from Stourbridge Junction to Gloucester (I think this was a Derby-Bristol working); a day turn working empty coal wagons from Kidderminster yard to Hendesford, then engine and van to Littleton colliery to pick up a coal train for Hartlebury. In addition there was a rest day relief and early and late spare turns to cover for holidays, so some driving turns did come up occasionally. The unlikeliest job that Stourbridge men were given, although I personally was not involved, was a footplate turn on a steam engine. Engines would sometimes have to be moved from Tyseley to the Severn Valley Railway, or were employed on rail tours, and when the opportunity arose former steam crews at Stourbridge jumped at the chance to get involved, especially Mick Jackson and Ken Skelding, two secondmen who relished a turn on the shovel. Unfortunately I was barred from steam work due to the fact that I was now required to wear glasses; I was all right in the cab of a diesel but not on the footplate. I tested bi-focals for three months and reported back to the Medical Officer who concluded that on the strength of this and other reports received, this type of spectacle would be suitable for diesel drivers.

Class '37' No. 37223 with 6T69, the 08.45 Washwood Heath to Brierley Hill Network Coal service, at Kingswinford Junction sidings on 15th April, 1987. The wagons will later be 'tripped' to Pensnett by the locomotive off 6T42, the Bescot-Brierley Hill Speedlink trip.   *David J. Hayes*

Class '47' No. 47503, with its train of continental bogie wagons, stands alongside the coal concentration depot at the LCP freight terminal, Pensnett on 15th April, 1987. This trip working was an extension of 6T42, the Bescot-Brierley Hill Speedlink trip.   *David J. Hayes*

Two years after being 'put-back' for the third time I reached a major milestone in my railway career; 35 years with both the GWR and BR. At the time there were four of us due to receive an award, myself, Reg Hill (a driver at Stourbridge), Alan Lawrence (train crew inspector), and Norman Wood, station manager at Kidderminster. I felt that all of us were a little reluctant to attend the presentation, given the way the industry had changed and how employees were being treated, but we relented and all-in-all we had an enjoyable day. Sadly, those who organised the event neglected to invite our wives; but perhaps that just about sums up the attitude of BR management at that time!

As a secondman I got on well with most of the drivers I worked with although one or two seemed to resent the fact that they had to have a secondman with them. One of the drivers that I worked alongside at this time was Bill Matheson and we developed a very good working relationship. Bill and I used to work alternate days driving and one of our turns was the afternoon working from Kingswinford Junction to Burton-on-Trent, returning empty coke wagons that had been tripped along the Pensnett branch from the LCP coal concentration depot. The road was still open through Dudley so it was out of the down loop at Kingswinford Junction sidings onto the main line, our usual traction, a class '47', making good progress against the gradient up to Round Oak. On our way we would cross Parkhead viaduct that spans a number of canals and locks. It's then through Blowers Green and past what was the junction of the Windmill End branch and into Dudley tunnel. At the other end we run through the site of Dudley station, where I had my first driving turn, past the Freightliner depot before swinging right onto the old South Staffs route through Dudley Port (Low Level) and Walsall. From Walsall we continue to Wichnor Junction and Burton where we put away the empties in Whetmore sidings. Usually we have some time to kill waiting for the return working so Bill and the guard normally slipped down to the 'Wagoners' for some liquid refreshment while I popped down to the local fish and chip shop for provisions. When they arrived back at the sidings our load was ready, full coke wagons for Pensnett. It's then back onto the main line where we retrace our steps back to Kingswinford Junction. After reversing our train into the sidings, the shunter unhooks the engine and we run light to Stourbridge Junction where we are relieved.

On 8th May, 1978 I am reinstated once more to driving and this time I keep the position until I retire. However, I now find myself in the shunting link working Brierley Hill steel terminal, a location which is now classified as an out-station of Stourbridge so men sign on and off there instead of at the main TCD at the Junction. This link worked the three turns at the steel terminal as well as trip and shunting work at Kidderminster, Langley Green, and Rowley Regis. I was in this link for about 12 months before moving into No. 2 link. As I had not driven main line locomotives and units within the last three months I had to undertake traction refresher courses. I also went on some route familiarisation training as well. Principally I worked dmus and believe me these units had not worn well. Poor maintenance seemed to be the major cause of most failures. Largely these were brought about by a loose generator belt and a flat battery, or leaking coolant systems, in fact cooling became such a problem that watering cans were made available at stations so that drivers could easily top up the system. Old Hill bank was still difficult to negotiate with these machines and time and time again assistance had to be summoned from Stourbridge Junction. With a '47' on the front the ailing dmu would be helped as far as Langley Green unless it was in real difficulty and then it would be all the way into New Street. Braking systems were not totally reliable either and when working the Town car special care had to be taken when approaching Foster Street station. The brakes failed on one of these units and the car went through the stop block to end up suspended over Foster Street, the incident being recorded for posterity by a number of photographers. The locomotives were more reliable, but faults occurred and drivers soon learnt their instruction manuals off by heart. When a locomotive failed the driver usually tried his best to get the line

Class '47' No. 47628 *Sir Daniel Gooch* shunting at Dudley Freightliner terminal on 30th April, 1985.   *David J. Hayes*

cleared without having to summon help; sometimes the failure could not be identified through reference to the manual and the driver would often call upon his own experience to tackle the fault and how it could be overcome. Obviously, despite the best efforts of the man concerned, if the locomotive refused to respond it was on the phone to summon an assisting engine.

The 1980s got off to a bad start with a strike in the steel industry that reduced enormously steel flows into the two main local distribution centres at Brierley Hill and Langley Green. The strike began in the public sector during January 1980 and by 11th February, 1980 five link turns and one spare turn had been suspended. As the dispute spread and the private sector became involved further turns were cancelled. The loss of work seriously threatened jobs, at least in the short term, and there was a real possibility of lay-offs. However, amendments to the roster, worked out week by week, managed to avoid men being laid-off, but the longer term effects of the dispute further weakened Stourbridge's position due to a continuing reduction in steel flows in the area and by June 1980 the TCD's complement of drivers was just 57 plus 13 secondmen. Nineteen-eighty though sticks in my mind for another reason: vandalism.

Trouble with football supporters had been a common feature for some time and the police regularly accompanied trains carrying these people, but what seemed to be on the increase were the incidents of stone throwing, and each end of Old Hill tunnel became notorious for such behaviour. However, it was at Monument Lane where I have the most vivid of memories. I was approaching at around 40 mph with a local evening dmu from Birmingham (New Street) when I saw three youths with bricks in their hands. There was nothing I could do other than duck down as the bricks hit the cab windscreen. Although shattering the screen the bricks did not penetrate and thankfully I was uninjured but I was very badly shaken and from then on I always kept an eye open at this spot. On the bright side, the 7.30 am Birmingham (New Street) to Worcester (Foregate Street) which continued to Henwick to reverse before returning with commuters for Birmingham and Lichfield, always seemed to be an enjoyable turn as was the afternoon freight from Stourbridge Junction to Gloucester.

Closure of the TCD looms and I am elected to the LDC

The 1980s was dominated by a continuous process of staff reviews at the TCD, however, there was also the introduction of variable day rostering resulting in selective strike action being taken by railwaymen angered by the proposed changes. On my part, I decide to stand for election to the Local Departmental Committee.

Nineteen eighty-two witnessed the introduction of variable day rostering or as it was known by the men 'flexible rostering'. Essentially, what this meant for Stourbridge drivers and drivers' assistants, as secondmen were now known, was a split shift system. For example four hours would be worked in the morning to cover the peak period between 6 am and 10 am and then in the afternoon returning to work to cover the peak period around 5 pm. This was rejected out of hand at Stourbridge but British Rail was undeterred and continued to press for some sort of flexible arrangements, the matter coming to a head when it was suggested by management that the eight hour day, the thing that railwaymen had fought so hard to achieve between 1917 and 1919, be abandoned. This was unacceptable and Ray Buckton, the then General Secretary of ASLEF, backed by the Executive Committee of the union, proposed a series of one day strikes, an action wholeheartedly supported by the men employed at Stourbridge. As the actions started to take effect, representatives from some of the industries affected urged the Government to take action to try and resolve the problem and this they did by bringing pressure to bear on the TUC. British Rail followed this up with a threat to issue dismissal notices to men taking strike action; clearly things were turning nasty. ASLEF turned to the TUC for help but to no avail and now isolated the union decided to call off its industrial action. So we went back to work knowing that the deeply unpopular flexible working arrangements would be waiting for us. On 6th September, 1982 BR introduced the new system much to the dismay of local railwaymen who had difficulty making head or tail of it!

In 1981, one of our long-standing members on the LDC, Denis 'Gus' Lamb, retired and was replaced by Andrew Gardner, a driver's assistant and the youngest man to serve on the committee for a very long time. The LDC at this time comprised Harry White (Chairman), Tommy James, Walter 'Bomber' Knowles, and the latest recruit, Andrew Gardner. By 1982 I had begun to seriously consider standing for election myself and knowing that a vacancy was due to arise in 1983 I put my name forward. At the time the votes were cast I was on holiday and when I returned I was given the news that I had been successful. Shortly afterwards, in the company of the other LDC members, it was into the lion's den to do battle over the new summer rosters and diagrams supplied by the office at Crewe. It was quite a baptism of fire as I had little time to prepare and even less time to get to grips with exactly what my role would be. However, I learnt quickly and was soon able to hold my own with the other more experienced men seated around the negotiating table. I read thoroughly ASLEF's interpretation of the conditions of service and soon found myself dealing with colleagues' complaints on a day to day basis. This proved a very challenging occupation for it soon became clear that it was impossible to please everyone all of the time and so on many occasions I found myself quite unpopular with one or another as I was unable to tell them what they wanted to hear. The other thing that I realised was that not all LDCs were treated equally, a fact which became very clear to me during my first joint meeting of local LDCs and management held at Stanier House in Birmingham. I also became Stourbridge's Health & Safety Representative and having attended a very demanding but thorough course at Aston University, I found myself well equipped to deal with difficult negotiations.

By 1983 many of the older drivers were looking to retire early while others were eager to take voluntary redundancy. Yet another staff review had indicated that some men could go but area managers decided to postpone the decision until the formal plan relating to Stourbridge's future was published in January 1984. They were obviously concerned that any reductions in staffing levels made now could prove premature and that the result might be that the depot would be unable to man all its diagrams. This reaction angered some of the men concerned who were not convinced by management's argument postponing their departure. Incidentally, this was not the only decision to anger the men at this time. There had been a proposal to introduce a drivers' assessment scheme whereby an individual driver's ability to carry out his duties would be judged by a footplate inspector accompanying the driver in the cab. Older men especially found this hard to take for here were some steam drivers who remembered the days when the driver was king. In my early days on the footplate, if an inspector wanted to ride on the footplate he would be asked to show his pass and once his identity had been established he would be invited onto the engine on the condition that he did not get in the way of the driver or his fireman. Ex-steam drivers were proud men and the thought of some young whippersnapper climbing into their cab to assess their driving after they themselves had spent years honing their skills to perfection was seen as quite an insult. I heard of one Old Oak Common driver in steam days, after arriving in Plymouth a minute or two late after a rough trip on a 'Castle'-hauled passenger train, being approached by an inspector who told him that he was late. 'Yes', replied the driver, 'very late'. The inspector, recognising the challenging tone in the driver's voice, decided that discretion was the better part of valour and after nodding to the crew, quickly went on his way. The authority of the driver, whose experience and knowledge of the job was second to none, was acknowledged at all levels; unfortunately, it is this experience which seems to be sadly missing from today's drivers.

January 1984 arrived and all local LDCs were called to a meeting at Stanier House to discuss the train crew depot plan for the Birmingham Division. The discussions soon confirmed Stourbridge LDC's worst fears; the TCD had been pencilled in for closure in the not too distant future, although management would not commit themselves to a definite date. However, with the amount of work at the depot declining and employee numbers reducing, closure was expected sooner rather than later. It was simply not cost effective to keep it open. Our LDC argued that if more work was put Stourbridge's way then more men would be encouraged to come to the depot, but we were not supported by the larger depots who obviously wanted the work for themselves. They had to protect their own work force but we did feel let down and isolated. What made things worse was that depot personnel at Stourbridge were not of one voice; some were in favour of closure while others were prepared to fight for it to remain open. We were very divided, and the divided soon fall. But it did seem that closure was a foregone conclusion and therefore the LDC had to set about trying to maximise benefits for our colleagues. But in the meantime everyday work still had to be carried out and as an LDC member I had to ensure that working arrangements met the requirements of the staff involved; a pretty tall order to say the least.

One of the biggest headaches was the flexible day rostering which was causing major problems on day to day diagrams. Drivers would often book-on as much as 30 minutes before the start of their diagram and finish long after their diagram had ended. This was to enable the hours worked to add up to the number required to complete the working week. But there was so much wasted time! It was a planning nightmare for the members of the LDC who were trying to work out rosters that combined diagrams of unequal duration to form a turn that would fit nicely into the eight hour day. Rest day relief turns were especially difficult as were Bank Holidays. Many men wanted to work the latter for the extra pay and a day off in lieu so there was never any shortage of volunteers. The difficulty was ensuring that all these willing hands were treated fairly but inevitably someone would complain and that meant reviewing the rosters to see if their complaint was justified. Mistakes sometimes would be made but often the men had simply lost track. Similarly Sunday work also had to be closely monitored. The LDC was therefore not only involved in depot negotiations and health & safety policy, but also responsible for planning men's working arrangements and ensuring that these arrangements allocated jobs as fairly as possible. Very interesting but sometimes I was at my wit's end trying to be seen to be fair to everyone all of the time. When in 1985 the LDC lost Andrew Gardner to New Street as a driver, I was thankful that Geoff Jackson was elected as his replacement as he was a former Stourbridge man who had gained a great deal of knowledge and experience while at Bescot. Geoff's contribution to the work of the LDC up to closure of the depot proved absolutely invaluable.

Returning to traction matters, turns worked by the depot were still a mixture of loco-hauled freight services and local dmus. Unfortunately, the reliability of the latter was still a problem and there seemed to be a constant stream of faults coming into the office for the attention of the fitters. The most persistent complaints were heater failures in the winter and coolant loss in the summer. Furthermore, the units stabled at Stourbridge were regularly being vandalised, and the number of fire extinguishers stolen was beyond belief. What remained of the trip workings were usually in the hands of Bescot type '2s', although the Stourbridge banker remained a type '4', usually a class '47'. At weekends as many as six to eight locomotives could be stabled in the west side sidings at Stourbridge. In the mid-1980s I had a pleasant Sunday afternoon job driving a dmu over the Severn Valley Railway (SVR) from Kidderminster to Bridgnorth to pick up around one hundred cyclists returning to Birmingham. I hadn't worked the Valley for ages so I welcomed aboard the local chargehand who acted as pilotman for the whole trip. Having crossed over to the SVR I passed the site of the old engine shed and memories came flooding back. It was hard to believe that almost 30 years ago I began my driving career at this very place working trips to the sugar beet factory. Running past the remains of the Hartlebury line at Bewdley, I recalled working a coal train from Alveley colliery sidings to Stourport and we had just run through Bewdley and had crossed over to the Hartlebury line. Beyond Burlish Halt the line steepens to 1 in 100 and suddenly the engine began to slip. I closed the regulator and started to apply sand but the slip continues and the sand threatens to run out. My mate had a bright idea, and jumping down to the trackside he started to shovel ballast onto the track. The wheels crunched through it, but it had the desired effect. Although this helped us out of our predicament the permanent way men responsible for that section were less than impressed by our actions and we heard later that they were very eager to meet whoever had been responsible for making a mess of their carefully manicured stretch of line.

Through Bewdley and past the underhung bracket signal. The signal still comprises two boards, the right-hand board is for the SVR whilst the left-hand one is now redundant, the Cleobury Mortimer/Tenbury Wells line having closed in 1965. Heading along the SVR we pass Northwood Halt and then Trimpley reservoir. At Arley we take the loop through the station. Arley had a signal box located adjacent the sidings to the rear of the station. I seem to recall that in my day Arley was very much in the hands of the Jones family, the signalman being the husband, the wife working as porter and general factotum as was required in those days at a country branch line station. Their son was also on the railway, he was a fireman at Kidderminster. Anyway, back to the 1980s, and having reached Bridgnorth it was into the refreshment room for a welcoming cup of tea and a chat about old times. I was then invited to have a look round the shed and the repair shop before returning to the cab of the dmu for the journey back to Stourbridge where I was relieved. The journey had brought back many memories of the places I used to call at, and the men who accompanied me, and also of one little gesture. On my last trip to Alveley colliery, with my usual fireman and guard Bert Rush, shunter Clive King's son presented me with a little bouquet of wild flowers to take home to my wife.

By 1985 I had progressed to No. 1 link, all passenger work on dmus, usually between Worcester, Birmingham and Lichfield, although working to Lichfield stopped for Stourbridge men when the winter rosters were introduced in January 1988. There were also ferry turns to Tyseley to exchange sets and for routine maintenance to be carried out on the units. Work had begun on the new Birmingham (Snow Hill) station and we were hopeful that some work would come our way, especially as it was largely Stourbridge men that manned the locals before services were withdrawn at the old station in 1967. But once more the requests from the depot were ignored. The winter of 1985-86 saw a fair amount of snow and it was not a pleasant task leaving home at 4 am to walk the two miles to the depot and then prepare stone cold units for the day ahead. Heaters were a nightmare, as was clearing snow and ice from siding points so that the dmu could get out onto the main line. However, there was a nice surprise at the end of 1985 when it was agreed with management that the depot would close over Christmas. As a result all units and locos had to be picked up by men from the main depots at the end of the day before the break and then returned to Stourbridge in time for work to commence on the morning after the holiday. Looking back, I remember as a 16-year-old at Stourbridge shed having to go into work in the shed offices at 10 pm Christmas Eve, Christmas Day, and Boxing Day. In the spring of 1986, I was awarded a special first aid certificate and silver salver for my action in administering help at Langley Green station to the passenger who had received severe head injuries at Smethwick. The certificate was signed by the General Manager of the LMR, Mr C. Beasdale and also the chairman of the Regional Ambulance Centre. The presentation came as quite a surprise.

In 1987 both Tommy James and Stan Roden vacated their posts on the LDC and I was elected Chairman. Both of these men had put a lot of hard work into the LDC and never conceded openly that more often than not they were fighting a losing battle, not only against management but colleagues at the other, larger depots. As usual the LDC, which now included Denis Stoneley, who had joined us from Bescot, were working upon the winter diagrams. This occupied quite a lot of time and on this occasion I had gone home for a bite of lunch. Suddenly I received an urgent call summoning me back to the depot immediately; Alan Peel, the train crew manager wanted to see me straight away. On arrival at the depot I met the rest of the LDC and we went into the conference room where we were greeted by the guards' representatives; clearly it was not good news. In many ways I expected what Alan Peel had to say; the depot was to close in the spring of 1988 subject to negotiations being satisfactorily concluded. The reasons given for the closure were predictable: the depot was no longer financially viable; lack of operational knowledge of new traction (this was a sore point as Stourbridge men were always denied training on new machines despite the fact that they were quite willing); the average age of the employees at the depot and the fact that many would be due for retirement in the near future. In view of the news a special branch meeting was held and a vote taken; a mere formality really. This was the last meeting of ASLEF members to be held at Stourbridge and after more than 100 years the branch was coming to an inglorious end. The ASLEF flag though would not come down without one last battle and, with the help of Jim Laws who worked on the personnel side at New Street, we set about getting the best terms that we could.

My own task was to identify all the entitlements train crews could get and where these could be sorted out. To ensure that I compiled the correct information I consulted a number of drivers who had already retired and with their help the final document proved invaluable in the months to come. My colleagues on the LDC were unstinting in their work and without their help, especially that of Geoff Jackson on the complex issue of redundancy payments, my task would have been enormous. ASLEF's own guide was consulted rigorously and that was nearly as worn out as I was when I completed the job and passed the document on to Glen Parish, the personnel manager for the Birmingham Division, for his comments, and to make any necessary amendments. This was the first document of this type that had been produced on redundancy and therefore this formed the basis for all negotiations both now and later. In January 1988 the final meeting involving Stourbridge depot took place at Birmingham International Conference Suite. In addition to our LDC there were those from Bescot, New Street and Saltley, also attending were representatives from ASLEF and BR's divisional management. Out of the 23 drivers at Stourbridge, 21 wanted to accept terms, the two remaining were undecided. Of the three drivers' assistants, two were seeking redundancy whilst the third had opted for relocation. It was this position statement that was communicated to ASLEF. Mr M. Whittle, secretary of Sectional Council B, opened with this question to management, 'Am I correct in saying that in regard to Stourbridge depot closing that all the men there will be able to finish if they so desire with full redundancy conditions and payments, and that men who wish to carry on at another depot will be allowed to do so?' The short reply to this was, 'Yes'. There was nothing more to say, and after attending the shortest meeting in my five years on the LDC it was back to Stourbridge to tell the men the outcome. The closure of Stourbridge TCD meant that arrangements had to be made to reallocate the work to other depots. Initially, it was agreed that Stourbridge men would continue to work the winter diagrams up to 11th April when the depot would close completely. However, we were advised that if the depot remained open until 9th July then the wage award due that month would enhance redundancy payments and improve pensions. The downside of this proposal was that as closure would come 12 weeks after the end of the winter timetable there would be no work for us to do as it was still the intention to transfer all our diagrams to other local depots as from 12th April. Despite the prospect of having to sit in the cabin for weeks on end mainly twiddling our thumbs, it was decided that the additional payments would be worth it. At the end of my turn on 11th April I put my dmu into the sidings and switched off the engine for the last time, and turning to the guard I said, 'Well that's me finished'. It was a very emotional moment and despite the fact that I felt let down, I could not keep a note of sadness out of my voice; 46½ years in one industry is one hell of a long time!

To commemorate the passing of Stourbridge depot it was decided to have a special badge made for everyone at the TCD on the day of closure; gold-plated with steam engine and dmu shown on Stambermill viaduct for the men; silver plated versions for wives and friends. After the last badge was cast the mould was destroyed. In the run up to closure a number of talks were held explaining to the men all aspects of redundancy; there was also investment advice. Soon the day was set for management to hand over the redundancy cheques. In the period of enforced idleness following the withdrawal of all diagrams from Stourbridge I did manage to check all of the first-aid boxes in the signal boxes, stations, and offices in the area, but mostly I just sat around waiting to book-off. As the last day approached I would often look back to my first day at the shed when as a young man I nervously crossed Stambermill viaduct before arriving at the shed to begin my career as a cleaner. I tried to picture all the men that I had worked with; the drivers who had taught me so much, and the firemen who worked alongside me in all weathers and on different types of trains. There were also the guards, the signalmen, and everyone else who contributed to the running of the railway. I remembered so clearly Tom Dovaston, my first shedmaster, who went out of his way to get me a job. At Stourbridge I was accepted into the railway family which represented not just a job but a way of life; we were Great Western men and proud of it, and I felt privileged to have worked with such men for the whole of my career.

The last day arrived and I booked-on at 9 am for the final time; no overalls and food bag today, but I still walked over to the cabin as usual. A few of the others were there, talking, drinking tea, but generally the mood was sombre; after all it was a funeral. Periodically our supervisor Allan Lawrence would come in and tell someone that they could go and one by one the cabin emptied, each man shaking hands with his colleagues before making for the door. I was not the last to leave, so as I turned to say farewell to the two men remaining, a lump appeared in my throat; was this really the end? Sadly it was, and I am not ashamed to admit that as I left, there was a tear in my eye as I realised that my days on the railway were over, and I knew that I would have great difficulty coming to terms with the enormity of it. But end they did and as I put my ticket in for the last time I remembered my shunting turns working over the place where I was now standing; what a busy place it was, its large marshalling yards and its South Wales expresses. It's hard to accept that so much had changed. But it was now home to my wife who stood by me through good times and bad, and there had been some bad times believe me. I walked through the door and there before me was my retirement cake specially baked for the occasion; it was now time to relax and smell the roses.

Early Trade Unionism and the Work of the Local Departmental Committee

Local Departmental Committees were established under the Railway Act, 1921 and were, in effect, the bottommost rung on the negotiating and consultation ladder. At the outset of the scheme, two LDCs were set up at Stourbridge Junction; one for staff included in Sectional Council No. 2, i.e. footplatemen and non-clerical shed staff; the other for those covered by Sectional Council No. 3, i.e. signalmen, guards, shunters etc. However, LDCs were not established for 'white collar' staff included in Sectional Council No. 1, or those embraced by Sectional Council No. 4 or Sectional Council No. 5 (the former included a wide range of miscellaneous occupations, e.g. loaders; carters; dock staff etc., whilst the latter was for Engineering, Signal and Telegraph Departmental staff). A Local Departmental Committee could only be established at a station or depot where the number of regular employees in a department or in a group of grades exceeded 75. Presumably, at Stourbridge, only staff covered by Sections 2 and 3 satisfied this criterion. Staff at stations where there were less than 75 still had a voice, employees being able to appoint representatives to discuss local matters with the company's officials. Local Departmental Committees were set up to meet a range of objectives and functions. These were laid down as follows:

Objectives
a)   To provide a recognised means of communication between the employees and the local officials of the Railway Company.
b)   To give the employees a wider interest in the conditions under which their work is performed.

Functions
a)   Suggestions for the satisfactory arrangement of working hours; breaks; time recording, etc.
b)   Questions of physical welfare (safety appliances, accidents, first aid, staff accommodation, etc.).
c)   Holiday arrangements.
d)   Publicity in regard to rules, etc.
e)   Suggestions as to:
     1. Improvements in method of organisation of work; 2. Arrangement of link working; 3. Transfers from link to link; 4. Labour-saving appliances.
f)   Investigation of circumstances tending to reduce efficiency or in any other way to interfere with the satisfactory working of the Railway.
g)   The correct loading of traffic to ensure:
     1. Safe transit. 2. Reduction in claims.

A Local Committee shall not introduce any arrangements inconsistent with the powers or decisions of the Railway Council or Sectional Railway Councils or of the National and Central Wages Boards.

According to Norman McKillop in *The Lighted Flame*, the LDC was the most difficult part of the new negotiating process to actually set in motion due to the reluctance of local managers to accept that they might be questioned about their actions. This said, there seemed little delay at Stourbridge where the first meeting of Sectional Council No. 2 Local Departmental Committee was held on 31st March, 1922. Perhaps the situation at Stourbridge was helped by the fact that there seemed to be a good working relationship between the men and the shed's management and that there may have already been in existence an informal negotiating process which predated the LDC by a number of years. Furthermore, organised trade unionism, in the shape of local branches of both ASLEF and what had been up to 1913 the ASRS*, had also been active in the area since the late 19th century. Although space precludes a complete review of the work of the Section 2 LDC at Stourbridge, what follows will hopefully enable the reader to form a clear picture of how this particular LDC operated and the sort of problems it was called upon to resolve. However, before moving on to this area, it may be useful to take a look at the situation before the birth of the LDC and although there is not a great deal of material available, that which has survived does give some insight into the early days of union activity in respect of membership and resolution of local issues.

ASLEF first established a branch at Stourbridge shed about October 1888 although by June of that year 18 enginemen (F.C. Currell, S. Rollings, W.E. Newton, T.M. Hackett, R. Johnson, J. Westwood, W. Downes, G. Constable, G. Jones, C. Clewett, S. Taylor, J. Callaway (who had become a member at Newport on 21st August, 1884), T. Turner, H. Rosier, E. Cooper, D. Davies, W. Brean and O. Mostyn) had already begun the process thereby becoming the founder members of the branch. By January 1889, there appeared to be 25 men in the union rising to 32 by October 1889. Ten years later membership had increased to 49.

Into the new century and membership increased substantially with the result that by June 1903, the union had 82 members, climbing to 124 by 25th August, 1908. Oddly, by 26th September, 1909 membership had apparently fallen to 94 (a full list is included in the Appendix). This temporary drop in the number of ASLEF men at the shed may be explained by reference to June 1907, when it had been rumoured that some 20-odd ASLEF members were considering defecting to the ASRS. Unfortunately, it has not been possible to substantiate this as no membership details relating to the ASRS at Stourbridge have so far been discovered. The ASRS itself was also active in the area during the late 19th century. For example, in December 1889, at a meeting held at the Exchange Hotel, Wolverhampton, members from several branches met to discuss reductions in hours and the abolition of Sunday working. Apparently, it was Stourbridge's Mr Webb who seconded a motion proposed by Mr W.F. Mee calling upon all railway servants to join the ASRS to add strength to their claim. Presiding over the meeting was Sir William Plowden, Liberal MP for Wolverhampton West.

Apart from Mr Webb's contribution mentioned above, very little else is known about the 19th century activities of the Stourbridge branches of either ASLEF or the ASRS. However, some things from the beginning of the 20th century were recorded and these have survived, albeit in sketchy note form. It would appear that early union meetings involving ASLEF members were attended by drivers and firemen only. This conclusion is based upon a note in the Minute Book which indicates that it was not until 29th May, 1904 that engine

* Amalgamated Society of Railway Servants. It is not clear if any of the other early trade unions such as the General Railway Workers' Union and the United Pointsmen's & Signalmen's Society were then active in the area. However, in September 1908, goods workers and platelayers held a joint meeting to hear addresses from delegates representing these grades on the Conciliation Boards. This was not a union meeting, although the men were urged to join the ASRS. It is thought that a local branch of the Railway Clerks' Association was not formed until 1912.

cleaners were invited to attend branch meetings. Earlier, on 31st January, 1904 the branch had sought permission from Head Office(?) to financially support the infant Labour Representation Committee, presumably a proportion of the dues collected from members being assigned to the appropriate fund. The first comment regarding operational matters was on 29th November, 1903 when reference was made to pilotmen and mates working turns of duty in rotation, although it was the 'walking' allowances which generated most emotion resulting in considerable discussion taking place at a meeting held on 25th September, 1904. To get the best turns of duty, some men were resorting to tactics unacceptable to the union, as the following quote illustrates:

> . . . that members of this station are sacrificing their principles, also the principles of their profession and our noble society (ASLEF), in walking from Stourbridge Junction to Stourbridge Engine House under the time allowed by the Company (25 minutes) the object being to secure a turn of duty in front of their fellow mates, which we consider a very dishonest act, and call upon all members of this branch to uphold their honour and the honour of our branch and Society by reporting at the club room all such cases that come under their notice for discussion at our meetings.

'Walking' allowances were also major topics of conversation at subsequent meetings and on 27th April, 1925 the employees' side proposed that the allowance from Stourbridge shed to Kingswinford Junction be increased to 55 minutes (including five minutes 'booking on' time) and 50 minutes for the walk back. At the same time, the employers were asked to revise the allowance to and from Brettell Lane to 45 minutes each way. Initially, these proposals were rejected but eventually the employers were forced to reconsider their decision and on 10th February, 1926 the new allowances were agreed. The issue also arose in January 1926, this time in connection with an allowance to the fireman on the 6.20 am Stourbridge to Wolverhampton and the fireman on the 6.30 am Saturday, Brettell Lane shunting turn. The matter was not immediately resolved, and it reappeared on the agenda of the meeting held on 3rd February, 1926. Here it was agreed to pay the minimum allowance of five minutes as the distance between the coal stage and the booking-off point in the new shed was over 100 yards (but no more than 440 yards). This allowance was laid down in Circular No. 4255 which quoted the National Wages Board agreement of 18th December, 1923.

At the end of 1951 the employees' side made an application for a 'walking' allowance between Dudley bus station and the goods yards at Dudley station, as well as between the nearest bus stop in Halesowen and Halesowen goods yard. On 8th January, 1952 the following allowances were agreed:

Dudley:	Birmingham Road bus stop to Dudley North Yard	15 minutes each way
Halesowen:	Shenstone Road bus stop to shunting yard	10 minutes
	Shunting yard to Basin sidings	15 minutes
	Basin sidings to Shenstone Road bus stop	15 minutes
	Shenstone Road bus stop to Basin sidings	15 minutes each way
Amblecote:	Church Road bus stop to Stourbridge shed	15 minutes each way

By October 1964, bus travelling times were agreed each way for men travelling from Stourbridge Junction to the yards at Kingswinford, Round Oak, Blower's Green, Dudley Goods, Lye, Halesowen, Rowley Regis and Oldbury & Langley Green.

Returning to pre-LDC days, the introduction of the steam railmotors at Stourbridge shed (and elsewhere on the Great Western system) just after the turn of the century, brought a sharp comment from the Stourbridge branch of ASLEF on 29th January, 1905. Clearly, members saw the rapid introduction of these machines on local passenger services throughout the GWR system as the thin end of the wedge in a move to drive down wage costs by paying the lowest possible rate to those men who were employed upon them. As a result, the local branch called upon the company to revise this policy. At this time a classification relating to the type of work carried out by drivers and firemen determined the rates of pay. Apparently, the company wanted to reclassify duties on railmotors in order that wage costs could be reduced. To justify maintaining the existing rate, the branch identified a potential danger to the travelling public of having an inexperienced fireman (a shunting fireman) in charge of the motor's boiler for a considerable amount of the working day without the benefit of a driver to advise him. The driver would of course, spend much of the shift in his compartment at the opposite end of the motor. In 1912 the classification of 'work' was abolished to be replaced by one which divided each grade into three groups, 1st class, 2nd class and 3rd class.

An interesting development came about in 1914 when it was decided, at an ASLEF branch meeting held on 7th January, to form an Advisory Committee. This became the intelligence gathering arm of the branch, its principal duty being to amass information relating to the welfare of those employed at Stourbridge. The members of this group were: J. Jones (Chairman); B. Corcoran; L. Read and A. Bartlett, whilst G. Tyler was co-opted onto the committee as Secretary. Of particular concern to the committee was the number of hours that enginemen were being asked to work. For example, one driver, T. Horton, during week-ending 20th February, 1915 worked 70 hours 32 minutes. Through the accurate keeping of records, the committee, when bringing something to the attention of John Preece, the shed foreman, or the divisional superintendent, was able to support its arguments with undeniable facts. Undoubtedly, the use of detailed records to illustrate manpower shortages and excessively long working weeks, was instrumental in the committee being able to persuade management to release scarce resources at a time when all stations would have been seriously short of labour. One such example occurred on 26th April, 1915 when it was agreed to increase the number of spare men at Stourbridge from eight to thirteen.

As mentioned above, the Local Departmental Committee came into being under the Railways Act, 1921, and during March 1922 the first members of the employees' side of this new committee were elected. The locomotivemen were represented by T. Jones, P. Bruton and J.N. Parker, whilst A. Weedner represented the shed staff. On the management side the four members would have been: Mr S. Giles, divisional superintendent (Wolverhampton), Mr John Preece, the shed foreman, Mr Tom Dovaston, John Preece's successor, but in 1922 the deputy foreman, and Mr R. Reynolds. At the initial meeting it was agreed that in order that the men's representatives could attend the LDC, turns of duty would have to be rescheduled so as to ensure that the two did not clash. It was decided that arrangements would be left in the hands of the employees concerned who would liaise with the appropriate foreman at the shed. The first operational issues to be raised at this LDC were personnel matters involving cleaners, firemen and drivers. At this time, the shed only had half its allocation of cleaning staff, a situation that probably reflected the company's desire to cut back on labour costs, a belief reinforced by the fact that Swindon had expressly forbidden Mr Giles to fill any vacancies which might arise. Furthermore, he had also been instructed to discharge any man that failed to pass (the fireman's examination?). The employees' side also brought to the attention of Mr Giles a proposal to employ four extra firemen to carry out duties currently undertaken by drivers. On this point, Mr Giles was quick to recommended caution; his warning was simple. Any action leading to the transfer of firemen to the shed could make the drivers they replace redundant. For them, this would be just a short step away from being moved to another station. Faced with this unforeseen consequence, the men's representatives thought twice about forcing the issue and decided instead to shelve the proposal temporarily.

However, they were more determined on the next question. At present, Wolverhampton men were being sent to work Stourbridge relief turns; not very popular with the men! Stourbridge's representatives saw this as a threat to local jobs, leading to redundancies and a loss of men to other sheds. To redress the situation, it was suggested that Stourbridge crews work the 5.20 pm class 'J' goods from Oxley Sidings to Stourbridge Junction and the 7.45 pm ex-Cannock Road Junction.* The implications of such a request persuaded Mr Giles that an answer without first weighing up all the pros and cons would be unwise, and therefore decided to postpone his reply until later. Instead, an undertaking was given that the proposal would be evaluated upon his return to Wolverhampton. After considering the suggestion, he wrote to the Stourbridge LDC on 4th April informing the employees' representatives that their application for the jobs had been unsuccessful. In making this decision, he was mindful of the impact that moving this work away from Wolverhampton would have on jobs at the shed. Apparently, Wolverhampton already had a higher proportion of redundant footplatemen on its books than Stourbridge, a situation which would have been made worse had the latter's request been granted.

By the end of 1927, the GWR appeared to be pushing for more economical working of its engines and men. At the LDC held on 11th November, 1927 the employees' side were asked to co-operate with the company to help keep unremunerative time as low as possible. To illustrate the problem, the company's accountants had drawn up a chart showing the relationship between 'Unremunerative Time' and total 'Engineman & Fireman's Paid Time'. This chart has been reproduced on page 213. Summarising, it can be seen that in the Wolverhampton Division the highest proportion of 'Time with Engine' was at Wellington with 79.6 per cent whilst the lowest was at Wolverhampton with 67 per cent. Stourbridge's time was 73.1 per cent; 2.1 per cent above the average for the Division. The average for the company as a whole was 71.6 per cent. The worst Division was Newport at 68.7 per cent; the best Newton Abbot with 77 per cent. Having put the proposal to the men, the employees' representatives were able to inform the management early in the New Year that the workforce was prepared to help tackle this issue.

---

* No further details regarding this train were included in the minutes. However, this may have been a class 'F' goods for a Pontypool Road crew on a Double Home turn? It is thought that the Wolverhampton crew would take the train as far as Stourbridge Junction where they were relieved by the returning Pontypool Road men. Stourbridge were suggesting, perhaps, that they work the train from Cannock Road Junction instead?

Agenda	Agreement
Item No. 1	
Application for alteration for boiler house coal bunker chute.	To be looked into.
Item No. 2	
Application for improved lamps on incline.	To be followed up with Engineering Department.
Item No. 3	
Application for 'Warning' signal at Blowers Green up road to be abolished.	Matter in order
Item No. 4	
Application for improved colour of distant signal arms.	In hand.
Item No. 5	
Application for slides for cabs of '51XX' and '55XX' class engines.	Slides being fitted.
Item No. 6	
Complaint of heavy working of levers on '51XX' class. Believed to be weighbar bracket brasses.	To be followed up.
Item No. 7	
Application for the general adaptation of the type of sand gear now fitted to '51XX' class.	To be submitted to Headquarters.
Item No. 8	
Application for additional time for preparation of '51XX' class	Not conceded. Referred to to Sectional Council
Item No. 9	
Top lubricator of '2109' class.	Boiler fitted with regulator in dome
Item No. 10	
Application for the alteration of the system of oil charging to stores from inside of shed to outside.	Agreed to carry vacuum connections to outside wall
Item No. 11	
Engineman A. Aimes and C.T. Smith's applications.	Refer back for local recommendation
Item No. 12	
Application for reversing lever catch handles of '57XX' class engines to be shortened by 2 inches.	Matter in order.
Item No. 13	
Engine tools.	Doors on shed being strengthened.
Item No. 14	
Triangle for turning engines.	Not practicable.
Item No. 15	
ATC battery box in the way on tank engines.	To be looked into.

Great Western Railway (Wolverhampton Division)
Analysis of Footplatemen's wages as percentage of total
Period Four - week ending 1st October, 1927

Station	Travel, Waiting Time, etc.	Show or Learn Road	Minimum Day or Week	Signing On or Off	Shed Duties	Total	Time with Engine	Allowances*
Banbury	8.1		1.8	3.2	3.9	17.0	68.5	14.5
Birkenhead	6.3	0.2	0.8	3.2	3.6	14.1	75.4	10.5
Chester	7.6		0.4	2.6	4.6	15.2	71.3	13.5
Croes Newydd	6.3	0.2	2.0	2.9	3.7	15.1	74.6	10.3
Leamington	8.3		1.6	3.6	1.0	14.5	75.6	9.9
Shrewsbury	6.4		1.1	3.4	6.7	17.6	68.7	13.7
Stourbridge	7.4	0.2	1.6	3.5	4.2	16.9	73.1	10.0
Tyseley	7.7	0.2	0.8	2.6	5.2	16.5	70.8	12.7
Wellington	4.2		0.9	3.2	0.5	8.8	79.6	11.6
Wolverhampton	6.7	0.1	1.1	2.8	7.2	17.9	67.0	15.1
Division Average	6.9	0.1	1.1	3.0	5.1	16.2	71.0	12.8
Whole line	5.9	0.4	2.2	3.1	5.3	16.9	71.6	11.5
Lowest Division							68.7	Newport
Highest Division							77.0	Newton Abbot

The sort of things discussed by the LDC can best be illustrated by reference to an actual agenda and the one relating to the meeting of a Section 2 LDC held on 26th November, 1931 has been shown opposite. Present at this meeting were, for the company, V.J.H. Webb (Chairman and divisional superintendent), T. Dovaston (shedmaster), R.E. Reynolds and J.H.Williams (Secretary). The employees' side were represented by J.W. Parker (Chairman), A.S. Dixon and J.W. Plant (Secretary).

The Section 2 Local Departmental Committee appeared to function at three levels (other Section LDCs probably followed a similar pattern). Matters to be aired were first submitted to the employee representatives who would meet amongst themselves to discuss these or any other topic which needed to be included on the agenda. This would then be followed by an informal meeting between the men's representatives and their immediate management at the shed. In the early 1950s, the informal meetings comprised, on the management side, J.H. Brown (shedmaster) and E.J. Jones, with L. Shutt, E. Harvey and H. Hardwicke representing the men. Sometimes it was necessary to call a formal meeting, this being differentiated from its informal counterpart by the inclusion of the divisional superintendent (Wolverhampton) or his assistant (at this time, Divisional representatives on the LDC were C.R.L. Rice or G.W. Robson).

The Local Departmental Committee was set up to discuss (almost) the whole range of railway topics; from personnel matters to locomotive modification; from the organisation of the links to the position of signals. All these, and more, were regularly to be found on the LDC agenda for it was here that the 'nitty gritty' of everyday railway life was discussed and argued over. When the LDC could not agree, the unresolved matter would be passed up the ladder to the appropriate Sectional Council, in the locomotivemen's case this would be Sectional Council No. 2 (later B). On at least a couple of occasions a Stourbridge driver served on this Sectional Council; in 1927 there was Charlie Broughton, whilst in the 1950s A.E. Ash held a seat. Usually, this was as far as the matter

* Allowances = Overtime; night work; mileage; holidays, and lodging.

went, but if it could not be resolved it would have to be referred to the head office of the union where bigger guns came into play. Occasionally, even if the two sides were in agreement, some decisions could not be made at the LDC, the problem being passed to headquarters (presumably Swindon together with any recommendation the Committee might think appropriate?). Union headquarters rarely became involved in LDC business. Finally, there were some items that were never subject to LDC discussion, in particular wage rates and the working week, these being subject to national negotiations. However, those items that were discussed do make interesting reading, even if the records sometimes raise as many questions as they answer. Consequently, it might now be helpful to take a more detailed look at some of the things that were raised at the Sectional Council 2/B's LDC so that the reader might develop a clearer picture of the sort of issues that had to be dealt with.

Personnel Matters

From time to time, problems involving the work force will occur in any organisation and Stourbridge shed was no exception. As a result, the LDC found itself dealing with a wide variety of personnel matters that somehow had to be resolved (not always to the satisfaction of the man making the complaint it might be said). An employee could feel that he was the victim of unfair treatment in respect of turn allocation, or have health, domestic or other personal problems that required special consideration in relation to the link or turns of duty he was employed upon. For example, in February 1934, fireman Sid Rollings' application to remain at Halesowen was turned down at a formal meeting of the LDC, whilst in August 1940, fireman Walter Guise's request to be put on 'light duties' on ill health grounds was referred by the LDC to Swindon. In 1955, driver Sam Bishop also claimed a transfer, due to continuing ill health, back to No. 9 link (it is thought that No. 9 link was the 'medical' link that was formed at the shed on 1st May, 1937. At the time, it was stated that to create a viable link there needed to be at least three drivers with health problems allocated to it, plus a number of others). In the same year driver Tom Howse experienced personal problems that required him to remain in his existing link (probably the working arrangements were more convenient). Questions could also arise in respect of vacancies at the shed. In September 1955, for example, the retirement of Bill Lane, the night shift chargeman engine cleaner, created a vacancy that was subsequently not advertised. This oversight was soon challenged. However, it turned out that as the majority of engine cleaners were youths under the age of 16 years and therefore could not be employed on nights (unlike in earlier years), there seemed little point in employing a second chargeman engine cleaner when there was insufficient cleaning staff to warrant the post being filled. The men were advised that if and when the full complement of cleaners was available, and night working recommenced, the position would be reviewed.

An interesting example of the LDC securing concessions for the men occurred late in 1951/early in 1952. On Sunday mornings, a number of footplate crews were needed to travel to such places as Old Oak Common, Southall, Oxford and Banbury, to collect local engines that had been stranded at these sheds after coming off unbalanced workings from the Black Country (during the war, from just before D-day until hostilities ceased, and for a time afterwards, many of these locomotives were used on Government stores trains). Most of these engines had to be returned to Stourbridge 'light'. Apparently, the LDC managed to obtain three reserved compartments for these men on the 8.00 am Shrewsbury to Paddington.

Use of Resources

One very important function of the LDC was the protection and enlargement of the amount of work that was allocated to the shed. There was always competition between sheds for jobs and the LDC at Stourbridge worked hard to protect its own. On 18th March, 1925 for instance, the employees' side made an application for the Great Bridge auto-engine to be worked by three sets of Stourbridge men, the proposal though, was rejected by the Divisional management at Wolverhampton (these turns were shared with Wolverhampton crews). Further examples pepper the LDC minutes, unfortunately, many of the items recorded are very brief outlines of what probably was a fairly long and complex discussion, consequently, trying to interpret these minutes accurately is often quite difficult. One item discussed on 1st December, 1950 related to Turn No. 618, a Stourbridge Junction to Pontypool Road freight service. Management was trying to find a more cost effective way of manning this train (possibly a mid-morning class 'H') as the Stourbridge crew would be relieved at Hereford to return 'on the cushions'. They therefore proposed that the turn be transferred to Worcester shed. How Worcester was to provide the crew is unclear; perhaps they came to Stourbridge 'on the cushions' themselves, or would they have arrived on a down freight from South Wales after relieving the Welsh crew at Worcester? In any event Stourbridge LDC were horrified; they could not see how this option could be more efficient. Furthermore, not only did this mean the loss of a job but also the shed would have to prepare the engine for use by the Worcester crew! That would really have rubbed salt into the wound!

A further example of the Stourbridge LDC fighting to protect jobs was in the early part of 1959. Inter-Regional trains working through Stourbridge Junction, in particular daily block trains from Bescot and Saltney Junction, and more recently the express parcels services between Bristol and Derby, were manned by LMR crews. Currently, the majority of these workings required Western Region pilotmen, a number of which were Stourbridge turns. What concerned staff members of the LDC was that eventually there would be enough 'foreign' footplatemen who knew the road to eliminate the need for the shed to supply pilots. The employees' side did, quite naturally, wish to avoid this and suggested that all block trains working through the area be manned by Wolverhampton or Stourbridge crews using engines from their respective sheds, although this would appear to imply a very inefficient use of resources. However, this does not mean that the employees' representatives closed their eyes to more productive ways of working; on the contrary, many suggestions were aimed at improving the utilisation of both men and locomotives (especially if this brought more work to the shed?). One such proposal involved an additional duty for No. 10 Bank Train (this working was the Halesowen to Rowley Regis, and Oldbury & Langley Green) which was put forward on 1st April, 1955. It was recommended that the empty tanks forming the Oldbury & Langley Green to Haverton Hill service be worked down to Stourbridge Junction yards by the Bank Train rather than send the train engine up to Oldbury light. The idea was rejected, mainly on the grounds that the absence of No. 10 Bank Train engine might cause delays to trips carried out by Halesowen Bank Trains Nos. 14 and 16 (No. 14 Bank engine was used to assist No. 10 from Halesowen up the steep climb to Rowley Regis, but how No. 16's duties would be affected is unclear).

Improved utilisation of locomotives was also the subject of an LDC recommendation made on 25th October, 1966, although on this occasion, it involved taking work off nearby Kidderminster. Originally, it was argued, Stourport Trip 72 (now Kidderminster Turn 5) was worked by Stourbridge when Kidderminster shed was closed to steam on 22nd June, 1964. Shortly afterwards, when the turn was diagrammed for a 350 hp diesel shunter, the duty was returned to Kidderminster. However, now that a type '1' diesel had replaced the 0-6-0 shunter on this work, it was suggested that it would be more efficient to transfer the turn to Stourbridge where the locomotive, after completing Trip 72, could be employed on Trip 5 thereby increasing its utilization from around 12 hours daily to approximately 22. Operating the diesel from Stourbridge would also have other advantages: it would avoid possible frost damage to the machine during winter months as at Kidderminster yard it would be left outside; it would also help eliminate complaints from Control about banking locomotive shortages at Stourbridge Junction (it would appear that delays to Trip 5 meant that the locomotive was often late returning to Stourbridge Junction to take over Trip 13 which was, presumably, the Banking Turn). However, the withdrawal of Kidderminster Turn 5 would also lead to unacceptable operational problems at Kidderminster, consequently, on 17th January, 1967 a reply was received via the station manager's office, Stourbridge, which explained that after due consideration by the line movements superintendent, it was considered that there was no justification for altering the present working.

A year earlier, two other instances highlighted the difficulties that were bringing Stourbridge into conflict with Kidderminster, both of which were referred to Sectional Council No. 2. The first of these involved the loss of Stourbridge Turn 4 and Turn 11 (two driver-only turns). Apparently, these two turns had been moved due to the dmu normally diagrammed for the 7.59 am Kidderminster to Birmingham (Snow Hill) having been transferred to Worcester to work local services into and out of Birmingham (New Street) via Bromsgrove. This was to enable steam working to be eliminated on the former Midland side of New Street station. The transfer of the dmu meant that steam power had to be reintroduced onto the 7.59 am ex-Kidderminster. The complaint, it is thought, revolved around Stourbridge's belief that the two driver-only turns had been allocated to Kidderminster to maintain that station's etablishment at the level agreed at the closure of the depot, and that this had been achieved at the expense of Stourbridge. This was flatly denied by management who pointed out that the diagrams now in operation had been introduced purely as a response to changes in the working environment. As far as losses and gains were concerned, Kidderminster's establishment remained unaltered whilst Stourbridge, although losing two driver-only turns, had gained one driving and one firing turn on steam.

The second complaint from Stourbridge LDC was in regard to the use of men from other depots. Seemingly, the problem arose when Kidderminster offered Control a passed fireman (who would be upgraded to driver) and a fireman as one set on an engine normally relieved by Stourbridge. As a passed firemen from the home depot had been available, it was argued that this action had deprived the Stourbridge man of an increased earnings opportunity. The matter had been initially discussed at Sectional Council level before being referred to a special joint LDC which was subsequently held on 14th October, 1965. Attending this meeting were representatives from the LMR Sectional Council No. 2; Stourbridge MPD Local Departmental Committee, and Kidderminster. After referring to an agreement made upon closure of Kidderminster shed relating to the provision of relief engine crews between the two depots, it was decided that whilst this agreement would remain unaltered, in order to avoid similar problems occurring in the future, spare Kidderminster men would be offered direct to Stourbridge.

Excursion traffic was also handled by Stourbridge and it was one particular aspect of this work that was subject to a complaint from the LDC on 2nd March, 1967. This was the working of mid-week West Bromwich Albion football supporters' trains starting from Stourbridge Junction that were travelling to 'away' destinations in and around London. Stourbridge men rostered for this duty would prepare the locomotive and then pick up the empty coaching stock from the carriage sidings. The train would then work 'all stations' to Birmingham (Snow Hill) where the 'home' crew would be relieved by Tyseley men. At their London destination, the crew would book-off until it was time to return to the West Midlands a few hours later. On arrival back in Birmingham, the train would be taken over by Stourbridge men, who had been sent to Snow Hill for the purpose, for the rest of the journey to the Junction. Consequently, to work the excursion required three sets of men. In view of the fact that a number of Stourbridge men still signed the road to London, the LDC suggested that it would be more cost-effective to allow the Stourbridge crew to work the excursion throughout. To the outsider, this would seem to be a fairly reasonable proposal, unfortunately, and here's the rub, the duty was rostered in accordance with Railway Staff Joint Council Minute L120 (1958) which, in the opinion of Geoff Jackson, Secretary of the Stourbridge LDC, was by this time both outdated and inappropriate. In essence, men from certain depots, e.g. Tyseley, were able to work weekday short rest turns (less than 12 hours between duties), something which Stourbridge crews had also been allowed to do prior to the ruling being made. What the LDC was now asking was that this agreement be reviewed to include Stourbridge. In his reply, Les Briers, Secretary of the Staff Side, Sectional Council No. 2, confirmed the interpretation of the ruling (that it applied to all depots on the LMR, except those that had been specifically excluded), but as it had been made by the Chairman of the

Railway Staff National Tribunal,* it could not be varied at Sectional Council level. Consequently, any application for a review would therefore have to be made to the Executive Committee at ASLEF head office.

Freight Turns

Although Stourbridge shed probably had no 'double home' workings after World War II, this was certainly not the case before 1939, in fact the shed had quite a number of these often unpopular jobs. One such turn was the 3.50 pm departure from Pontypool Road to Oxley Sidings. This was the return working for a Stourbridge crew from the double home link and was certainly not their favourite duty. The men's complaint was all about the departure time and the excessive amount of hanging around at Pontypool Road that this implied. In view of this, it had been requested that the train be rescheduled to leave at 9.00 am. Mr S. Giles, the divisional superintendent at Wolverhampton, subsequently carried out an investigation but concluded that it was not practicable for the train to depart at the suggested time as a load could not be made up by this time. To resolve the problem, it was suggested that the job be withdrawn from Stourbridge and given to Pontypool Road. Although initially this was arranged, Stourbridge men must have had a change of heart for they withdrew their objection. The possible loss of this double home turn clearly meant more to the link than the time wasted waiting for the afternoon departure to roll round.

When management wanted to introduce new work, this too was subject to consultation through the LDC. On 29th June, 1949 it was agreed that Stourbridge crews would work the following turns:

1.50 am Stourbridge Junction to Hereford (Barton) booked to arrive at 3.58 am (Tu-Sat). (This was the 9.40 pm Victoria Basin to Cardiff class 'D' freight.)
Return as ordered.
12.45 am Stourbridge Junction to Hereford (Barton) booked to arrive at 2.27 am (Tu-Sat), and the 1.05 am Sunday departure arriving at Hereford at 3.17 am. (The former was the 10.00 pm Bordesley Junction to Llanelly class 'C' freight, the latter the 9.50 pm Saturday class 'E' freight Bordesley Junction to Cardiff.)
Return with the 3.20 am Hereford (Barrs Court) to Stourbridge Junction booked to arrive at 5.51 am (this was the 9.20 pm Mon-Sat ex-Llandilo Junction class 'D' freight.)

A month later, on 25th July, 1949, another new turn came Stourbridge's way:

2.20 am Stourbridge Junction to Worcester Tunnel Junction booked to arrive at 3.33 am (MX). (This was the 11.20 pm Priestfield to Pontypool Road class 'F' freight.)
7.02 am Worcester Goods Yard to Kingswinford Junction booked to arrive at 9.09 am (MX). (This was the 2.25 am ex-Didcot class 'F' freight.)

* Negotiations comprised two elements; (1) matters arising from the conditions of service and (2) proposals to vary national agreements. In the former, unresolved minor issues were decided by the Railway Staff Joint Council (RSJC), whilst more important issues were ultimately ruled upon by the Chairman of the Railway Staff National Tribunal (the successor to the National Wages Board). On national agreements, proposals had to be raised by the union head office and discussed first at the Railways Staff Conference. If unresolved, the matter would be referred to the RSJC. Where no decision was reached at this stage, minor matters would have to be decided by the Chairman of the RSNT. However, major items would first go to the Railway Staff National Council and if unresolved, would be passed on to the RSNT.

Locomotive Modifications

As can be seen from the agenda shown above, locomotive problems did, understandably, account for a large percentage of LDC business. Many of the issues raised entailed fairly minor alterations or modifications, although some suggestions implied more work to be done than others. On 13th February, 1951 the following memorandum was submitted by the employees' side to Mr H. Brown, the Stourbridge shedmaster:

> On the '28XX' engines the main exhaust steam pipe and the vacuum brake train pipe turn from the sides to the middle of the engine right underneath the crank shaft making it a difficult and dirty operation for a driver to climb up to oil the eccentrics and axleboxes. We suggest that both pipes should be kept to the sides, or alternatively, that the inwards turn of the pipes should be taken a little further towards the front of the engine. It is also difficult to climb up the back of the shaft to oil the big-ends and eccentrics on the '66XX' class engines because of the position of the brake rod and train vacuum pipe. We think the brake rod and the vacuum pipe should also be kept to the side of the engine.

These observations were duly forwarded to the district motive power superintendent at Stafford Road, Wolverhampton for comment. His reply came back on 12th May, 1951:

> No great difficulty or inconvenience should be experienced with the former but the latter is regarded at this stage as being inconvenient and sketches are being prepared for submission.

Signalling

Signals passed at danger is one of the major concerns on today's railway, a problem which many drivers working in the Stourbridge area are very familiar with. Signal SJ89, which at one time had been passed 11 times in 10 years while at 'danger', had made Stourbridge Junction joint fourth in a list of 22 'danger' blackspots across the country. However, signalling difficulties are not something that can be solely associated with the late 20th/early 21st centuries, the failure to act quickly perhaps, but not the problems themselves which have stalked railway operation since signalling was first introduced. One such incident, which had horrific consequences, occurred on 8th October, 1952 when the Perth-Euston 'sleeper' passed two semaphore signals at danger in patchy fog before crashing into a local train at Harrow & Wealdstone. Seconds later, a northbound express struck the wreckage. As a result of this double collision 112 people died at the scene or later from their injuries. Apart from the Brierley Hill disaster in 1858 (see *The Railways of Stourbridge*, p.168-169), no major tragedy has so far happened in the area (and hopefully never will!) but the reference to the semaphore signals is interesting, for in certain circumstances these could be very misleading as the following examples from the LDC minutes of the 1950s testify.

Often difficulties arose from the position of street lamps in relation to semaphore signals and one such problem was experienced with the Langley

Green up home signal. However, it was the Stourbridge South up advanced starter signal, which was located near the Worcester Lane road bridge in Pedmore, approximately half way between Stourbridge Junction and Hagley, that was a real concern. Near this road bridge was a street lamp situated immediately behind the signal and when this was on, and if there was the slightest hint of mist or fog, the signal appeared to show a green aspect. This combination of conditions had regularly led to a misleading visual effect for train crews and many had not realised their mistake until they had almost passed by.

In 1957 enginemen were reporting that they were having difficulty locating the Blowers Green sidings up main home signal at night. Apparently, a powerful electric light in the yard of 'Thompson's Limited' in Peartree Lane was right behind this signal. Consequently, footplate crews were often only picking out the signal when almost level with the down starter just 30 yards from the signal in question. It was suggested that the troublesome signal be lowered to bring it in line with the dark background of the nearby road bridge thereby eliminating the glare of the lamp.

Other problems for drivers and firemen were created by the poor illumination or siting of signals. An example of the latter occurred in 1951 when the position of the shed signal for engines leaving the 'old' shed was considered not conducive to safe working. Another complaint arose at one of Stourbridge's furthest outposts, that is, the yards and station at Halesowen. By 1956 the station layout had been remodelled with the up main line having become bi-directional with the original down main line acting as a loop controlled by catch points and a disc signal, the former being located just below the down main starter. It would seem that whilst shunting from the loop, some enginemen had become confused by the position of the down main starter causing a number of derailments on the catch points. It was suggested that the signal be repositioned on the platform side of the up/down main line.

The question of inadequate illumination of signals can be illustrated by reference to one report which highlighted the fact that the Stourbridge North up advanced starter; the Stourbridge North down branch inner home and loop; and the Stourbridge South up main home, were all poorly lit. This complaint was quickly acted upon by the Divisional management and the signal inspector was instructed to investigate immediately. The ensuing report confirmed the men's complaint that the lamps were well below standard and that immediate remedial action had been taken. It would appear that poor quality lighting oil was causing a crust to form on and around the wicks thereby reducing the effectiveness of the lamps at night. Both the oil and wicks were replaced.

The Links

The LDC was also heavily involved in the allocation of turns of duty to the links; sometimes a controversial area. At an LDC held on 29th July, 1928 the employees' side stated that the recently introduced 6.41 am Stourbridge

Junction to Snow Hill had been placed in the '36XX' link (more details about the links can be found in Chapter Three) without any consultation with the employees. Clearly, the men's representatives were more than a little put out by the fact that this new job had been allocated without first seeking agreement through the LDC. Apparently, at an employees' informal meeting, 26 men had voted on the issue, the majority (in fact it was 14 to 12) being in favour of this service being placed in the 'Metropolitan' link ('Metro' for short). In spite of this vote, management upheld the original decision, presumably taken by the roster clerk, informing the men at a meeting held on 23rd August, 1928.

Link working was possibly the most discussed item on an agenda and at one meeting on 29th October, 1935 considerable time was spent on agreeing the transfer of turns from one link to another, e.g. the 1.30 am Oldbury relief was moved to the Senior Bank link in place of the 4.45 am spare turn; the 10.30 am Control special transferred to the same link to replace another Control special that had been cancelled, and so on. Another meeting held earlier, on 16th August, 1934 agreed the following changes: the Friday freight to Pontypool Road to be placed in the Double Home link; the 9.30 am and 10.30 am Control specials and the 4.45 am spare turn to be allocated to No. 1 Bank link; the 6.15 am Bewdley and 8.59 am Dudley shunting turn to be put in No. 2 Bank link; the 5.30 am Kingswinford trip working placed in the Shunting link in place of the 6.15 am Bewdley; the 3.00 am spare turn to be changed to a midday spare turn in No. 2 Bank link. It appeared to be, at times, a very complex business!

The employees' side of the LDC regularly made applications for the reallocation of services from one link to another, although many of these proposals failed to get management agreement. However, on the assumption that the application would be successful, the employee's side would normally produce a list of those men that would be affected by the change. For example on 19th July, 1927 it was proposed that the 7.00 am Stourbridge Junction to Birmingham (Snow Hill) passenger service be allocated to the 'Metro' link which would have meant that driver Charlie Broughton and fireman B. Love would also have moved into the 'Metro' link. Two years later driver Broughton was again featuring in the LDC discussions having applied for a transfer from No. 2 Passenger link to No. 1 Passenger (it is thought that the decision regarding this application was taken at Divisional level). By this time, not only was driver Broughton a member of the Sectional Council, but also very prominent in local politics, consequently a move into the top link would have given him more time to carry out his political and trade union commitments. (Incidentally, in November 1943 fireman Joe Broughton had his turns altered so that he could carry out his Council duties more effectively.) The jobs in No. 1 Passenger link were exclusively passenger (although in 1934 the link was allocated a freight turn which probably gave rise to much discussion at the LDC meetings) and therefore the hours worked were far more conventional than those in No. 2 Passenger which would have had a number of inconveniently timed freight turns. The success of this application would have led to four other drivers being moved through the links: engineman Sokell into No. 2 Passenger; engineman Fiddler into the Double Home link; engineman Steele into No. 1 Bank 'A' Section); and engineman Wall out of the shunting link and into No. 2 Bank. The promotion of driver Wall would, however, have left a spare fireman in the shunting link so it was suggested that the junior fireman in the link, H. Lavender, drop back into the shed link firing to F. Winnall, a job that had previously been a spare turn.

In August 1928 the men's representatives put forward a proposal to move the following from the 'Metro' link to the '36XX' link: the 11.35 am passenger relief, the 2.12 pm Stourbridge Junction to Wolverhampton (Low Level) passenger service (the 9.45 am ex-Paddington which ran under 'B' head lamps from Kidderminster), and the 4.25 pm Stourbridge Junction to Hagley local, (it is thought that this was a railmotor service. After returning to Stourbridge empty the 'motor formed the 4.38 pm to Wolverhampton (Low Level) which ran via the Wombourn branch). Had this request been granted then enginemen H. Woolridge, S. Hall and E. Elt, together with firemen S. Bishop, H. Taylor and G. Saunders would all have followed suit.

Not all employee transfers between the links were permanent. At times the demands placed upon the shed to supply engine crews would have stretched manpower resources to the limit, especially at holiday times. In April 1929, possibly in anticipation of the forthcoming Easter Bank holidays and the need to supply additional crews for excursion traffic, a plan was drawn up by the employees' side of the LDC that would enable the two senior firemen in each link to move into the link immediately above for the duration of the holiday period only (drivers were not mentioned). This proposal suggested the following changes:

Into No. 1 Passenger link	R. Garbett and H. Brown
Into No. 2 Passenger link	R. Kendrick and J. Griffiths
Into the Double Home link	A. Wassell and P. Hamblett
Into No. 1 Bank link	S. Gough and J. Eveson
Into No. 2 Bank link	J. Watkins and L. Doyle

In addition, two firemen would be allocated to the passenger pilot turns whilst the next five senior cleaners on the shed would be rostered on firing turns, one of whom would have fired to passed fireman B. Vaughan.

World War II

With the outbreak of war in 1939, the LDC found itself having to deal with hitherto unknown difficulties. Consequently, issues relating to the conflict soon found their way on to the agenda. On 15th August, 1940 the employees' side expressed their concern at the lack of ARP equipment at the shed. This complaint resulted in 11 sets of helmets and respirators being delivered in the following October. These must have been for use by the breakdown gang as it was in their vans that the equipment was stored. An attack by marauding enemy bombers was always a possibility so local railwaymen had to ensure that adequate air raid procedures were in place. In the event of night time raids, the location of the shed could be given away by the careless disposal of fires, the glow from which might be seen by German pilots flying overhead. Consequently, great care had to be exercised by tired men after a long shift. At the shed, it was agreed that nine men (it is thought that these were recruited from the cleaning staff) were trained in aircraft recognition and fire-damping, a set of three men being allocated to each shift. These men received enhanced rates of pay for the additional duties. A hut was even erected for use by these teams, this being sited on the bank overlooking the shed and 'spotters' (aircraft not trains) using it were able to communicate with their colleagues in both the shed and at the coal stage. Bells were fitted in the air-raid shelters to signal the 'all clear', and special 'shelter wardens' were appointed. No air-raid precautions would be complete without sandbags and at least 36 of these essential items were, on one occasion, ordered from the stores at Wolverhampton. ARP sheets were also issued to engine crews for fixing to locomotives and, in July 1942, a request was made to provide these for Nos. 8742 and 5734.

In 1942 the membership of the formal LDC was as follows: for the company: Messrs Snell (Chairman and divisional superintendent); Morris (shedmaster); Reynolds (roster clerk) and Bolding (Secretary), whilst the employees were represented by Harry Chant (Chairman and driver); Len Shutt (driver); Tom Jenkins (coalman) and Bert Homer (Secretary and driver). However, by 1943 the membership had been widened, probably to enable issues normally dealt with by the Section 3 LDC to be included. This situation may have arisen due to war-time conditions? The LDC now included, on the management side, Messrs A. Harrison, J. Kinsey and R. Bullaston (all Goods Department) whilst the employees' side was increased by the inclusion of B. Noblett (Goods Department).

Industrial Change

The early 1950s brought with it the first signs that the traditional operation of the nation's railways was about to change; a new (but not necessarily better) age was about to dawn and with it came the demise of the steam locomotive. On 6th May, 1955 the LDC met to hear the latest proposals regarding motive power at the shed, proposals that were a clear indication that the days of steam at Stourbridge were numbered, and soon the talk of diesels began to fill the messroom. Diesel traction, however, was not new to the men as ex-GWR railcars had been in use in the area since the mid-1930s. Oddly, these machines were not mentioned in the LDC until it was proposed to introduce a new diesel link in 1943 when the shed had by this time two or three of these cars in its allocation. But it was not the arrival of the odd machine here and there that occupied the minds of drivers and firemen; it was the prospect of widespread dieselisation and the effects that this would have on men's jobs.

As the years wore on, it became increasingly clear that changes in the railway industry were going to have major implications for jobs at Stourbridge and the rest of the local stations. Traditional freight business was being lost to the roads (as was passenger traffic), thereby jeopardising jobs at the yards, putting all grades of railwaymen at risk of redundancy or redeployment. Dieselisation threatened accepted manning levels as well as those shed jobs dependent on the steam engine, e.g. coalmen, tube cleaners, firedroppers, boilersmiths, etc. All these changes were tied up with the West Midlands Rationalisation Plan. At a staff consultation meeting held on 11th May, 1965 the Stourbridge representatives asked the question, quite rightly, what was the future of Stourbridge Motive Power Depot? The answer probably did little to reassure the men for although it was stated that the shed would be one of the last places for steam, jobs clearly depended upon staff requirements of the new, perhaps some would say, 'streamlined' railway. On 8th June, 1965 Geoff Jackson, the Secretary of the employees' side of the LDC, sent a memorandum to Mr Williams, the divisional manager of the London Midland Region based in Birmingham asking: '. . . is it the intention to slowly squeeze Stourbridge out of existence as these diagrams mean the loss of route and diesel knowledge to Gloucester and Salop . . .' Mr Jackson was referring in particular to the loss of two turns of duty involving the Monday Only, Margam freight, and the daily Rowley Regis-Llandarcy tank train, both worked by Stourbridge crews as far as Gloucester. Also, perhaps, 'specials' over the Severn Valley line conveying RAF personnel. A reply eventually came from Mr Gregory, the shedmaster at Stourbridge, who explained:

> . . . the changes referred to arose through freight train alterations and cancellations which necessiatated considerable revision of the enginemen's balances between Stourbridge Junction; Worcester and Gloucester, and these revisions were based upon formulating the most economical workings. The main freight train alterations were as follows:

09.35 (D)	Llandarcy	- Rowley Regis	Cancelled
20.40 (SO)	Llandarcy	- Rowley Regis	Cancelled
22.52 (D)	Rowley Regis	- Llandarcy	Cancelled
07.43 (SO)	Rowley Regis	- Llandarcy	Cancelled
08.40 (SX)	Oldbury & L.G.	- Ripple Lane	Cancelled
09.15 (SO)	Rowley Regis	- Thames Haven	Cancelled
09.40 (SX)	Thames Haven	- Oldbury & L.G.	Cancelled
13.08 (SO)	Ripple Lane	- Regis Regis	Cancelled

> The 08.45 Stourbridge Junction to Margam which became unbalanced in consequence of the 09.35 Llandarcy to Rowley Regis being discontinued was incorporated into Worcester enginemen's diagram to absorb uneconomical working caused by the cancellation of the 08.40 from Oldbury & L.G.

By August 1965, it was forecast that closure of the steam shed would be at the end of 1966 or early in 1967, although a booking on/off point would still be required to cater for well in excess of 100 enginemen. However, in reality, the long term future for Stourbridge looked rather grim. Earlier, in November 1963, the Stourbridge Junction-Worcester (Foregate Street)-Hereford section was the subject of downgrading proposals, whilst the closure of many of the intermediate stations on the route, as well as a reduction in local services, was high on the operational agenda. The existence of Stourbridge Town station was also hanging in the balance, but a report in the Spring of 1965 offered hope by stating that the line was just about self-supporting. Unfortunately, the rest of the decade was a story of closure after closure; of job loss after job loss.

When it was finally decided to close the shed to steam on 11th July, 1966 around 180 jobs were initially identified for footplate crews at Stourbridge, consequently a number decided to leave the service or apply for jobs elsewhere. Of the few remaining conciliation staff at the shed, a number were allocated to the train crew block that was to be built at Stourbridge Junction, whilst others were transferred or resettled. Fitting shop jobs were also reduced, although many men left the service when it became known that jobs were to disappear. Those that did remain continued to maintain the diesel locomotives and dmus at the shed and after closure, at Stourbridge Junction. Incidentally, the fitters were not covered by the LDCs at Stourbridge. This group was represented by their elected shop steward at meetings with BR management. In 1956 this representative was G. Skelding, however, when promoted to foreman in 1961, the now vacant shop steward post was filled by B. Castle who continued to represent the fitting shop personnel at Stourbridge until maintenance duties were removed from the station in the late 1960s.

The other major casualty during the 1960s was the freight handling operation, the first victim being Kingswinford Junction marshalling yard which closed on 16th September, 1963. Unfortunately, further wholesale closures were on the cards and soon the spectre of unemployment began to loom large as reductions in the local infrastructure appeared inevitable. With the closure of Amblecote goods yard in 1965, Stourbridge's importance as a freight centre quickly faded and it came as no surprise when it was announced that the marshalling yards at Stourbridge Junction were soon to follow. The shut down of the yards was confirmed at an LDC early in February 1968, it being explained that the general downturn of freight on the rail network had resulted in a considerable reduction in the level of traffic being dealt with at Stourbridge. The development of steel and oil block trains in particular had considerably reduced throughput at the yard with the result that the facility was now severely under-utilised. Moreover, with 66 per cent of the wagons passing through the yards having already been handled at Bescot (Walsall), there seemed little justification in maintaining a marshalling facility especially as the remaining traffic (about 70-80 wagons per day) could easily be accommodated at the Walsall site. A joint meeting was arranged between Sectional Council LDCs 2 and 3 and the divisional operating officer, Mr R.M. Taylor, to discuss the closure, but it was stressed that as this matter was officially being dealt with at Sectional Council level, any talks which did take place must be considered 'unofficial'. However, it was clear that nothing could be said or done that could save the yard and it was taken out of use from 6th May, 1968. Although freight handling in the district had been dealt a severe blow it had not been entirely eliminated, the Stourbridge LDC being able to take some comfort from the news, on 1st April 1965, that it was proposed to open a Full Load (steel) Concentration Depot on 31st May, 1965 on the old Moor Lane Depot site. This became Brierley Hill Steel Terminal on 31st March, 1966.

The New Era

The work of the LDC was not confined to the steam era, and the fight for Stourbridge jobs continued well after the shed and yards had been closed. However, it was an increasingly difficult task, trying to negotiate in a harsh climate of reduction, closure and rationalisation, and what was left of the Stourbridge-based operation was under constant threat. On the other hand, from the 1960s, the men's representatives were possibly more professional in their approach than their predecessors (this is not being disrespectful to them or their efforts on behalf of their colleagues) who perhaps did not have the benefit of a well prepared, union-sponsored educational programme aimed at providing a good background knowledge of the negotiating machinery and the conditions of service. In other words, the employees' side was now more than adequately equipped for the arena in which they were required to operate. It was still an uphill struggle and one which was ultimately doomed to failure, but there were some successes as will be seen below.

Although the larger Motive Power Depots in the area, e.g. Bescot, obtained the lion's share of the work on offer, Stourbridge LDC was able to argue convincingly that certain jobs should be allocated to their own TCD. Competition between Bescot and Stourbridge for work, in particular Sunday ballasting turns, was the source of a number of disputes between the two depots one of which gave rise to a complaint from the latter's LDC on 30th July, 1980 regarding loss of earnings due to Bescot men being employed on engineering work throughout the length of Old Hill tunnel on 13th July, 1980. Apparently the Appendix to the meeting of Sectional Council B (footplate crew) dated 1st February, 1977 had outlined how Sunday ballasting work in the Stourbridge area should be allocated. It would appear that according to Stourbridge this condition had not been applied. The LDC had apparently done its homework! Incidentally, during the early 1970s Stourbridge's Sectional Council LDC No. 2 (footplate crew) and No. 3 (guards) obtained a ruling at Sectional Council level which stated that the area to be worked by Stourbridge men would conform to the Area Manager's administrative district which was from Eagle Crossing to Stourbridge via Dudley; Handsworth to Stourbridge via Smethwick West; and Stourbridge to Cutnall Green.

Finally, by the mid-1970s, there was an air of desperation about the station, a situation that can probably be summed up by the following extract from quite a lengthy letter from the Secretary of the LDC to J.E.Cox, Secretary of Sectional Council No. 2, dated March 1976:

> What is Stourbridge's future . . . no proposals in the pipeline to close it, but they still keep cutting away at every pretext. Other major depots in the area, Saltley, Wolves, Bescot and New Street, are only fighting to retain or get more jobs. We at Stourbridge are fighting for survival and losing hands down, our complement today is only 39 Crewe diagrams Mondays only; 37 Tuesday to Friday, so if you take away 12 passenger, 8 shunt trips, 3 pilots, 1 ferry and 3 rest day relief, what is now left is 10 freight turns . . .

Stourbridge depot's future? Sadly not very bright, for the writing was well and truly on the wall. The end came on 9th July, 1988 when train crew working ceased and the TCD closed.

Chapter Eight

Accidents and Incidents
on the lines around Stourbridge

The railway, especially in the early years, could be a very dangerous place to be for both employees and public alike. Accidents and incidents happened quite frequently and were usually reported in the local papers; some of course, including the Brierley Hill disaster, can be found in *The Railways of Stourbridge*. This sequel has enabled others to be reported, especially a major collision which took place at Cradley, and an update on the fate of Frederick Cook, the guard at the centre of the Brierley Hill incident.

The worst accident to be covered by this chapter occurred in the early evening of Wednesday 8th December, 1869; the place, Cradley on the Stourbridge Extension Railway. The ensuing tragedy came about when a passenger train and a coal train collided just outside the station. The 4.45 pm express from Birmingham (Snow Hill), which comprised one first, one second, two thirds and a guard's van next to the engine, had made its first stop at Smethwick Junction where two LNWR through carriages, a composite and a third brake, were attached to the rear. The train was then booked to run non-stop to Stourbridge Junction before continuing to its destination. The report mentions the destination as South Wales, although the driver actually stated that it was an express to Worcester. The train therefore, may also have been conveying through carriages for Cardiff. The express, driven by Henry Richardson, left Birmingham two minutes late; the train was further delayed by about two minutes at Smethwick Junction whilst the LNWR through carriages were attached. On the section between Rowley and Cradley Heath, the speed was maintained at around 25 mph over the falling gradient. About 1¼ miles from Cradley the driver sounded the engine's whistle to alert the guard, John Carter, and remind him to apply his handbrake. The express, which had by this time lost another two minutes and was therefore now running about six minutes late, was given a clear road through Cradley when the driver suddenly saw someone holding a red light on or near the up main line just beyond the station (it later transpired that this was Porter, the guard of the coal train). Immediately he closed the regulator, however, it was too late to stop the train and just before the impact, Richardson jumped for his life. Luckily he survived the crash, although his fireman, Charles Tasker, was far less fortunate, being killed instantly.

The reason for the accident was only too apparent; the coal train had left the down sidings located just beyond Lyde Green Lane bridge at Lane's End and was attempting to cross to the up line when it was hit by the express. At the time of the collision many of the coal trucks were still in the siding, however, several, together with the engine, straddled both main lines. The violence of the crash knocked the goods engine down the embankment, whilst the three or four wagons behind it were smashed to smithereens. The express engine was running tender first, the force of the collision sending the tender spinning into an adjacent siding. The adjoining guard's van was wrecked, although the carriages escaped quite lightly, as did the passengers, only Thomas Hall of

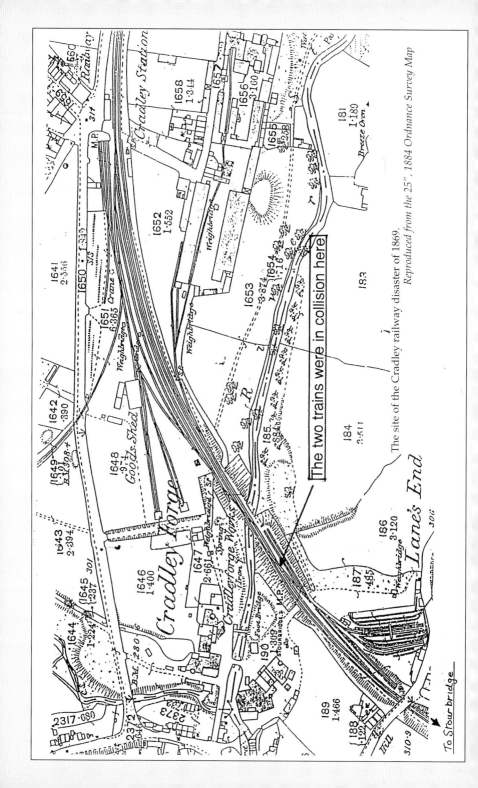

The two trains were in collision here

The site of the Cradley railway disaster of 1869.
Reproduced from the 25", 1884 Ordnance Survey Map

To Stourbridge

Burford sustaining serious injury. The crew of the coal train, Daniel Porter (guard), Thomas Page (driver) and Phillip Smart (fireman), were uninjured although severely shaken, the latter having to be sent home in a cab to recover. However, it was a porter travelling on the express who had the luckiest escape, moving out of the guard's van behind the engine to another part of the train at Smethwick Junction! Had he not done so he would surely have suffered a similar fate to that of the unfortunate Charles Tasker. Amongst the passengers was Mr J. Ward-Armstrong of Hereford, a divisional engineer with the GWR, who immediately lent his experience to the task of clearing the wreckage. There were also two medical men on board, Mr Lamb of Stourport and a gentleman from Stourbridge. They too rendered assistance. Immediately after the crash a message was sent to Stourbridge informing the staff there of the pile-up. Straight away the station master, Mr Phillips, commandeered an engine and sped to the scene where he remained on duty all night. The telegram also brought assistance from around 150 railway workers taken to the spot by special trains.

In addition to the passenger locomotive which ended up on its side, only the guard's van and the following two carriages actually left the rails, although the track itself was severely damaged with rails twisted and bent and sleepers splintered and pulled up. It was the first priority of the permanent way men to get the tracks cleared to allow some sort of service to be reinstated and to this end the gangs set about their task with vigour. By around 10 o'clock on the Wednesday night their efforts had been rewarded, for by this time most of the wreckage had been moved. By 11 pm, one line had been returned to work whilst the other came back into operation between 2 and 3 o'clock Thursday morning. During Thursday all wreckage was loaded into wagons and sent to the Locomotive Department at Worcester.

So how did this tragedy occur? The newspaper report indicated that Thomas Page, the driver of goods engine No. 251 (formerly No. 30, an OW&WR double-framed, six-coupled tender goods engine, withdrawn October 1903), had been instructed not to come out of the siding until two passenger trains had gone by, that is, an up stopping passenger train and the ill-fated express. Apparently, the former had passed some 15 minutes before the accident. Furthermore, it would also appear that the company's operating instructions had been breached insofar as the siding should have been locked thereby preventing the coal train from leaving. So, who was culpable? The evidence given at the ensuing Inquest has been summarised below.

The Inquest into the tragedy opened at 10 am on Friday 10th December, at the Vine Hotel, Cradley before Mr Bayley the Deputy Coroner. Mr Sermon, from the offices of Messrs Whately of Birmingham attended on behalf of the GWR along with John Locke, inspector on the Stourbridge Extension of the GWR. Also present were a number of employees of the GWR and passengers who were there to give evidence, although the two injured men, Henry Richardson, the driver of the express, and Thomas Hall, a passenger, were not fit enough to attend. During the hearing, it soon became clear that the case revolved around the actions of five men; the three man crew of the goods train together with William Marston, the signalman, and William Davies, yard foreman at Cradley station. The Inquest continued throughout the day, however, as all the evidence could not be heard, in particular that of one of the key witnesses, the injured driver Henry Richardson, the Inquest was adjourned until Tuesday 21st December at noon, although, this too was destined to be cut short. Apparently, the Coroner had been informed by the surgeon who was attending Richardson that he would not be fit enough to give evidence for another three weeks. But for the late arrival of Captain Tyler, the Government inspector, who had been carrying out an inspection at the scene of the crash, the Inquest would have been adjourned there and then. However, the Coroner wished to delay the adjournment until after the appearance of Captain Tyler who may have wished clarification of evidence already given. Upon arrival the Captain assured the Coroner that further delay was unnecessary and the Inquest was adjourned until 17th January, 1870 at 1.00 pm.

The cause of the accident appears to have stemmed from the fact that formal operational orders at Cradley were ignored and that signalling arrangements, in the form of hand held flags by day and lamps by night, could be misinterpreted. John Locke stated that printed instructions had been given to Marston, the signalman, on 5th May, 1869. These informed him that a train must not be allowed to pass the signal box if the keys to the points and stop-blocks were missing. The instructions were certainly still in force on the day in question, although Marston appeared undecided as to whether or not he had seen them, first stating that he was not aware of the instructions relating to the keys and then immediately changing his mind saying that they had been in the box a month and that he had read them. However, he did not sign to this effect until after the accident. Even more worrying was his admission that he did not fully appreciate their meaning until later on the night of the crash! Perhaps this goes some way to explain why the instructions were regularly disregarded by the signalman, as well as the yard foreman who claimed that he had never seen a copy of the duty paper requiring the keys to be in the signal box until after the accident!

The evidence indicates that on 8th December, Marston first gave the keys of the points and stop-blocks to George Civil, a checker at Cradley station, at about 2.00 pm. These were in turn given to William Davies at 3.30 pm. At this time the points and stop-blocks were locked and presumably were then unlocked by Davies. A few minutes after 4.00 pm shunting of the coal train into the sidings began with Marston and Davies exchanging signals to control the movements. At about 4.20 pm Davies indicated to Marston that the coal train had safely entered the sidings. Here it should have remained until at least five minutes after the express had passed by. At this point the company's regulations were certainly broken as although a stopping train and an express were due neither the points or stop-blocks were locked to prevent the coal train from leaving the siding. Davies then left the sidings to work in a different part of the yard (possibly Cradley station goods yard, although it could have been Netherend sidings just to the south of the crash scene), keeping the keys with him rather than returning them to the signal box. A further transgression! Apparently, due to an alleged heavy workload, together with the walking distances involved between the yard, sidings, and signal box, the practice had developed whereby the points and stop-blocks were simply left unlocked until all trains booked to leave the sidings had gone and only then were they locked and the keys returned to the signal box. When Davies left the sidings just prior to the accident he supposedly pushed the stop-blocks on to the line, although these of course were not then locked. The yard foreman was seemingly of the opinion that the mere positioning of these on the line indicated that the line was not clear and that no departures must take place without his sanction. For the coal train to get out on to the main line these blocks would have to be moved, an action that all three train crew denied. So were they moved or were they simply not put on? Unfortunately, the answer to this question was never actually established. Furthermore, Page, the driver of the coal train, was reputedly told by Davies not to go out on to the main line until the passenger train had gone. About 10 minutes later Davies again approached Page to tell him not to leave until the express had passed. In view of this, why did the crew take the coal train out?

Firstly, there appears to be some doubt as to what was actually said between Davies and Page. Secondly, each member of the train crew stated that the engine's whistle was sounded one or more times to attract the attention of the signalman. This was done to inform him that the train was ready to leave. Shortly afterwards a white light was seen on the platform near to the signal box at the place where the signal was normally given. The guard, driver and fireman all saw the white light which meant 'proceed'. The guard stood at the side of the engine and waved his lamp to the footplate crew authorising them to start the train. If the crew are to be believed, the stop-blocks were not across the track as stated by Davies and therefore they believed that they were at liberty to move out as they had been given the 'proceed' signal from the box. Once the signal had been confirmed by the guard, the footplate crew drew the train steadily out on to the main line with the subsequent disastrous results. The fireman (Smart) said in evidence that he had never known a guard on this goods train direct them on to the main line while the blocks were in the state that they were on the night in question. However, he did understand that it was acceptable to go out if instructed to by the guard, even if the yardman, or anyone else having charge of the stop-blocks, was not there. The driver subsequently corroborated the fireman's evidence. The guard admitted that he knew that the express was due but believed that it should have passed by the time the coal train was about to leave.

There is no doubt that the crew saw a white light, and that this was interpreted as the signal to go out on to the main line. So why did the signalman give it when he knew of the imminent arrival of the express? He certainly was aware that it was due as he had signalled the line clear from Cradley to Hayes Lane. He subsequently received the 'train on line' signal from the box at Corngreaves Junction which he acknowledged with one beat of the bell. The express then passed at about 5.13 pm. Earlier, he had also signalled trains at 4.13 pm and 4.38 pm (both goods trains), and at 4.51 pm (the local passenger?). The last one was at 5.07 pm (the express?). Unfortunately, another local version of the rules seems to have come into play after he had signalled the line clear for the passage of the express. The signalman stated that he did leave the box with a white light in his hand, but this was merely for the purposes of illuminating his path along the line toward the sidings to see if it was clear (after he had already signalled the 'all clear'!). He did not wave the lamp, as he would normally do if signalling a train out of the sidings. However, it was pointed out that should a white light be shown, whether it be stationary or waved, it would be taken by a train crew as a signal that the line was clear to proceed as the distinction was not made in the rule book. Furthermore, another crucial factor was that neither Page or Smart seemed to be sure if the express had passed. If it had been on time it would have gone by: unfortunately it was late! The footplate crew were expecting to leave the sidings after two trains had passed through. Whilst they had been in the sidings two trains may have done just that, i.e. those signalled by Marston at 4.38 pm and at 4.51 pm. It was very foggy that evening and by the time the accident happened darkness had fallen. Could the crew have thought that these were the trains they were waiting for and after these had gone, they perhaps mistakenly thought that the line was clear, an assumption confirmed by the showing of the white light?

When all the evidence had been presented the Coroner summed up, the jury hearing that the duty of the guard was to have control over the loaded trucks and having satisfied himself that the line was clear, the signal to proceed having been given (or so it was thought), to instruct the driver how and when to proceed. Clearly, the jury thought that Porter had not discharged this duty for after retiring to consider their verdict, they returned to inform the Coroner that they had found Daniel Porter, the guard, guilty of negligence and returned a verdict of manslaughter against him. Porter was then advised by the Coroner that he would be committed for trial at the next assizes to be held at Stafford, bail being set at £50, plus two sureties of £25. As an application for bail was not made, Porter was taken into police custody. Turning to Davies and Marston, the jury recommended that each be censored, the former for leaving the stop-blocks unlocked, the latter for not having the keys in his box when the express was due. Perhaps these two can think themselves lucky that their punishment was not more severe. No blame was attached to the footplate crew. It was also suggested that a siding signal be installed which would be controlled from the signal box and that this should be interlocked with the signals on the main line.

Porter was later charged by the police with unlawfully causing the death of Charles Tasker and appeared before Magistrates early in February 1870. However, it was here that the tale took an unexpected twist. The JP, Mr Moore, told John Locke, the inspector on the Stourbridge Extension, that he could not see how the prisoner was to blame for the accident as he was acting in response to a mistake made by someone else and thought that he was behaving correctly in taking the white light as a signal to proceed. The JP's view concurred with that of Locke's. With that the Bench retired and having been absent from the court for about two minutes returned to inform the prisoner that they had decided to dismiss the case against him. However, Porter still had to face trial at the Assizes on the Coroner's warrant and this he did on Saturday 12th March, 1870. The presiding judge, Mr Justice Lush, informed the jury that the Grand Jury, whose job it was to decide which cases should proceed to trial at the Quarter Sessions, had thrown out, quite properly in his opinion, the bill of indictment presented before them against Daniel Porter. That being so the prosecution had not offered any evidence on the Coroner's inquisition and therefore, His Lordship instructed the jury to find a verdict of 'not guilty' against the accused.

Clearly, it is dangerous to assume that the verdict of the Coroner's Court will always be upheld at the Assizes. The above illustrates this view. However, the most striking example must be the one involving one Frederick Cook, the guard at the centre of the tragic accident at Brierley Hill in 1858 (see *The Railways of Stourbridge*, p.168-169) who was found guilty of manslaughter at the ensuing Coroner's Court. Cook was committed for trial at Stafford Assizes at the end of November 1858, Mr Baron Bramwell presiding. In view of what had been decided at the Coroner's court, that which was to follow must have come as quite a surprise to those involved.

From the outset, His Lordship left no one in any doubt that he held very different views to those of the Coroner's jury. In fact the propriety of putting Cook on trial at all on the Coroner's inquisition was strongly questioned. As a result of the judge's very decided opinions on the subject, the Grand Jury ignored the bills of indictment presented before them. This decision may also have had something to do with the non-appearance of Captain Tyler, the Government Inspector of Railways whose experiments at the scene of the crash and his ensuing evidence were major factors influencing the Coroner's jury to reach their verdict. This is what Mr Kenealy, the leading Counsel for the prosecution, seemed to be saying later in the week after the judgement had been announced. Counsel for the prosecution were initially convinced that there was a case to answer, however, following His Worship's revelations, both Messrs Kenealy and Hill were in agreement that they should exercise their discretion not to proceed. Cook was subsequently arraigned before the court on the Coroner's inquisition in order that a verdict of 'not guilty' could be formally recorded. So what caused the prosecution to change their minds? The answer to this lies in His Lordship's interpretation of the evidence, in particular the value of the 'scientific' contribution.

At 10 am, Tuesday 30th November, the learned Baron began his address to the Grand Jury. In essence what His Lordship was saying was that whilst he did not know if anyone was responsible for the lamentable consequences of the accident at Brierley Hill, he was certain that Cook could not be properly convicted of manslaughter. It was pointed out that the prosecution's case was shown to rely very heavily on the 'scientific' evidence as opposed to positive statements by some of the witnesses examined at the Inquest. Therefore, this might be regarded as speculation against fact. The judge opened his address by directing the jury to ignore the evidence relating to the journey from Wolverhampton to Worcester during the morning; also the management of the railway company and all the other rubbish with which this case has been encumbered may be very properly omitted, pointing out that their sole and only duty was to say whether Cook was guilty of manslaughter or not. The verdict of manslaughter will depend on what caused the deaths of the deceased. The judge went on to say:

If there had been no other train coming up the incline the accident would not have happened; but for that he is not responsible. If the coupling chains were whole and had not been broken the portion of the train would not have become detached and would not have gone down the incline; now, is he responsible for that? . . . I do not think you will have any evidence before you that there was anything to induce anybody to believe that the particular coupling chain which must have broken to cause these carriages to become detached would break or were in any way insufficient. I do not see any reason for supposing that he is responsible for the breaking of the coupling chains. If they were bad it was not his fault . . . you ought not to hold this man responsible for the accident unless you find that there was some deficiency in the coupling chain attached to the carriage which separated from the rest, so that the guard either knew it, or in the course of his duty ought to have known it, or that it was his duty to rectify or call attention to it . . . I cannot find any ground for believing that such are the facts.

His Worship then commented on the 'scientific' evidence:

I do not say it is so in this particular case, but very likely he may be one of those who are made scapegoats in order to satisfy public indignation against the authors of this disastrous calamity. It is certainly fair to say in favour of this man that it is a very different thing to get quietly into a train, when they know and when they feel that in their experiments they will come to no trouble and then see what they can do to stop a train - that I say gentlemen, is very different from what a man can do in the alarm and hurry of the moment, when he knows that an accident is impending . . . if this man mismanaged the brake . . . because he got so frightened that he lost his head, this would not be manslaughter. I think it right that you should also bear in mind that, after all, the speculative evidence - for that is really what is meant by what is called 'scientific' evidence - only goes to show what the guard ought to have done on the night in question, when these gentlemen did not know what the condition of the rails on that night was. . . there is positive evidence that he was doing his best to stop the train when the accident occurred . . . But a man is not guilty of manslaughter merely because he does not do that which some more clever, stronger, or more cool-headed person might do. [*Staffordshire Advertiser*, Saturday 4th December, 1858]

At around midday the Foreman and several members of the jury entered the court and spoke to the judge. Minutes later the Clerk of the Court rose and announced 'Not a true bill against Frederick Cook for manslaughter', repeating the same for all 14 cases in which death occurred. On hearing these announcements, Mr Motteram, who had been instructed to defend Cook, applied for his client's immediate discharge from custody as apparently it was not customary to try prisoners on the Coroner's inquisition when the Grand Jury had thrown out a bill of indictment that had been presented before them. Moreover, as Cook had been in prison ever since the conclusion of the Inquest, Counsel argued that it was only right and proper that he should be released immediately (it would seem that Cook having been committed on a Coroner's inquisition had been unable to procure bail; had he been committed by Magistrates, bail would not have been a problem). Having listened to Mr Motteram's request the judge pointed out that the decision not to proceed was in the hands of Prosecuting Counsel who subsequently requested 24 hours delay in order that their position could be reviewed. Cook was then liberated on his own recognisance to appear before the court the following morning. However, a few hours later Messrs Kenealy and Hill, having reconsidered the case, informed His Lordship that, 'it would not be expedient to present the case upon the Coroner's inquisitions'. Shortly afterwards Cook again appeared in court where he was arraigned on the Coroner's inquisition in order that the verdict could be formally recorded. After addressing the Petty Jury, His Lordship confirmed that he could not properly convict Cook of the charges against him and accordingly a verdict of 'not guilty' was recorded in each of the 14 cases. With that Cook was discharged a free man. It would seem that the only guilt here is that of the author who did not follow the proceedings through to the Assize Court thereby giving the impression in *The Railways of Stourbridge* that Cook's guilt would be a foregone conclusion.

In the early years in particular there were many incidents involving individual railway employees and all too often these had fatal consequences. In the local area between 1866 and 1871 shunter Timothy Bowers; parcels porter W. Stokes; and an unnamed fireman all lost their lives whilst carrying out their duties. However, even if an accident was not fatal it often had life changing consequences. Take for example engine driver Drake who in April 1865 lost a leg when he was hit by the brake van of a passing freight as he dismounted from his engine at Stourbridge station. He lived but his career was over!

The branch from Stourbridge Junction to Stourbridge was built in the late 1870s. Part of this line had to be laid through a sandstone cutting, the rock having to be blasted out. This was particularly dangerous work and in November 1878, two men were very seriously injured whilst blasting was being carried out. Altogether, six men had been involved in accidents since construction began. The work also put to flight some of Stourbridge's oldest inhabitants. A group of rooks, that had for many years made their homes in the elms near Job's Lane, decided enough was enough and left the area for trees anew.

The congestion at the original Stourbridge Junction station has been referred to in *The Railways of Stourbridge*, however, this next incident serves to illustrate further the sort of problems local railwaymen had to deal with. November was always associated with thick fog and it was on 17th November, 1878 that these conditions led to a collision at the main line station. The Town service had just arrived in the down platform and was coming slowly to a halt when it ran into the rear of the stationary 7.09 pm departure for Wolverhampton (Low Level) (the 2.15 pm ex-Paddington). The train from off the Town branch ordinarily terminated some way down the platform, but on this occasion the fog was so dense that the driver lost his bearings and failed to appreciate just how far he had travelled. Unfortunately, he only realized where he was when the collision occurred.

The dangers of working with animals has already been highlighted in *The Railways of Stourbridge* but another incident can be recounted here. On 3rd September, 1887 William White, a shunter at Stourbridge, was loading horses into a horse box at 8.45 am when one of them kicked the gate open. A piece of ironwork on the gate struck White on the right temple. Luckily, there was on hand James Barnett, passenger guard and member of the Stourbridge Railway Ambulance Corps (SRAC), who was able to apply first aid to the badly bleeding wound. This was the fifth case attended by Mr Barnett and the twenty-fifth dealt with by the SRAC.

On 23rd February, 1889 passenger guard Willoughby came across an unusual case of vandalism on the last train from Birmingham to Kidderminster. Presumably the guard was walking along the platform at Stourbridge Junction when he saw a man in one of the compartments cutting off the leather straps (presumably on the blinds or windows) and throwing them out of the window. At Hagley, Police Constable Holloway boarded the train but just as he was about to make an arrest the train moved off. The man, who was later named as Joseph Wood, leapt from the compartment and was later found unconscious and clearly the worse for drink. Wood was subsequently dispatched to Kidderminster Infirmary. On the subject of vandalism, a boy by the name of William White received 12 strokes of the birch for firing a gun at a train on the Stourbridge Extension during March 1889.

In the 1890s there were several very serious accidents on the local railways. The first involved Thomas Daniels who was severely injured when the turntable he was repairing at Brettell Lane crushed him. A month later, in early September, Harry Turner was killed at Stourbridge goods yard when a tree he was unloading by crane slipped and fell on him. On 16th October, 1891 there was a collision at Stourbridge Junction which provoked further editorial comment in the *County Express* regarding the need for improved facilities due to the increased amount of traffic now handled at the station. The accident involved the Town shuttle service which collided with an empty stock train standing on the up line. Apparently, the points had not been switched over to allow the Town service to cross over from the up line on to the branch and therefore the train had simply continued along the main line. The results of the accident were that the Town engine had to be replaced and passengers arrived at Stourbridge Town station some 30 minutes late.

Walking along the track itself is obviously a particularly dangerous thing to do so it can come as no surprise that any one choosing to do so will probably be involved in a very nasty accident. At 8.00 pm on 19th March, 1894 Thomas Haden was walking on the down line of the Stourbridge Extension towards Lye when he was run down by a train from Birmingham. The impact threw the body on to the adjacent track where a goods train carrying out shunting duties ran over it twice more. Shunting was also responsible for the death of chief yard inspector Thomas Tyler aged 54 on Monday 30th January, 1897. The deceased was probably talking to the station master, Mr Cope, when he stepped on to the line and knocked down by an engine and carriages. Mr Tyler had probably momentarily forgotten that shunting was taking place in the immediate vicinity.

On Monday 23rd January, 1899, at about 8.30 in the evening, a collision occurred to the south of the original Stourbridge Junction station. A freight train bound for Kidderminster received the right of way and began to leave the up loop between the station and Chawn Hill bridge when it collided with a tender engine running light on the main line after taking water at the station. The impact caused the light engine to leave the rails, damaging the stonework of the bridge and leaving the tender overhanging the parapet. To get the engine away from the bridge, three goods locomotives were coupled together and these in turn were hooked up to the stricken engine. Unfortunately, their efforts only resulted in a drawbar snapping. Eventually, five engines succeeded in pulling the locomotive back on to the track. By 6.00 am the following morning the line had been cleared.

Moving forward to 1903, an incident occurred which, although not directly attributable to the railway itself, could have had terrible consequences. About 100 yards to the south of Brettell Lane station the railway line crosses the Stourbridge canal. Near here, and just to the west of the railway bridge carrying the Great Western main line from Dudley to Stourbridge, the canal passed the large brick works of G.K. Harrison and the iron works of Roberts & Cooper, both companies having access to the canal via Wheeleys basin. Spanning the entrance to this basin was a small bridge which carried the towing path. It was here, on Saturday 14th November, 1903 that there was a spectacular collapse or 'crowner-in' of the towing path which caused the immediate flooding of nearby works and mines. However, not only did the cave-in drain the canal for around three miles, the water pouring into the abandoned mine workings below, the disturbance also threatened the foundations of the railway bridge. Shortly after the 'crowner-in' occurred two passenger trains began to cross the bridge at the same time. The immediate fears of onlookers was that the combined weight of the trains, added to the possible damage to the bridge's foundations, may lead to a terrible disaster; thankfully, both trains made it to their respective sides. As both the bridge and the adjoining embankment might have been weakened by the subsidence, a close eye was kept on both structures by local railway officials. However, the damage was not considered dangerous enough to suspend services, although a flag man was stationed at each end of the bridge and a speed restriction was introduced for all trains crossing.

The year before the outbreak of the Great War witnessed a number of accidents and incidents on the railways around Stourbridge, two being in the Lye area. On Friday 4th April, 1913 a labourer by the name of Henry Aston was crushed to death in the private siding of G.K. Harrison's brick works located in Dudley Road, Lye. Apparently, just before 8 am the man had been moving a tar sheet between two trucks when the wagons moved crushing him. The body was freed by the foreman, Samuel Sergeant. Three months later on 12th July, passenger guard Alfred Woodward was almost decapitated in an accident at Engine Lane road bridge just beyond Lye station. It would appear that the guard had been in charge of the 8.15 pm Birmingham (Snow Hill) to Stourbridge Junction service which had left Lye at 8.55 pm. On arrival at Stourbridge he was found to be missing and after a search along the line his body was found alongside the track under the bridge. At the Inquest the Coroner concluded that the double doors on the guard's van had not, for some reason, been bolted properly and had sprung open causing the man to fall to his death. Incidentally, during 1913/14 Engine Lane bridge was the scene of three fatalities in 18 months, the last being on 5th September, 1914 when Rupert Oliver, a passenger on the 11.05 pm departure from Stourbridge Junction, was killed when his head hit the bridge, presumably whilst leaning out of a carriage window.

As readers will undoubtedly be aware, the Earl of Dudley's Pensnett Railway was an extensive network of lines which linked local collieries to the large steel

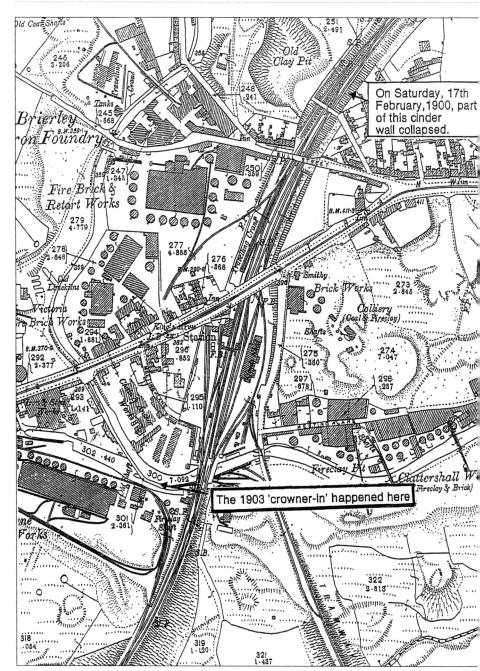

On Saturday, 17th February, 1900, part of this cinder wall collapsed.

The 1903 'crowner-in' happened here

Map showing the sites of two Brettell Lane incidents in 1900 and 1903.
Reproduced from the 25", 1919 Ordnance Survey Map

Two views of an accident at Amblecote goods yard on 24th April, 1905. A 32 wagon train ran out of control down the steep bank leading into the goods yard. The engine crashed bunker-first into the goods office.   *R.S. Carpenter and Gordon Dean Collection*

works at Round Oak. This railway, in common with the nearby GWR, experienced a number of accidents, one of these was on Tuesday 28th January, 1913. The accident involved the Pensnett Railway's own locomotive *Countess*, a Manning, Wardle 0-4-0 tender engine built in 1859. *Countess* was heading towards the Himley coalfield from Pensnett when the driver, William Mace, saw a line of trucks, that had somehow been released from a siding, quickly catching up with him. Realising that a collision was inevitable, Mace opened the regulator in the hope of increasing the engine's speed so that when the wagons did catch him up the force of the impact might at least be reduced. The collision happened shortly afterwards and Mace was thrown from the cab on to the ground. With no one at the controls *Countess* picked up speed and headed towards No. 4 pit smashing to smithereens a platelayers' vehicle which happened to be on the track in front of it. The next obstacle suffered a similar fate, a wagon full of slack being smashed to pieces. After a journey of 1½ miles the engine passed the disused No. 8 pit where a little way beyond a set of catch points guarded a short dead end siding. The catch points did their work and *Countess* left the main line and derailed, causing serious damage to the engine. However, after the post-accident inspection, it must have been decided to repair the engine for it remained in stock and was not scrapped until 1924.

Also on the Pensnett Railway, there was a serious runaway incident on Thursday 29th March, 1917. A train comprising 26 wagons, some of which were loaded, was descending the steep Barrow Hill incline at Pensnett when the locomotive's brakes failed. The driver, unable to bring the train under control, jumped for his life. At the bottom of the incline the runaway crashed into a line of stationary trucks forcing one of them through the 14 inch wall of the nearby engine shed whilst others were smashed to match wood. The locomotive was extensively damaged although thankfully there were no injuries to any railway personnel.

It was reported in the *County Express* that a serious collision occurred near Stourbridge engine shed on Friday, 9th July, 1920. However, the story was far from complete and it was only when a copy of the official Ministry of Transport report was kindly supplied by the Darlington Railway Centre and Museum that the full picture was revealed.

The accident happened at around 9.40 am. A goods train, No. 1 Bank - the Round Oak early service, was passing Engine House down home signal (located 598 yards north of Stourbridge Junction North signal box) when it was ran into by a light engine. As a result of the collision the guard of the goods train, Mr Martin, had to be rushed to Corbett hospital where he was treated for serious head injuries. Eight wagons and the brake van were derailed and one other wagon was damaged whilst the tender of the light engine was stove in. Additionally, a number of chairs, sleepers, and point rods were broken or damaged. The goods train, drawn by No. 1015 a '360' class, 0-6-0 tender engine weighing in total 69 tons, had consisted of 12 loaded and eight empty wagons with a four-wheeled 15 ton brake van. The light engine was a '388' class 'Standard Goods' 0-6-0 tender engine No. 497, total weight 72 tons. The incident also involved a second light engine, 4-4-0 No. 3531 a '3521' class rebuild which weighed 80½ tons.

The incident primarily revolved around the working practices of the three block posts to the north of Stourbridge Junction station: Middle signal box approximately 70 yards beyond the station; North signal box, about 100 yards north of the Birmingham junction; and Engine House signal box, the most northerly of the three located just to the south of Engine House sidings. Ordinarily No. 1 Bank was due to leave the north end of Stourbridge Junction down yard at 9.10 am, however, on the day it was running 10 minutes late. On duty in Engine House box was signalman Lowe who accepted the train from North box at 9.22 am, the train coming to a halt at Engine House down home signal at about 9.25 am. After standing for several minutes the signal was pulled off allowing the goods train to start off towards Brettell Lane. After having travelled around 275 yards, at a speed of four or five miles an hour, the collision took place.

A few minutes after the goods train had passed North box, Charles Barnett, the duty signalman, received a telephone message to say that a light engine (No. 497) was ready to leave the north end of Stourbridge Junction up yard, running to Stourbridge shed. He therefore set the road from the up yard to the down main line, over the trailing crossover opposite his box. The engine duly came to a stand, clear of the trailing slip points, some 30 or 40 yards north of the signal box. The light engine was not offered to Engine House box as Barnett had not received the 'out of section' signal for the goods train. However, Barnett was then offered, from Middle signal box (located 647 yards to the south), an engine (No. 3531) that had just been detached from a passenger train which had arrived at the Junction station at 9.33 am (possibly a service from Malvern Wells). This too was scheduled to run to the shed. Barnett immediately accepted the passenger engine (No. 3531) under the 'line clear to clearing point' bell signal, a special bell signal authorised at certain signal boxes on the Great Western's system a number of block posts were grouped closely together. However, this engine should only have been accepted under certain circumstances and it was clear from the position of No. 497 on the down main (about 220 or 230 yards ahead of North box's outer home signal) that Barnett acted irregularly in accepting No. 3531.

Barnett's intention had been to draw up the passenger engine as far as North signal box where it would couple up to No. 497 so that both could run to the shed together. The procedure that should have been adopted was first to bring No. 3531 to a halt at the outer home signal; then draw it up to the inner home, and finally, after clearing the inner home, to exhibit a hand held danger signal at the box itself. In his evidence Barnett stated that the outer home was pulled off before No. 3531 reached it; after passing the signal the arm was returned to danger and the inner home cleared. Barnett then obtained his red flag and went to the window of his box. However, this view conflicted, as will be seen later, with the evidence of Kimbell, the fireman on No. 3531. The driver of No. 3531, Mr Phillips, stated that the Middle box starting signal was pulled off when he was about 25 yards from it running slowly without steam. Steam was then applied and shut off again as he passed the starter so as to be ready to stop at North box outer home. About 200 yards or so beyond Middle box, Phillips' fireman, who was in a better position to view the North box home signals than his driver standing on the right-hand side of the footplate, informed his driver that the North box outer home was off and steam was reapplied. Kimbell had first seen North box outer home in the off position as soon as his engine had passed the Middle box starter and stated that he had also seen, at the same time, the inner home in the off position. Obviously this contradicted Barnett's statement.

The first indication that Phillips had that No. 497 was ahead of them was a warning from Kimbell that another engine was on the road. No. 3531 had not at this point passed the inner home and on hearing Kimbell's shout, the driver shut off steam and applied the steam brake. Fearing a collision he gave a brake whistle as a warning before operating the sanders. The driver's prompt action enabled the engine to be brought to a halt just beyond North signal box about 10 yards behind No. 497. Then, to his amazement, he saw the driver and fireman of No. 497 on the ballast, their engine heading off towards Brettell Lane.

A few moments earlier there had been panic on the footplate of No. 497. The fireman, seeing the approaching light engine and thinking that it was a passenger train, shouted a warning before immediately leaping off the engine. Price, the driver, concluded that the approaching engine was travelling too quickly to avoid a collision so he decided to open the regulator in an attempt to move No. 497 away, however, his nerve failed and he too decided to jump. But before doing so he attempted to shut the regulator. The footplate, though, was slippy from recent rain fall, and as he reached out for the handle he lost his footing. As a result the regulator remained open. On the trackside both men realised that a collision had been avoided and seeing their engine heading away they ran after it, intent on returning to the footplate. Unfortunately, No. 497 could not be caught and with no one at the controls the engine quickly overhauled the slow moving goods train, hitting the brake van at a speed of between 20 and 25 miles per hour.

News of the collision quickly reached Stourbridge shed and the breakdown gang, together with Jack Preece, the shed foreman, were soon on the scene together with Mr A.E. Murphy (station master) and inspector S. Wilkes. The breakdown gang immediately set to work and in about 40 minutes the up line had been cleared. Shortly afterwards single line working was introduced. The clearing of the down line took considerably longer and it was several hours before normal running was achieved. At the Inquiry Major G.L. Hall, who carried out the investigation into the accident, concluded that Price, a man with 24 years' service with the company, seven of which as a driver with a previous good record, must shoulder most of the blame. However, the action of Barnett was also a contributory factor and he too was seen to be blameworthy. The signalman's action was undoubtedly influenced by the imminent approach of two passenger trains, one from Wolverhampton on the up main, the other from Hereford on the down main heading for the Stourbridge Extension. To avoid any delay to the ex-Hereford express Barnett wished to clear the Birmingham line facing points as soon as possible, even if this meant the incorrect operation of the home signals to enable the light passenger engine to pass through Stourbridge North junction as quickly as possible. This action seriously compromised safe working and fortunately, the up passenger train had passed the down goods just before the collision occurred. In conclusion Major Hall considered that whilst certain automatic safeguards would have prevented the mistakes from occurring, existing operational conditions meant that signalmen should have no special difficulties carrying out their duties as long as the Block Telegraph regulations, supplemented by the additional precautionary instruction with regard to acceptance at locations such as Stourbridge, were adhered to. Installation of automatic safeguards, i.e. a track- or treadle-operated lock on either the block instruments or on the relative signals as a safeguard against irregular acceptance, and incorrect signal operation respectively, were therefore not recommended.

Track maintenance men need to keep their wits about them for any lapse of concentration when working on or near a busy main line can spell sudden death, more so when there are few, if any, formal safety measures in place. And so it was, on Tuesday 11th March, 1924 that platelayer John Coley met his end in front of a light engine whilst working on the track near Lye station. At the ensuing Inquest held on Thursday, 13th March, John Cornaby, the sub-ganger for the section, told the jury that they were engaged in reballasting sleepers near Bromley Street bridge, on the Cradley side of Lye station, with another member of the team, John Green. Initially, Coley was unaware of the approach of the engine until warned by Cornaby who suddenly noticed it steaming towards them some 40 yards away. Coley tried to reach the outside of the track but was hit before he was able to do so. The gang had been employed some 40 feet away from a signal which was 'on' when they commenced work. However, whilst going about their business the signal was pulled 'off' although this went unnoticed. Shortly afterwards the engine arrived, the sound of its imminent arrival being drowned by noise from nearby factories (there were galvanising works and a forge adjacent to the line). There was a slight curve to the line going towards the bridge but immediately beyond it straightened out affording a good view at least as far as the Cradley Park branch. This persuaded Cornaby that a look-out was unnecessary; how wrong he was. Frederick Wright, who was driving the engine, in his evidence at the Inquest told the jury that he had left Cradley West signal box at 4.05 pm, his engine running tender first. Apparently, he had earlier arrived at Cradley from Lye and had not seen any men working on the line at Bromley Street bridge, nor had he seen them on his return. On arrival at Stourbridge shed he was informed of the incident and on inspecting the engine found evidence that suggested an accident had taken place. His fireman, Sidney Harris, corroborated his story. The jury returned a verdict of 'accidental death', the Foreman adding that a flag-man should be posted when platelayers were working at a bad curve. In response to this suggestion, Mr W. Mullard, permanent way inspector at Stourbridge, pointed out that had a look-out been requested by the man in charge one would have been supplied. Clearly this discretionary aspect of the sub-ganger's responsibilities had on this occasion led to terrible consequences.

Moving forward a couple of years, two incidents are recalled that happened in the vicinity of Old Hill just before Christmas of 1926. The first occurred on Saturday, 18th December and brought traffic between Birmingham and Stourbridge to a complete standstill. A goods train bound for Bordesley Junction had entered Old Hill tunnel when the engine failed about halfway through. Station staff at Rowley Regis & Blackheath, realising that something was wrong, immediately stopped all trains on the down line, i.e. those heading towards Stourbridge Junction. On the up line traffic was also halted, the principal casualty being the Hereford to Birmingham (Snow Hill) service conveying through carriages from Cardiff. This had been stopped at Old Hill. Great Western officials then proceeded to the tunnel where they found the engine driver desperately trying to restart his train, however, his efforts were to no avail and a locomotive from one of the halted trains (possibly the 4.25 pm ex-Birmingham to Stourbridge Junction) was sent to the rescue.

The second incident occurred two days later, on the night of Monday 20th December, when an empty auto-train and a passenger train collided in Old Hill station, the latter being the 7.18 pm from Birmingham (Snow Hill) to Kidderminster, arriving at Old Hill at 7.47 pm. Apparently, the Kidderminster train had been given the signal to depart by the guard when the auto-train, travelling on the same line, crashed into the rear carriage with such force that the latter was lifted about two feet into the air shattering many of the windows and throwing passengers around the compartments. The front end of the auto-train was also badly damaged. Thankfully, injuries to staff and passengers were, by and large, mostly minor although 10 passengers (nine women and a sailor returning to Quarry Bank from Devonport on leave) had to receive first aid on the platform. This assistance was given by a number of trained railway workers who were travelling on board the train at the time. The last coach of the passenger train was subsequently uncoupled and shunted into a nearby siding together with the trailer from off the empty working. The passenger train then continued on to Kidderminster about half an hour late.

The reporter from the *County Express* arrived at the scene some 40 minutes after the accident and attempted to obtain an official explanation as to the cause of the collision. However, Mr Maybury, the station master, remained tight-lipped, having been instructed by the divisional superintendent, Mr A. Brook, not to divulge any information to the press. Undeterred by this wall of official silence the reporter approached a number of eyewitnesses in order to try and piece together the events which led up to the incident. It would appear that normal working arrangements at Old Hill allowed the auto-train to cross from the up line to the down line whilst the Kidderminster train was still in the platform. Presumably, the former had earlier arrived from Dudley and was preparing to return to the town along the Windmill End branch. The auto-train was manned by its full complement of guard, driver and fireman, although it was the presence on the platform of Mr Ernest Farmer, a foreman at Old Hill, that probably helped mitigate the effects of the collision. Seeing that a crash was imminent he shouted a warning to the driver of the empty train. Unfortunately, the warning came too late and whilst the driver was able to reduce his speed he could not prevent a collision.

On the Tuesday following the accident an Inquiry was held at the scene of the crash. To the disappointment of the *County Express*, officials would not release any information, neither was it divulged if a Board of Trade investigation would be necessary. The newspaper concluded that the possible cause of the accident stemmed from a misunderstanding on the part of those in charge of the auto-train. Having crossed over, the crew were under the impression that the Kidderminster train had left. In fact it had only just begun to move away when the collision occurred.

Those who have read *The Railways of Stourbridge* will probably recall the accident between the 11.30 pm Dudley to Stourbridge auto-train and the 9.50 pm class 'E' Victoria Basin to Cardiff freight train which happened on the night of Friday, 17th July, 1936. Previously, lack of space had meant that many of the details concerning the collision had to be omitted, however, the opportunity has now arisen to take a closer look at the crash which illustrates just how fragile the relationship was between the railwayman and his working environment. The accident claimed the life of auto-train driver William Meredith, fortunately those accompanying him: fireman Horace Reynolds; guard Mr B. Male; and three passengers, Mr and Mrs Pierce, and Jim Davies, a railway porter, all escaped serious injury. The goods train was manned by a Worcester crew comprising guard Charles Wilkes, who himself had a miraculous escape by jumping from his van moments before impact; fireman Frederick Hopcott; and engine driver Finch. The collision occurred 190 yards to the north of Stourbridge North signal box, the on-duty signalman, Charles Bonser, playing a crucial role in the night's events.

The goods train consisted of 36 wagons, the leading three being vacuum brake fitted, and a 25 ton brake van. It was hauled by '43XX' class 2-6-0 No. 8332. The total weight of the train was judged to be about 480 tons, the overall length being around 816 feet. The auto-train consisted of one 70 ft 8-wheeled bogie coach weighing 32 tons propelled by '48XX' class 0-4-2T No. 4853. The driver was in the driving compartment of the coach where there was a mechanical control to the engine's regulator and a vacuum brake valve which operated the vacuum brake on all wheels of the coach, and through a combination valve, the steam brake on the coupled wheels of the locomotive. In the engine's cab was the fireman who was able to apply the steam brake independently, in an emergency, by operating a release which would override the control of the vacuum brake.

As the Cardiff goods neared Stourbridge Junction North signal box engineman Finch found the inner home signal for No. 2 goods loop 'off'. The home signals were located on a single post, the arm controlling the up main line being uppermost whilst below were two smaller arms for No. 1 and No. 2 goods loops. These signals were located 10 yards to the north of the signal box. The goods train passed the signal box at 11.47 pm, running slowly for the turnout into the loop where Finch was expecting to see the train meeter. As the engine passed the signal box the driver was unable to see a light from the up main to No. 2 goods loop starting signal located 90 yards further on. He shouted to the signalman but was unable to attract his attention; neither could he see him at the window. Pulling up at the signal the driver blew his whistle. (The signal was a bracket holding four signals: on the main post was located Stourbridge Junction North up main starting signal whilst below was the distant for Stourbridge Junction Middle box. On two small dolls on the left of the bracket were two starting signals controlling admission to No. 1 and No. 2 up goods running loops). Moving to the fireman's side of the cab Finch looked out and saw that the signal arm had not dropped to the correct angle, nor was there any sign of a light (neither green or red). Thinking that either the points or signals were out of order he sent his fireman to the signal box to inform the signalman and obtain instructions. Shortly after the fireman had departed, the driver noticed that the up main advanced starter, some distance to the south, had cleared. He then looked above him at the up main starter and saw that it too had been pulled off. He concluded that the signalman intended the goods train to move forward as far as the south end of the yard where the train could reverse into the loop. However, his fireman had not returned so he waited. Moments later the auto-train struck the goods train, the time being about 11.51 pm.

In the brake van at the rear of the freight, about 190 yards to the north of the signal box, the guard suddenly heard a noise and saw a light approaching from around the curve. Realising it was another train and that a collision was inevitable he jumped for his life. The approaching train was the ill-fated 11.30 pm Dudley to Stourbridge Junction auto which had left Brettell Lane station at 11.47 pm (four minutes late). A few moments earlier driver Meredith had seen Engine Shed signal box's distant signal set at 'caution', however, it cleared just in time to avoid delaying the train's progress. Crossing Stambermill viaduct at between 30 and 35 mph the driver shut off steam about half way across. Fireman Reynolds was busy adjusting the reversing gear when he heard the driver sound his whistle. Then the vacuum fell sharply as the brakes were applied. He straight away pulled the release to enable the steam brake to be applied more quickly but almost immediately came the collision. The driver, although taking prompt action to avert a collision, had seen the tail lights of the freight train too late, his range of vision being seriously restricted by the curvature of the line. He had been running under clear signals, consequently, he had no reason to suspect that the line was occupied.

On duty in North box that night was Charles Bonser, a man of 34 years service with the GWR, 29 of which had been as a signalman. For the past 11 years he had been employed in the North box. At about 11.45 pm the signalman had spoken to a driver of one of two engines involved in a crew change immediately outside the signal box, one engine being in the down goods loop, the other on the down main. The driver of one of the engines had asked the signalman to telephone Engine Shed box with a message about a block book that was being sent there on the engine. However, he was unable to put the call through. He then accepted the Cardiff goods and after setting the road and pulling off the signals, he watched the engine pass whilst still trying to contact Engine Shed box. At that moment he received a telephone call from the shunter in the down yard requesting that one of the locomotives standing on the down side outside his box be sent back into the yard. After setting the signals for the light engine, he looked across to the up yard and saw what he thought was the red tail lamp of the Cardiff train at its usual spot in the loop. Unfortunately, it was not the tail lamp of the 'Cardiff' but one on the brake van of another freight train which was in the second siding beyond No. 2 up goods loop, a guard coming on duty having just lit the lamp and the side lights. Consequently it never dawned on him that the 'Cardiff' was still occupying the main line immediately outside his box!

Having mistakenly concluded that the freight train had passed safely into the loop the signalman returned the goods loop signal to 'danger' and accepted the auto-train; he did not look through the front windows of his box to ensure that the line was clear. At that moment into the signal box walked the fireman off the goods train (although Bonser denied this) and asked if it was all right for the freight to continue along the main line. However, before the signalman could answer the collision occurred. The impact completely wrecked the driving compartment and leading end of the auto-trailer, the headstock being forced in and the sole bars pushed outwards. The bogie centre casting was broken and the bogie itself was shoved back about two feet. The brake van on the goods train suffered a great deal of damage, most of the woodwork was smashed although its main structural members stood up well. The track was littered with debris. Five box-vans and wagons immediately behind the guard's van were derailed, two of the wagons somersaulting to land with their wheels in the air, the two others fouled the down main line. One of the buffers was broken off and hurled over a bank 15 yards high. It then continued through a hedge before hitting a door post of a house some 25 yards away. The Stourbridge breakdown gang arrived almost straight away and after working throughout the night, services were resumed at around 5.50 am.

When questioned at the ensuing inquest Bonser stated that he was unaware of the reason why the goods train had stopped at the starting signal explaining that two light engines had used the same road earlier in his shift without a problem. Furthermore, this stretch of line was without a track-circuit and consequently there was no electronic indication that the main line was still occupied. After the accident the signal was checked and it was found that although the signal wire may have been in need of slight adjustment, a normal, sharp pull of the lever would have led to the signal arm moving to its correct position. However, by pulling the lever slowly the signal arm might not fully come 'off'. In the light of the evidence the inquest jury returned a verdict of 'accidental death'. The report to the Ministry of Transport, submitted by the investigating officer Colonel A.C. Trench, placed responsibility for the accident on signalman Bonser in that he had signalled 'Out of Section' for the goods train without ensuring that the train had entered No. 2 up goods loop. Driver Finch was also criticised for not blowing his whistle a second time after he had brought his train to a standstill.

Accidents on the railways were not of course confined to the early years and there are many dreadful examples of such occurrences stretching right up to the present day. Locally, there were a number of accidents on the Town branch, in particular the spectacular crash in April 1977 (see *The Railways of Stourbridge*, p.181), however, there were also incidents elsewhere with 1950 being a particularly bad year. During that year it seemed that hardly a month went by without some misfortune or other occurring upon the local network. For example on 21st April the first of two collisions involving a passenger train and a freight train happened at Stourbridge Junction. A Worcester-bound freight (probably the 5.15 am, class 'F', Oxley sidings to Worcester goods yard) was making its way past the station by way of the up goods running loop when it was in collision with carriage stock being shunted out to form an early morning

A series of photographs which show an accident at Stambermill viaduct on 6th September, 1965. *Above:* An ex-LMS Stanier '8F' class 2-8-0 is involved with clearing up operations as the steam breakdown crane recovers a mineral wagon. *Below:* A member of the breakdown gang sets about a mineral wagon with a cutting torch.   *(Both) E.J. Dew*

Above left: '57XX' class 0-6-0PT No. 3788 and its train at the bottom of the bank adjacent to Stambermill viaduct having crashed through the stop block on the up loop headshunt.   *E.J. Dew*

Above right: The 45 ton breakdown crane begins to lift wagons and debris up to the lineside at Stambermill.   *E.J. Dew*

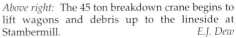

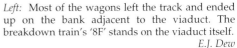

Left: Most of the wagons left the track and ended up on the bank adjacent to the viaduct. The breakdown train's '8F' stands on the viaduct itself.   *E.J. Dew*

What is believed to be the last victim of the old bridge over Foster Street at Stourbridge Town station. When the portion of the bridge that carried the platform was removed, the 'low bridge' warning was taken with it, consequently this unfortunate result in October/November 1957.   *Keith Tilbrook*

passenger service to Birmingham (Snow Hill). Luckily there were no personal injuries but there was severe damage to the freight engine. Also damaged were three carriages, a nearby signal and a length of track. Before the stricken engine could be moved one of the cylinder blocks (probably on the driver's side) had to be dismantled. The engine was then lifted clear by the breakdown crane which had been summoned from Wolverhampton (this was a 45 ton maximum lift steam crane based at Stafford Road. Stourbridge was only equipped with a 6 ton hand crane). The carriages were moved in similar fashion. The collision caused inevitable delays to traffic, the 16 carriages being prepared for early passenger trains either being damaged or blocked-in at the carriage sidings. In spite of this, only one Birmingham (Snow Hill) local service was actually cancelled.

Two months later there was another collision, but this time it was just inside Dudley tunnel. On 13th June Billy Robbins was at the controls of the ex-GWR diesel railcar working the Old Hill to Dudley passenger service. The car had left the Windmill End branch and after crossing Blowers Green junction it pulled up at Blowers Green station, the last stop before Dudley. With everyone aboard, the guard gave two rings of the bell and with the signal in his favour Billy Robbins started off towards the tunnel; unfortunately, unbeknown to the driver, the preceding freight (possibly the 3.00 am, class 'F', Pontypool Road to Oxley sidings) had been brought to a halt at the signal just outside Dudley station, the rear portion still in the tunnel. When the signal cleared the goods train started forward, then suddenly there was huge bang just as the last wagons were leaving the tunnel; the railcar, unable to stop in time, had collided with the rear of the slow moving freight derailing the brake van, and the wagon immediately in front. At the Dudley end the tunnel curves to the left so Billy Robbins could not have seen the red tail lamp on the guard's van until the last moment, so even though the goods train was moving and the railcar's brakes were immediately applied it was impossible to prevent a collision. When the end of the train emerged from the tunnel with the last two vehicles off the rails Tom Upton, a driver of a light engine waiting for the road to Stourbridge, sounded his whistle furiously in an attempt to attract the other driver's attention. At the same time Bill Taylor, the signalman in the South box, hurriedly returned the signal to 'danger', but it was too late, the engine had passed by, the driver unaware of what was happening behind him. As the derailed brake van left the tunnel the goods guard, Jack Griffiths, and three LMR guards from Saltley depot who were learning the road, jumped clear. The wagon in front of the van, which was carrying about a ton of iron, hit the end of the platform and breaking free from the rest of the train was thrown across the tracks blocking both up and down lines completely. The brake van itself ended up on the platform. By now Billy Robbins had brought the railcar to a standstill outside the tunnel entrance and after disembarking all of the passengers, guided them away from the tracks to the safety of the adjacent bank. The derailment was eventually cleared five hours later. So how did the accident occur? At the time Blowers Green station was being rebuilt and it was the contractor who set the chain of events in motion. When the signal cleared it was not pulled 'off' by the signalman in Blowers Green box, but by the contractor's men dropping a large baulk onto the signal wire. This activated the signal arm giving the road to the driver of the railcar.

Early in November there was a third accident involving a passenger train but this time a stationary engine caused the problems. The locomotive had finished shunting at Langley Green and was returning 'light engine' to Stourbridge shed when it was diverted into the down loop just before Rowley Regis station to allow a following passenger train to overtake. However, it was this simple manoeuvre that led to the collision as for some unknown reason the engine overran the points thereby fouling the main line. By now it was too late to halt the approaching passenger train, the 5.34 pm from Birmingham (Snow Hill), and it collided with the locomotive's front end. The footboards of the carriages also hit the engine and these splintered upon impact. When the passenger train came to a halt it was possible to detach the engine and shunt it into a nearby siding. The Stourbridge breakdown gang had been summoned and on arrival dealt with the other locomotive and carriages. In the mean time single line working had been introduced under the supervision of the district inspector's staff from Snow Hill. Obviously serious delays ensued and these continued until well after midnight when the line was cleared. The two engines involved in the collision were both towed back to Stourbridge to await inspection and, if possible, to be repaired in the shed's fitting shop.

Luckily, these three incidents were free from tragedy, but on 28th September platelayer Joe Cox was the first of two local railwaymen to be killed in very similar circumstances. The 10.24 am auto-train was approaching Stourbridge Junction from the direction of the Town station when driver Charlie Grange saw Mr Cox walking very close to the line with his back to the train. Apparently the platelayer had been sent up to the Junction by sub-ganger Jim Clarke for a crossing bolt. The man seemed totally oblivious to the impending arrival of the train even after the driver had rung his bell once; twice; and then a third time continuously. It was all to no avail, and unable to stop, the auto-train ran the unfortunate man down. The following month also witnessed a fatal accident to a railwayman. This time it was one of Stourbridge's own drivers. Although no one actually saw Henry Surrell meet his death, an examination of 2-6-2T No. 5193 by Bill Heighway, a fitter at Stourbridge shed, discovered ample evidence that this was the engine which had hit Mr Surrell. The locomotive had earlier worked a Wolverhampton (Low Level) to Stourbridge Junction passenger train, arriving at the latter at about 4.40 pm. Mr Surrell had been walking back from the shed along the line and after crossing the viaduct was probably run down about 100 yards further on. Not surprisingly, on that dark, wet and windy afternoon, neither the driver, Herbert Hobbs, nor his fireman were aware of the fate that had befallen their colleague. Also in November a third railwayman died but on this occasion it was from natural causes. It is thought that the train involved was the 6.25 am empty train from Stourbridge Junction to Brettell Lane which then formed the 6.37 am passenger train to Birmingham (Snow Hill) via Dudley and Great Bridge. The train duly arrived at Brettell Lane at 6.30 am and was met by lady porter Vera Rodgers. The porter entered the guard's compartment and found the guard, Len Timerick, sitting in his accustomed place pen in hand. Having not received a reply to her greeting she found to her horror that Mr Timerick had died at his post.

The penultimate incident in this chapter has been recalled by Ramon Williams which occurred whilst he was firing to the late Teddy Roberts (Top 'em up Ted) in the early 1960s:

We left Kidderminster goods yard one dark winter's morning with about 60 empty coal wagons from Stourport power station being returned to Cannock colliery via Ryecroft Junction. On the front was an ex-LMS '8F' so my mate, Ted, was on the left-hand side of the footplate. Passing under what was then Offmore Farm bridge, Ted shouted over to me to take a look out of the cab to see if I could make out what was in front of us. I could just about see a pinpoint of light, then, as we got closer I realised something was across the track. I shouted a warning to my mate who immediately put on the brakes; we couldn't stop in time and the train slid into an agricultural tractor. The train bounced back upon impact; the guard, who was on his feet in his van with a cup of tea in his hands, was thrown to the floor. We stopped in a cloud of steam and I got down from the footplate holding my Bardic lamp and went to the rear of the train to meet the guard whilst the driver went to inspect the damage at the front end. On my way down I noticed that the train had parted in three places and that two wagons had come off the rails. Having spoken to the guard I returned to the engine and reported the situation to the driver. Thankfully, the tractor driver had been off his machine and was unhurt, but the tractor was a mess. I put on my coat, picked up some detonators and started to walk the three miles to Blakedown signal box. In accordance with the rules, I placed the detonators on the up line to warn any approaching train that the line was obstructed; the guard carried out a similar operation to the rear of the train. After placing the detonators, a light engine came along and even though the detonators went off, it did not stop. By the time I reached Blakedown, the guard had already reported the incident at Kidderminster. I sat in the box for over two hours while the track was cleared and we were able to limp into Stourbridge. Two days later the Crewe inquiry team met in a room at Kidderminster station and my driver, the guard, the driver of the light engine, and myself were called in to give our version of events. It was discovered that on the Sunday, new track had been laid and the ganger in charge had forgotten to replace the crossings for road traffic. Consequently, after opening the first gate, the tractor driver drove through onto the track and got stuck on the down line. The conclusion of the inquiry was that the ganger was 50 per cent to blame for the accident, as was the tractor driver, who should have opened both gates before attempting to drive through. Had he done so, he would have seen that the rail crossings were missing. The driver of the light engine was suspended for three days and sadly, the tractor driver passed away a few months later having never quite recovered from the experience.

To bring this chapter to a close the story steps back in time over 130 years to December 1872 and an accident on the Amblecote incline, the steepest part of the branch line which joined the Great Western main line to the iron works of Messrs John Bradley & Co. and Messrs Firmstone & McEwen. The accident happened on Friday 20th December, 1872 at around midday. A rake of empty wagons being hauled up the incline by the stationary winding engine, separated into two when a coupling parted. This caused about a dozen vehicles and the brake van to roll back towards the yard. Trains working down the incline were headed by a 'powerful' brake van; this would then form the rearmost vehicle on trains heading up towards the main line. However, even this was not sufficient to bring the wagons to a halt. At the bottom of the incline, just beyond the spot where the line began to rise, was stationed a pointsman, and it was about 50 yards past this man that the coupling snapped. On seeing the wagons hurtling towards him the man reacted quickly, switching the points over thereby directing the runaway off the branch and into a nearby siding. In the siding stood two wagons loaded with iron wheels and two with coal; it was these that felt the full force of the crash. The impact smashed to matchwood the wagons loaded with wheels, whilst the two full of coal were thrown on top of the adjacent 10 ft high cinder bank. At the same time the brake van was split in two and many of the following wagons were wrecked. The man at the brake stuck to his task courageously only leaving his post moments before the crash. Although damage to rolling stock was great there were no injuries to staff, even the man that jumped from the brake van escaped unscathed. Without doubt the pointman's prompt action contributed to the lack of serious injury, for had the wagons continued unchecked they would have smashed through the gates which guarded the crossing on the High Street which on Fridays was heavily used by both pedestrians and vehicles. The newspaper commented at the time that 'the incline is a very dangerous one, and the fact of the line crossing the street is both inconvenient and hazardous'. This was a view that probably summed up local feeling and the incident was certainly not the last to occur on this very steep stretch of line (see *The Railways of Stourbridge*, p.23).

Postscript

Since opening on 1st October, 1879 'Stourbridge Town' has seen many changes over the years, although its existence was never really threatened until the 1970s when an operating loss of around £30,000 per annum almost sounded the death knell for the country's shortest branch line. Fortunately, the storm passed and the future of the branch appeared secure, especially after a £380,000 investment led to the building of a brand new station in 1994. However, recent developments mean that Stourbridge Town station may once again be under threat.

The source of the concern was the unveiling by the Secretary of State for Transport, Alistair Darling, of the Strategic Rail Authority's 'Community Rail Development Strategy' (CRDS) on 22nd November, 2004. The CRDS covers mainly local and rural lines and provides a broad framework for developing passenger usage and reducing operational cost. The Strategy lists 56 routes which the SRA proposes to designate as Community Rail lines, the future of which will depend upon effective partnerships being forged between local authorities, community groups, and passengers themselves. Central to the plan is the involvement of local communities in the support and development of these routes. One of these lines is of course the Stourbridge Town branch, one of three West Midland routes covered by the CRDS. Initially, seven routes: the St Ives Bay line; the Looe Valley line; and the Tamar Valley line, all of which are in Cornwall; the St Albans Abbey branch; the Grantham-Skegness line; the Penistone line; and the Esk Valley line, will be used as pilot schemes.

All of the lines identified in the plan have running costs which are said to be increasing whilst passenger numbers are reducing. On the Stourbridge branch, peak time services appear to be well used, unfortunately, during off-peak times there are many empty seats on the class '153' single diesel car which plies its trade up and down the branch in excess of 140 times a day (excluding Sunday). The SRA is encouraging partnerships to come up with imaginative ideas to reduce costs and encourage usage. Perhaps the introduction of the Parry People Mover will be the line's saviour? At the other end of the line is Stourbridge Junction and there appears to be no sign of flagging passenger numbers there. Car parking, such a problem at the site during weekdays, is set to be eased by the provision of additional facilities nearby.

Returning to the Town station, the signal box was closed on 25th August, 1935 however, it would seem that the building remained, surviving as a storage facility until the 1950s. Keith Tilbrook recalls the box being used by Charlie Millward and his Permanent Way gang for storing their tools; it was even used by Keith's father, Bill Tilbrook, who would leave his bicycle there when he was working in the signal box at Stourbridge Junction. Stourbridge Town box was eventually sold for a nominal sum, in accordance with the 'disposal of redundant materials to staff' arrangements, to a member of the local S&T gang who later found use for it at his house as a garden shed. Keith has also pointed out that in the early days of the single diesel units on the branch these machines were often strengthened at peak times by the addition of a driving trailer or occasionally, another single motorised unit. Furthermore, it was not unknown for the Town services to be worked by a three-car suburban set, with the first class section locked off, whilst on occasion just the driving end trailers of the set would be used, the middle car having been knocked out. Finally, at least once a three-car Cross-Country set, complete with buffet (closed), was also put into service.

In Volume One there was a reference to the late Ernie Payton. Ernie has informed us that he is still very much alive! We would like to apologise to him for any distress caused to family and friends.

Appendix

Local ASLEF Members on 26th September, 1909

Index

References to Volume One are shown in Roman type, Volume Two in italics.

255